WHAT IS ISLAM?

WHAT IS ISLAM?

A Comprehensive Introduction

Chris Horrie and Peter Chippindale

CONTENTS

THE KORAN (QUR'AN)

Quotations from the Qur'an are given in brackets, for example (20:50). The first number refers to the chapter (or *surah* in Arabic) and the second refers to the verse.

Modern editions of the Qur'an reproduce the Book exactly as it was revealed to Muhammad. It therefore contains what appears to be punctuation, grammatical and other human errors. In most editions these 'errors' are indicated in brackets. Square brackets are used, in addition, to enclose clarifications made by non-Muslim editors.

Part 1

FAITH

1. THE UNIVERSAL RELIGION

'There is no god but Allah.
Muhammad is the messenger of Allah.'

Recitation of these two phrases in the presence of two witnesses is all that is required for conversion to Islam. Each year millions of people – mainly in the Third World – make this simple declaration and, by accepting the strict obligations of Islamic law, join the fastest-growing body of religious believers in the world. The exact number of Muslims is difficult to estimate, but all authorities agree that the population now is at least 1,000 million.

Islam is thus the second largest religion after Christianity, which already has over 1,000 million followers divided between Eastern Orthodoxy, Catholicism and Protestantism. And in practice, as many Muslims point out, Christian belief in the highly secularised countries of Europe and North America is often nominal. Therefore, they claim, Islam probably has the largest number of 'true believers'.

Unlike Christianity, Islam could never become a purely private religion of personal conscience and ethics. Rather it is a complete way of life governing dress, economics, business ethics, rates of taxation, justice and punishment, weights and measures, politics, war and peace, marriage and inheritance, family and domestic life, the care of animals and livestock, sexual relations within marriage, education, diet, cookery, social behaviour, forms of greeting and rules of hospitality. Even the way in which a glass of water is to be drunk is governed by Islamic religious law.

Islam's approach to the great religious issues of life and death, the origins and fate of the universe, and the nature of mankind and God (Allah) is both simple and uncompromising.

It holds there is only one merciful, eternal and all-powerful Allah. He is the Lord of everything in existence, including the whole of mankind. He brought the universe into being in an act of creation approximately 8,000 years ago and He will bring it to an end when He wills. The end of the universe will be followed by a Day of Judgement when all mankind will be resurrected, individually called to account, and sent either to Paradise or hell for all eternity.

Allah has made this known to all mankind through a series of Prophets, starting with Adam and ending with Muhammad ('The Last Prophet' or 'The Seal of the Prophecy').

Allah's final message to mankind was given to the Prophet Muhammad and has been set down in the Koran (Qur'an) which, together with certain stories about the life of Muhammad, dictates everything that a man should know and do in order to enter Paradise.

The spread of Islam has always been based on the strength and simplicity of this religious conviction, with its emphasis on ideas of punishment and reward in the afterlife. It is therefore easy to see why the poor of the Third World – where Islam is growing fastest – should seek solace in the idea of Paradise after death.

But there are also political and social reasons for the religion's continuing success. Islam is a powerful conservative force, bolstering traditional family life and protecting individuals and communities against the enormous and often destructive changes imposed on Third World countries by contact with the developed capitalist or former Communist world.

The recent growth of Islam has been particularly marked in African and Asian countries where there was contact with Christian colonial powers. At independence the elites in most of these countries embraced Western or Soviet ideas of secularism, economic development and either liberal democracy or socialism. Now, after decades of political instability, growing poverty and social disintegration, the dream of Western or Soviet-style development has almost without exception ended in disillusionment.

It is against this background that the Islamic 'Reformation' known as 'fundamentalism' – literally a return to a simplified and basic form of Islamic law – is taking place.

Western reaction to Islamic fundamentalism has been marked by revulsion against the reintroduction of Qur'anic punishments such as amputating a hand for the crime of theft. Beneath this is a revival of the ancient European fear that Muslims plan to conquer the world.

These fears are understandable, but are exaggerated because of a basic and widespread misunderstanding of the Islamic duty of *jihad* (Holy War), one of the few aspects of the religion widely discussed in the West.

It is true that all Muslims are obliged to fight to the death in defence of Islam and that the Islamic epoch began with the declaration by Muhammad of *jihad* against the pagans of Arabia. But this Qur'anic duty is entirely defensive. Aggressive war, either to gain worldly power or wealth or to forcibly convert unbelievers, is expressly forbidden in the Qur'an: 'There is no compulsion in religion; truly the right way has become clearly distinct from error' (2:256).

At the same time there is a clear obligation of self-defence, and a duty to fight those who oppress fellow Muslims. The Qur'an says: 'And fight in the way of Allah with those who fight you . . . and kill them wherever you find them, and drive them out from whence they drove you out . . . and fight with them until there is no persecution, and religion should only be for Allah, but if they desist, then there should be no hostility except against oppressors' (2:190–193).

In reality the distinction between war in the name of self-defence and aggressive war is blurred and Muslim states tend to be as warlike as any others. Nevertheless they do require at least a pretext of aiding oppressed co-religionists, and this has always been a factor in conflicts between them in the modern world. But even in conditions of peace, it is unlikely that fundamentalist Islam could ever compromise with the secular societies of the West, or accept Western political ideas and institutions. In particular the cherished Western ideals of nationalism and individual freedom have no place in Muslim thought.

The very word *Islam* translates from Arabic as 'submission' or 'obedience' (to the will and laws of Allah as set down in the Qur'an) and the word *Muslim*, with the same Arabic root, means 'that person or thing which obeys Allah's law'.

It is this trenchant denial of individualism, and the requirement to submit to Divine authority in every minute aspect of life, which seems so alien to the Western mind.

In Islam the issues of 'freedom of choice' and 'human rights', which form central pillars of modern Western political philosophy, hardly arise. The only free choice to be made is whether to obey the eternal laws of Allah and gain salvation, or to disobey and risk eternal damnation. And the only important human right is to be able to follow unhindered the laws given by Allah through the agency of Prophethood.

Whilst the central creed of Islam is simple monotheism – accepting Allah as controlling the fate of all the universe – the second inseparable belief is the Prophethood – Allah communicating with mankind through a series of divinely guided messengers.

2. THE PROPHETS

Muslims believe all races and nations have had their own Prophets. Islam is therefore not a religion of human speculation and discovery, but of Divine revelation of Allah's pre-existing laws, centring on the oneness and unity of Allah, His omnipotence and mercy. In line with this, He has also taken care to warn against the dangers of worshipping false gods of any kind.

Unfortunately, mankind has repeatedly ignored or forgotten this message from the Prophets and lapsed into paganism and polytheism. Sometimes Allah has punished us for this – for example in the time of Noah (Nuh), when all but the true believers were drowned by the flood. But, in most cases, in His mercy, He has sent further Prophets to clarify His message, reveal further elements of His law, or warn of the dangers of disobedience.

There have been an extraordinary number of Prophets. Muhammad said Allah had sent 124,000 Prophets before him and 25 Jewish-Christian Prophets from Adam to Jesus (*Isa*) are mentioned in the Qur'an.

Other religions based on the Prophethood – such as Judaism, Christianity and the effectively extinct monotheistic religions of Arab Sabianism and Persian Zoroastrianism – are said to be 'Muslim' in the sense that followers accept monotheism and parts of Allah's law.

However, followers of polytheistic religions, paganism and godless ethical cults such as Buddhism, Confucianism, Taoism, Humanism and Marxism are rejected as *kafirs* (non-Muslims). But even *kafirs* are believed to be 'Muslim' by nature, though in a condition of *kufr* (hiding from Allah) through their own choice. And it is this act of deliberately hiding from the Truth which condemns *kafirs* to eternal damnation, as those who hide from Allah also hide from His mercy.

THE JEWISH HERITAGE

Judaism is particularly important to Islam and is the religion it most closely resembles. The Qur'an states that the Prophets Jacob (Yacoub) and Abraham (Ibrahim), who founded Judaism, were the first human beings to fully submit to Allah's law.

Islam's claim to be the true religion of Ibrahim is based on the events surrounding his willingness to show obedience to Allah by sacrificing his son. Both religions agree that Allah, in His mercy, allowed him to sacrifice a ram instead.

The split comes over which of his two sons he was prepared to kill, and was therefore saved. Jews believe it was his younger son Isaac (*Ishaq*), and both religions then agree that Ishaq's twelve sons founded the twelve tribes of the original Jewish nation. Jews therefore claim Allah intervened directly to bring the Jewish nation into being, and that the original Jewish nation was Allah's chosen people, and He was God of the Jewish nation alone.

The Qur'an directly contradicts this. It says that Ibrahim only had one son, Ishmael, at the time of the proposed sacrifice and that Ishaq was born afterwards as a reward to Ibrahim for his obedience. Ishmael (Isma'il) went on to found the Arab nation, proving Allah chose the Arabs to be particularly blessed and, in particular, to receive the final revelation via Isma'il's direct descendant, Muhammad.

But the Qur'an is quite clear that Allah is the god of all mankind and not either the Israelites or Arabs alone. It chides the Jews for refusing to accept the Prophets Jesus (*Isa*) and Muhammad and continuing to believe they are His chosen people.

The second chapter (*surah*) of the Qur'an, much of which is directly addressed to the children of Israel (Banu Isra'il), says: 'Surely those who believe, and those who are Jews, and the Christians, and the Sabians, whoever believes in Allah and the last day and does good, they shall have their reward from their Lord, and there is no fear for them, nor shall they grieve' (2:62). In other words, the Sabian Arabs, Jews, Christians and 'whoever believes', regardless of nation, have the same God – Allah.

The same *surah* warns Banu Isra'il about their failure to accept the Prophethood of Jesus (*Isa*) and Muhammad: 'What! whenever then an apostle came to you with that which your souls did not desire, you were insolent so you called some liars and some you slew . . . Evil is that for which [Banu Isra'il] have sold their souls – that they should deny what Allah has revealed, out of envy that Allah should send down His grace on whomsoever of His servants He pleases; so they have made themselves deserving of wrath upon wrath, and there is a disgraceful punishment for the unbelievers' (2:87–90).

After this dire warning Allah tells the Jews to sincerely repent in which case He will be merciful: 'O Banu Isra'il, call to mind My favour which I bestowed upon you and made you excel amongst the nations . . . And [unbelievers] say: Be Jews or Christians, you will be on the right course. Say: Nay! we follow the religion of Ibrahim . . . we believe in Allah and in that which had been revealed to us, and that which was revealed to Ibrahim and Isma'il and Ishaq and Jacob (Yacoub) and the tribes, and that which was given to Musa and Jesus (*Isa*), and that which was given to the Prophets from their Lord, we do not make any distinction between any of them, and to Him do we submit' (2:135–136).

But even those who fail to heed this message and remain practising Jews are awarded a greater status by Islam than followers of pagan or polytheistic religions. Throughout history Muslim rulers have given their Jewish subjects 'protected persons' (*Dhimmi*) status, free to follow their own religion unmolested, as the Qur'an commands toleration of Biblical religions.

Historically *Dhimmi* Jews in the Arab world not only enjoyed this considerable freedom, but also greatly influenced

Islamic culture and commerce and sometimes reached high office in the state. Although the Jews of the Muslim world were discriminated against from time to time, they escaped the terrible persecutions periodically inflicted upon them throughout most of Christian Europe.

Most Muslim Middle Eastern countries retained large *Dhimmi* Jewish populations until the establishment of the state of Israel in 1948, since when many Arab Jews have emigrated there. Life for those remaining, still a sizeable number until recently in Syria, Iraq, Egypt and Morocco, has become more difficult.

JESUS – PROPHET OF ISLAM

Christianity, like Judaism, is described throughout the Qur'an as essentially a misguided form of the 'religion of Ibrahim', the true version of which is Islam. The main error of Christians is their misunderstanding (sometimes described by Muslims as wilful slander) of the significance of the Islamic Prophet Jesus, Son of Mary (*Isa ibn Maryam*).

Jesus (*Isa*) is regarded by Muslims as the Jewish Messiah, sent by Allah to lead them back to the true path of Ibrahim and take their place amongst the rightly guided Islamic nations. He is described as a Prophet of the Highest Order (*rasul*), a status otherwise reserved only for the most important Prophets including Ibrahim and Muhammad himself.

The Qur'an confirms *Isa*'s miraculous virgin birth, his performance of symbolic miracles, and the validity of the Gospels as genuine revelations from Allah, but the Book dwells on his rejection by the Jews. His significance as the founder of Christianity is of secondary importance to the central story of relations between the Jews and the Prophets.

Nevertheless, the Qur'an reveals Allah to be astonished and angered by the Christian idea that *Isa* was His son: 'And they say: The Beneficent God has taken a son. The heavens may almost be rent thereat, and the earth cleave asunder, and the mountains fall down in pieces, that they ascribe a son to the Beneficent God. And it is not worthy of the Beneficent God that He should take a son' (19:88–92).

The fifth *surah* of the Qur'an deals with the story of *Isa* at length and parts are directly addressed to Christians as fellow 'People of the Book'. The *surah* warns that the Christian concept of the Holy Trinity is a form of polytheism and bluntly denies the divinity of *Isa*: 'Certainly they disbelieve who say: Surely Allah is the third of the three; and there is no God but one God, and if they desist not from what they say, a painful chastisement shall befall those among them who disbelieve. Will they not then turn to Allah and ask His forgiveness? And Allah is Forgiving, Merciful. The Messiah, son of Maryam, is but an apostle . . .' (5:73–75).

The same *surah* shows that *Isa*, like any mortal, will be tried by Allah on the Day of Judgement. It even reports the conversation which will take place between Allah and *Isa*: 'And when Allah will say: O *Isa*, son of Mary, did you say to men, Take me and my mother for two Gods beside Allah, (*Isa*) will say: . . . I did not say to them aught save what Thou didst enjoin me with: That serve Allah, my Lord and your Lord' (5:116–117).

Because *Isa* was crucified he is not only a Prophet but also an Islamic martyr. There is some debate amongst Muslims about the fate of *Isa* after his death. The Qur'an says he did not die – probably a reference to the privilege of martyrs who are said to remain in a state of bliss until the Day of Judgement. But some Muslims have interpreted this as a literal denial of *Isa*'s crucifixion and there is even a popular belief that *Isa* returned to the desert, performed additional miracles and lived to be 120 years old.

Although Christians are discussed far less frequently than Jews in the Qur'an, there are signs that, despite their errors, they are believed to be closer to Islam. A passage in the fifth *surah* addressed to the Muslims says: 'And you will certainly find the nearest in friendship to those who believe to be those who say: We are Christians . . . And when they hear what has been revealed to the apostle [Muhammad], you will see their eyes overflowing with tears on account of the truth that they recognise; they say: Our Lord! we believe, so write us down with the witnesses' (5:83).

The original Arabian and Assyrian Christian Church was certainly much closer to Islam than modern Christianity. Many

early Christians subscribed to Arianism, a Christian heresy
which, like Islam, believed Jesus (*Isa*) to have been merely
human.

All that divided Arians from Muslims was acceptance of the
finality of Muhammad's Prophethood and Qur'anic law. But
Arianism was crushed after the adoption of a coherent
Trinitarian doctrine by the Roman Church at the Council of
Nicea in the third century AD.

Despite these similar beginnings, Christianity and Islam
began to diverge in the Middle Ages. Countless wars between
Christian and Muslim states left a legacy of bitterness and
mutual ignorance expressed as a growing theological gulf.

The idea that the Holy Trinity is just a sophisticated version
of One God monotheism was so alien to Muslims that most
believed it was the simple polytheistic worship of Allah, His
wife Maryam and His son *Isa*. Medieval Christian reverence
for sacred relics like fragments of the Cross led, with some
justification, to the accusation that Christians had become
pagan symbol worshippers.

Veneration of icons was denounced as pagan idol worship
(classical Islam forbids attempts to represent Allah in pictures).
The adoption of the pre-Christian Roman solar calendar and
the celebration of Christmas at the winter solstice similarly led
to the belief that Christians practised pagan sun-worship.

But Christians, like Jews, have still enjoyed protected
Dhimmi status within Muslim states for many centuries. Cut
off from the mainstream of Christianity, *Dhimmi* Arab
Christian Churches – such as the Egyptian Copts and Syrian
Maronites – have preserved an older, more original version
of their religion, whilst absorbing and enriching Islamic
culture.

Ironically, in the light of the recent Muslim–Christian civil
war, this process was most developed in Syria and Lebanon,
where Islamic sub-sects such as the dominant Alawite group
adopted parts of Christian doctrine. Until the Second World
War, *Dhimmi* Christian communities within Muslim territories such as Syria – including the Lebanese Maronites – were
unmolested by Muslim rulers.

PAGANS AND POLYTHEISTS

Ancient history shows that Islam's central idea of one all-powerful god – monotheism – is relatively new as a force in world religion. The earliest men and women almost always believed in a hierarchy, or family, of gods controlling different aspects of worldly life. And, until the conversion of the Roman Empire to Christianity, followers of monotheistic religions were a small minority.

Today the position has been almost exactly reversed. Polytheism – in the shape of formal religions at least – remains as a major force only in the Hindu and Sikh religions of the Indian sub-continent.

Muslims are implacably opposed to polytheism, the practice of which is a form of *shirk* – either the 'association' of Allah with another god, His division into parts, or the denial of His absolute command of the universe. *Shirk* is Islam's one unforgivable sin – 'far error' as it is put in the Qur'an – and the penalty is eternal damnation.

Surah 4 is quite clear about the penalty: 'Surely Allah does not forgive that anything should be associated with Him . . . and whoever associates anything with Allah, he indeed strays off into far error . . . These are they whose abode is hell, and they shall not find any refuge from it' (4:116–121).

The sin of *shirk* also applies to Buddhists, Shintoists, Confucianists and followers of tribal religions of Africa because of their worship of idols and the graves of ancestors. The atheistic philosophies of Marxism and Humanism, which propose that God is the creation of the human imagination, are also guilty of *shirk* in the highest degree because they elevate man to a position above Allah.

In recent decades many 'fundamentalist' Muslim scholars have, in addition, denounced the nominally Christian societies of the West as pagan. Passive agnosticism and religious scepticism is widely regarded as *shirk* because of the implicit denial of Allah's omnipotence. The 'worship' of material goods and money, faith in scientific progress, problems of drink and drugs, sexual permissiveness, widespread gambling and the spread of superstitious cults (such as astrology) are all seen as signs of the growing paganism of the Western world.

Thus, although Islam recognises 'Biblical' Judaism and Christianity as being worthy of toleration and respect, the other major world religions, ethical systems, political ideologies and secularised versions of Christianity and Judaism are all fiercely rejected as being, in effect, pagan.

And the struggle against paganism is central to Islam's mission, just as the struggle against the corrupt pagan aristocracy of Mecca and Arabia dominated the life of Allah's last and greatest Prophet – Muhammad.

3. THE LIFE OF MUHAMMAD

The exact date of Muhammad's birth in Mecca is unknown, but it is thought to have been no later than AD 570, the year the city's territory was invaded by the Christian Emperor of Ethiopia.

His father was called Abdullah, which means 'servant of God' and his mother Aminah ('peaceful'). Both were members of the Hashim clan, a sub-division of the Quraysh tribe which had lately abandoned its nomadic life as desert Bedouins and risen to dominate the trading city of Mecca.

Although the Hashemites could trace their ancestors back to Isma'il and Ibrahim, it seems they had largely lapsed into paganism, although some clan members were Christian or Jewish.

Muhammad had a sorrowful early childhood. His father was dead by the time of his birth and his mother died before he was six, meaning he was raised as an orphan. According to Quraysh law he was to be given to a Bedouin foster mother and sent off into the desert, and would be unable to inherit from his father's estate. So almost from the beginning of his life he was both poor and something of an outcast from Meccan society. Although there are hundreds of traditional 'reports' or 'sayings' (hadith) about Muhammad's early life, many are regarded by Muslim scholars as pious inventions or allegories invented centuries after his death.

But it is known for certain that when he was eight Muhammad was sent to live with his uncle, a merchant called Abu Talib. From the age of twelve Abu Talib took him with him on his long trading trips, which sometimes lasted for many months. Muhammad first worked as a camel driver but, as both his horizons and business acumen expanded, he became known as The Trusted One (al-Amin) for being fair in his dealings and honouring his obligations.

The most important *hadith* about his early life, and the ones with some of the largest degree of unanimity, are about a trip to Syria, where he was recognised by a Christian monk as Shiloh – the non-Jewish Prophet whose coming was foretold in the book of Genesis.

The relevant verses, which form a central part of Islam's mission to the Jews, tell of events immediately before the end of the world. 'And Jacob (Yacoub)', Genesis reports, 'called unto his sons [The Israelites] and said, Gather yourselves together, that I may tell you that which shall befall you in the last days ... The [Prophethood] shall not depart from Judah ... until Shiloh come; and unto him shall the gathering of the people be' (Genesis 19:1–10).

It seems that Muhammad, from an early age, believed himself to be Shiloh, the first and last non-Jewish Prophet who would bring the final message and warning to mankind in the 'last days' before the end of the world.

It may have been for this reason that he became something of a mystic, spending long periods of isolated meditation in the desert. From his early twenties onwards he began to have religious experiences and visions of various sorts, but was on the whole confused by their significance. He is also reported to have become an expert on the Jewish and Christian religions and to have engaged in long religious debates with both monotheists and pagans.

At the age of 25 Muhammad's social status changed markedly. He had been employed by a wealthy widow, Khadijah, to run her trading interests and, after they had prospered, she asked him to marry her. He accepted, even though she was forty, and became a person of prominence and wealth. She was not only his first convert but just as importantly she was to prove a faithful, understanding and supportive wife and the marriage was happy. The couple had only one surviving child, a daughter called Fatima who in later life became a fanatical Muslim.

At that time Mecca was a tumultuous melting pot of Christianity, Judaism and the various pagan religions practised by the desert tribes and Meccan clans. Khadijah's family had been exposed to monotheism, which was growing in popularity in its various forms and it is known that her uncle was a practising Christian.

In contrast, the pagan clan cults of the Quraysh in the city had become decadent, especially in their shameless worship of material goods and worldly wealth and the consequent huge disparities between rich and poor, which Muhammad, with his varied background, was able to appreciate.

These problems, springing from the difficult transition of the Quraysh from nomadic poverty to sedentary merchant wealth, concerned him greatly, and social injustice – especially the treatment of orphans like himself – is the theme of many of the early *surahs* of the Qur'an.

The cults of the pagan desert Bedouin clans, who visited Mecca only occasionally, were equally divisive, degenerate and cruel. Human sacrifice and female infanticide were widely practised. Each Arab tribe or clan had its own gods and worshipped idols or natural features in its desert sanctuaries (*harams*).

The most important of these was the House of God (*Ka'bah*), located in Mecca itself. When Muhammad was a young man it contained 360 pagan idols, worshipped by dozens of separate tribes and clans. His clan, the Hashemites, had the honour of guarding it, through tradition which held that the monument had been rebuilt by their ancestors Ibrahim and Isma'il after the original – believed to have been built by Adam at the beginning of time – had fallen into disrepair.

In its narrowest sense the whole of Muhammad's mission can be summed up by Allah's Qur'anic command to 'Purify my House [The *Ka'bah*]' (2:125), by smashing the pagan idols within and revealing its true purpose – the worship of Allah alone. And when he began to preach the need to 'purify' the *Ka'bah* his activities led to bitter civil war.

But before this Muhammad had begun to receive Allah's final message to mankind in the form of the Qur'an through miraculous revelations which did not come until he was – by the standards of the time – already an old man.

THE QUR'AN

Muhammad received his first revelation during the month of *Ramadan* in the year AD 610 when he was about forty years old. He was engaged in one of his regular periods of solitary meditation in a cave known as Hira near the top of Mount Jabal Nur, near Mecca, when he received a visitation from the Archangel Gabriel (*Jibreel*).

Muhammad had experienced religious visions before, but this was quite different. *Jibreel* commanded him to 'Recite in the name of your Lord', and the Prophet lost control of himself and, Muslims believe, began to speak the actual words of Allah.

In the 23 remaining years of his life Muhammad received a total of 114 separate revelations which were compiled as the Qur'an (the Arabic for 'recitation') after his death. Muhammad was illiterate so he would repeat each revelation afterwards. Some were written down on whatever was available, from parchment to palm leaves and animals bones, but the majority, in the tradition of the times, were memorised.

A year after Muhammad's death they were collected together by his secretary, Zayd, under the supervision of a committee, shown to many of the Prophet's companions, and agreed to be accurate.

But by about thirty years after his death a number of different versions were circulating and being recited, so a definitive 'canonical' version was issued and sent to the four main Islamic cities of Basra, Damascus, Kufh and Medina. Two of these original copies still exist today. One is in Tashkent in Uzbekistan and the other is in the Topkapi palace in Istanbul, Turkey.

The text is divided into 114 *surahs*, each containing the words of one revelation. The number of verses, or *ayas*, varies from three to 286 and totals 6,239. Each has a title, and 86 have sub-headings indicating they were received in Mecca, whilst another 28 were received in Medina. The Meccan *surahs* are shorter, more mystical and warn about the dangers of paganism. The Medinan *surahs* are in general longer and deal in great detail with aspects of Allah's law such as the rules for declaring war, accepting converts, divorce proceedings and the mandatory punishments for various crimes.

The structure of the Qur'an is unusual and, apparently, illogical. In general the longer Medinan *surahs*, given last, are at the front of the Book and the shorter Meccan *surahs*, the earliest, at the back.

There is no logical explanation for their order but at the same time Western scholars, attempting to reorganise them on this basis, have found that no other order works without splitting the *surahs* up into scattered verses. Sunni Muslims hold that the order was dictated by *Jibreel* to give the Qur'an an esoteric inner meaning reflecting the Divine rather than human order of things.

Acceptance of every word of the Qur'an as the literal word of Allah is a binding obligation on all Muslims. The idea that Muhammad (or any other human or spirit) was the author of the Qur'an, or any part of it, is rejected absolutely.

At the heart of the Qur'an is the simple, repetitive warning that mankind must renounce paganism, accept Allah as the One God of all mankind and live according to His laws. This message is directly addressed to the pagans, Jews and Christians of Mecca, amongst whom Muhammad lived, complete with threats of dire consequences if they failed to mend their polytheistic ways. The first revelation received by Muhammad (by tradition, *surah* 96) deals with this very theme.

In *surah* 96 Allah describes an unnamed pagan Lord who has prevented his servants from praying to Him and calls on them to take up arms. 'Does he not know that Allah does see?' the *surah* asks. 'Nay! if he desist not, We would certainly smite his forehead, A lying, sinful forehead. Then let him summon his council, We too would summon the braves of the army. Nay! Obey him not, and make obeisance and draw nigh to Allah' (96:14–19).

In another early revelation Allah openly threatens Muhammad's brother-in-law Abu Lahab, who, as head of his

Hashemite clan, had disowned Muhammad and annulled the marriage between his son and Muhammad's daughter Fatima. Allah also shows himself to be equally angry with Abu Lahab's wife, who had ridiculed the idea of Muhammad's Prophethood: 'Perdition overtake both hands of Abu Lahab, and he will perish. His wealth and what he earns will not avail him. He shall soon burn in the fire that flames, And his wife, the bearer of fuel, Upon her neck a halter of strongly twisted rope' (111:1–5).

A sceptic might think the Allah revealed in *surah* like this is too suspiciously spiteful and parochial to indeed be the God of all mankind. But Muslims still remain absolutely adamant that Muhammad had no role in writing a *surah* such as this.

The main argument used to defend the Divine authorship of the Qur'an is the incomparable quality of the writing. Much of it is composed in rhyming Arabic and the language is particularly beautiful and graceful. The lengthy *surah* 81 is held up as an example of absolute mastery of the classical Arabic poetical style and does not resemble anything which could have been composed by anyone with Muhammad's rudimentary education.

The *surahs* were given in Arabic and, since it would be a sin to alter the word of Allah, Arabic remains the sacred language of Islam. Non-Arabic-speaking Muslims can use translations but the Qur'an is so important to them that many learn Arabic just so they can read it in its original form.

Muslims and non-believers alike agree that the full power and beauty of its writing can only be appreciated in the original. But for Muslims it goes further than that. Translations can only be 'interpretations' which cannot truly say what is said in Arabic. The combination of the words and rhythms in the original language – the way the Qur'an sounds when recited – is also an important part of its power.

Muslims think of the Qur'an as a complete philosophy, a comprehensive description of the universe and the entirety of the law by which mankind must live. The longer and later Medinan *surahs* stress Allah's merciful nature more fully, with extensive friendly practical advice on personal and family matters.

The Qur'an is also the focus of Islamic art. Many individual copies of the Book are major works of art in their own right – with sublime Arabic calligraphy on superb hand-made paper, and high quality decorative leather and metalwork. Figurative art is forbidden by classical Islam, especially the creation of images of Allah and the Prophets, and the astonishingly fine decorative art found in many mosques is largely based on Arabic calligraphy, woven into patterns repeating passages from the Book.

Even the most sceptical non-believer, Muslims insist, is forced to admit that the Qur'an is a book of immense beauty and importance – not least because it has now almost certainly become the most widely read and memorised book in the world. The preface to one of the most widely available Qur'an in English, the Tahrike Tarsile translation, puts it like this: 'The Qur'an's miracle lies in its ability to offer at least something to non-believers and everything to believers.'

Learning large parts of the Qur'an by heart is an important part of Muslim religious devotion and children start memorising it at an early age. In many Muslim countries learning the Qur'an by heart forms the basic curriculum of primary school education. Muslims who memorise its contents in their entirety are given the honourable title of *al-hafiz*.

THE DAWN OF ISLAM

After receiving the first *surah* of the Qur'an, Muhammad acted with enormous caution. He realised the pagan Quraysh rulers of Mecca, to whom the blood-curdling threats of the early revelations were directly addressed, would eventually oppose him by force, so for three years he preached privately to the immediate members of his own family. According to tradition his wife Khadijah was the first to accept his Prophethood, followed by his cousin 'Ali and servant Zayd.

Islam first came to the attention of the Quraysh in either 611 or 612 when Muhammad began preaching to the Hashemite keepers of the *Ka'bah*. The Quraysh and some Hashemite elders denounced him as mad, but no action was taken.

The Quraysh's wealth was based on the dozens of pagan cults who used the *Ka'bah* as their central shrine. They sold idols and Mecca's position as a trading city was largely based on contacts made with the visiting tribes. New religions were welcomed as good for business. At first Islam was seen as just another money-making cult and Muhammad was encouraged to use the *Ka'bah* alongside the others in a spirit of fair play and toleration.

But in 613 Muhammad began preaching to the public at large, rejecting all other religions, demanding the removal of idols from the *Ka'bah* and therefore threatening trade. As Quraysh hostility grew Muhammad showed himself to be a skilful politician as well as a learned theologian.

Steadily he gathered around him the elders of minor clans and middle-ranking merchants through preaching a return to the religion of Ibrahim. Whilst the Quraysh continued to ridicule him, calling him a madman and an impostor, Muhammad remained protected by the complex laws of pagan religious toleration, tribal kinship and blood feud and they were reluctant to act against him.

The confrontation with the Quraysh began in 616. Having fully converted some of the smaller Meccan clans and many individual Christians and Jews, Muhammad began to use his position as one of the Hashemite keepers of the *Ka'bah* to preach to pagan Arabian tribesmen as they arrived to worship in its precincts. The other Quraysh tribes now moved to silence him. Their first offer was to make him King of Mecca if he stopped preaching. When he refused they punished him by boycotting merchants belonging to his Hashemite clan.

This caused some of the Hashemite elders to turn against Muhammad and his followers. Some were forced into brief exile in Christian Abyssinia (modern Ethiopia), where the Emperor, Negus, attempted to convert the Muslims to Christianity, but failed.

Negus was nevertheless impressed by their honesty and sincerity. According to tradition, when the Muslims described how the Quraysh had defiled the *Ka'bah* he wept until his beard was soaked and promised not to help the Quraysh if the Muslims attempted to overthrow pagan rule.

THE NIGHT JOURNEY

In 619 Muhammad and the Hashemites arrived at a tactical compromise which lifted the trade boycott and allowed him to return to Mecca. It was also at about this time that Muhammad received one of his most remarkable revelations – the Night Journey – described in the 17th *surah* and in numerous *hadith* attributed to him.

In the *hadith* Muhammad describes how he was sleeping next to the *Ka'bah* when he was woken by *Jibreel* and told to mount a winged animal 'smaller than a mule but larger than an ass'. The animal took him to the ruined site of the Temple of Solomon in Jerusalem, where all the Prophets – including Adam, Musa, Ibrahim, Ishaq, Isma'il and Jesus (*Isa*) – were assembled. Muhammad said he prayed with all the Prophets and was then asked by *Jibreel* to drink cither wine or milk. He chose milk and was told this was the right path for himself and his followers.

The Angel *Jibreel* then carried him up in the sky and showed him the gates of heaven, where reality begins and ends. Here he received the command from Allah that he and his followers pray fifty times a day, every day. After some discussion with Musa, Muhammad thought this too often and begged Allah to reduce the number to five – a request which Allah, in His mercy, granted. Muhammad then returned to Mecca on the back of his winged beast.

The site of this miraculous happening, which graphically demonstrates the kinship of all Prophetic religions as well as confirming Muhammad as the last Prophet, is now marked by the Dome of the Rock mosque in Jerusalem, Islam's holiest shrine outside Mecca. The Night Journey is also commemorated in the annual festival of the Night of Ascent (*Laylat al-mi'raj*), one of Islam's most important Holy Days.

Following the Night Journey, Muhammad became certain that war with the Quraysh was inevitable and prepared to leave Mecca. He and his followers switched their missionary efforts to the neighbouring, rival city of Medina, 250 miles to the north.

Between 619 and 621 Muhammad converted virtually all the tribal leaders of Medina, many of whom were previously Jews.

With his position greatly strengthened, Muhammad returned to Mecca and began preaching the need to overthrow pagan Quraysh rule.

Outraged by Muhammad's boldness, the Quraysh now demanded his expulsion from the Hashemite clan, which would have removed the protection he enjoyed as one of the keepers of the *Ka'bah* and enabled the Quraysh to execute him without fear of a blood feud amongst the clans.

Fearing for their lives, Muhammad and his followers fled from Mecca into desert exile, arriving in Medina on 16 September 622.

THE *HIRAJ*

Muhammad's flight into exile (known as the *Hiraj*, the Arabic word for 'emigration') is the most significant episode in the Prophet's life apart from the revelations he received which made up the Qur'an.

It marks the point in the Prophecy when Allah demanded not just a reform of the religious life of Mecca, but a total break with it. It also marks the start of *jihad* (Holy War – both spiritual and physical) against the pagan Quraysh and, ultimately, all those oppressing Muslims and opposing by force the spread of Allah's word.

The date of this declaration of war was later chosen as the first year of the Muslim calendar, with 622 the first year of the Age of *Hiraj* (*Anno Hijarae* – AH).

By this time most of Medina's population regarded themselves as his followers. Many, in addition, had signed military treaties with his followers in Mecca promising military aid. They now eagerly awaited Muhammad's declaration of war. But instead, after receiving fresh revelations, he decided to first convert the nomadic Bedouins in the surrounding desert.

Muhammad was now following the classical pattern of Arab politics and warfare, based on short-lived confederations of nomadic tribes united around a specific military objective and rewarded afterwards by the fair division of booty.

These confederations, often brought into being by a charismatic figure such as Muhammad, developed quickly. The difficulty was in uniting the first two or three tribes. After that united tribes had such a military advantage the others were forced to join or face destruction.

Between 622 and 628 Muhammad set in motion the biggest tribal avalanche Arabia had ever seen. The tribal chieftains (*shayks*) rapidly converted to Islam and joined Muhammad's army. The process was helped by Islam, being an entirely new religion free from the feuding associations of both the localised pagan cults and the 'foreign' monotheist doctrines of Judaism and Christianity.

Muhammad showed himself to be a brilliant military leader in early skirmishes with the Quraysh and this, along with further revelations promising Allah's support and certain victory, is likely to have persuaded yet more *shayks* to join.

In just six years Muhammad assembled an army of 10,000 Arabs – a huge force for those times – and marched with the people of Medina against Mecca. The force was so overwhelming the city was taken without resistance.

Muhammad issued a general amnesty to the Quraysh and urged them, without pressure, to convert to Islam, which they slowly did. The conquest of Mecca also gave him control of the *Ka'bah* and he resumed his preaching to pagan pilgrims as they visited the shrine. Conversion was rapid and only nine months after the occupation of Mecca his army had grown to 30,000.

Muhammad's next move was a great expedition to Tabuk, on the trade route to the wealthy north-western Arabian territory of Syria, where Damascus had been Mecca's main rival as the predominant Arabic trading and cultural centre. More clans and tribes were converted on the way, whilst settlements of Jews and Christians were offered 'protected minorities' *Dhimmi* status so long as they did not oppose Islam.

Muhammad died at Mecca on 8 June AH 11 and AD 632. Although Syria, Palestine and north Arabia had not been subjugated, at his death he was the greatest military leader the Arabs had ever known. The basis for Arab–Islamic domination of the whole of the Middle East in the centuries that followed had been firmly laid.

However, even before Muhammad's death, there was unease amongst his original followers in Mecca that the religion might easily be corrupted by rapid growth and worldly success. Satan had been defeated on the battlefield, but might he not now work within the religion, as he had done many times before, to turn it into an idol-worshipping mockery?

4. THE FIVE PILLARS OF ISLAM

Any person may become a Muslim by sincerely accepting Islam's basic 'creed': 'there is no god but Allah; Muhammad is the messenger of Allah'. This creed is a contracted form of all the core beliefs of Islam, known collectively by the Arabic title *shahada* ('witness').

But to remain a Muslim they must then accept four obligatory duties, known collectively as the *ibadah*, the Arabic word for 'state of submission', sometimes translated as 'holy slavery'.

The obligations of the *ibadah* were revealed to Muhammad during his period of exile and warfare and clarified by further revelations when he was ruler of Mecca and Medina.

The basic function of the *ibadah*, then as now, is to discipline followers for the purpose of spreading the religion of Islam and weeding out hypocrites and 'lukewarm' converts. The obligations are arduous, and the practical effect is to force the believer to build his entire social and business life around devotion to the religion.

The *ibadah* consists of: ritual prayer five times a day, every day (*salat*); payment of a tax for relief of Muslim poor (*zakat*); fasting for the entire month of *Ramadan* (*sawm*); and pilgrimage to the *Ka'bah* and other holy places of Mecca (*hajj*).

Together the *shahada* and *ibadah* are known as the Five Pillars of Islam. Muslims may disagree over some of the finer points of Islamic law, or the significance of events in Muslim history. But the entire body of believers accept the Five Pillars in their entirety. They must be rigorously observed by Muslims to avoid being sent to hell on the Day of Judgement.

THE CREED (*SHAHADA*)

The simplest form of Islam's creed, the *shahada*, is recited in Arabic as: '*la ilaha illa allah; Muhammadon rasul Allah*' (There is no god but Allah; Muhammad is the messenger of Allah). This phrase, known as *kalima*, must be recited in the presence of two witnesses to be accepted into the body of the religion. Thereafter it is recited during prayers, various religious ceremonies and whenever Islam is challenged by non-believers.

The first half of *kalima* – 'There is no god but Allah' – is known as *tawheed* (the unity). This is by far the most important Muslim article of faith and denial. The second half – 'Muhammad is the messenger of Allah' – is known as *risallah* (acceptance of Prophethood). It implies acceptance of Muhammad and all the Prophets as infallible messengers of Allah.

But the *shahada* does not stop at *kalima*. Acceptance of *shahada* involves unquestioning acceptance of seven articles of faith – *tawheed*, *risallah*, and five others: belief in angels (*mala'ikah*); belief in the infallibility of the Qur'an and other Prophetic books such as parts of the Bible (*kutubullah*); belief in the Day of Judgement (*yawmuddin*); acceptance of predestination of worldly affairs by Allah (*al-qadr*); and faith in life after death (*akhriah*).

Acceptance of all seven beliefs of the *shahada* without question is the first and central obligation of the Five Pillars of Islam. Denial of any part of the *shahada* amounts to the crime of apostophy (reversion from Islam), punishable under Qur'anic law, in extreme circumstances, by death.

Denial of the *shahada* by a sincere Christian or Jew may be forgivable on the Day of Judgement, but the open denial by a Muslim will certainly lead, as well as punishment in this life, to eternal damnation in the hereafter.

THE UNITY (*TAWHEED*)

Tawheed is the belief in the oneness and unity of Allah. Although it is summarised as 'there is no god but Allah', the phrase has far greater significance than the literal translation implies. 'Allah is greater than anything else, or anything which can possibly be imagined' would be closer to the real meaning of *tawheed*.

The concept is expressed by Allah Himself in the Qur'an as: 'Say: He, Allah, is One. Allah is He on Whom all depend. He begets not, nor is He begotten. And none is like Him' (112:1–4).

Comparing Allah to other gods or humans claiming to represent Him is again rejected by Muslims as the unforgivable sin of *shirk*. The importance given to the sin of *shirk* originates in the mission of Muhammad (and Muslims would say all the Prophets) to the pagans, known as 'The Associators' (*mushrikun*).

ACCEPTANCE OF PROPHETHOOD (*RISALLAH*)

All Muslims must accept that Muhammad and all the other Prophets were chosen by Allah to deliver His literal word to all mankind. Their central mission was to lead humans back from their degeneration into paganism to the 'true path' given to the first Prophet, Adam, at the beginning of time.

Muhammad in turn, according to *hadith*, said he was the last of the 124,000 Prophets, all of whom gave the same basic message of *tawheed* to all the nations in their own languages.

The idea that Muhammad was the final Prophet, or 'The Seal of the Prophecy', is central to Islam, underlining its claim to be the true version of Judaism and Christianity. Allah himself confirmed Muhammad as the last Prophet in *surah 5* (by tradition the last revelation) which states: 'This day I have perfected your religion for you, completed my favour upon you and have chosen for you Islam as your way of life' (5:3).

But Muslims are not permitted to worship Muhammad, or any other Prophet, as Divine or godlike as this would be the sin of *shirk*. The common Western description of Islam as

Muhammadanism (probably a confusion with Christianity or Buddhism which are both named after their founders) is an absurdity.

ANGELS AND SATAN (*MALA'IKAH*)

In common with classical Christianity and Judaism, Islam teaches that all mortals (animals as well as humans) are a combination of 'clay' (*hayula*) – tangible but lifeless physical material and 'spirit' (*jinn*) – the intangible, immortal soul which brings the 'clay' to life.

Spirits ('genies' or *jinn* in Arabic) existed as Divine light (*Nur*) before the material world and mankind came into being and the first man, Adam, was fashioned from clay by Allah. But he only came to life when he was invested with a spirit. After the creation of the human race those *jinn* which were not given human form became angels.

Both men and angels were created by Allah to serve Him but, apart from angels not taking human form, there is another important difference between them. Whilst Adam and his offspring were given the freedom to obey or disobey Allah, reaping the appropriate reward or punishment on the Day of Judgement, angels have no free will and are incapable of sin. They can only do Allah's bidding.

Allah has an army of billions of angels – at least one for every human – and His omnipotence is expressed through them.

The angels are arranged in an aristocratic hierarchy with the Archangel Gabriel (*Jibreel*) at the top. All have specific functions, some move the sun and moon around the sky, others deliver thunderbolts that destroy wicked tribes. The angel Israfil has the job of sounding the trumpet which will herald the Day of Judgement whilst the angel Isra'il, the angel of death, sees to it that we die at the time allotted in Allah's plans.

A whole host of angels known as the Honest Recorders (*Kiraman Katibin*) have been given the job of accurately recording the thoughts, words and actions of every man, woman and child on earth. In this way Allah is able to know what every mortal is thinking or doing at any time. The constant presence of Allah's angels is an important part of any Muslim's thinking and controls his behaviour.

Allah cannot allow any man to talk to Him directly or to see His form. Inevitably they would compare Him with something or somebody else – the sin of *shirk*. So instead He has spoken to Prophets through angels who are incapable of sin or error and can be relied upon to deliver His words completely and truthfully. The status of a Prophet can usually be judged by the rank of angel who summons a Prophet to receive revelations. Ibrahim, Jesus (*Isa*) and Muhammad, for example, were spoken to through Archangel *Jibreel* himself.

SATAN (*IBLIS*) – THE FALLEN ANGEL

The only angel ever to disobey Allah is Satan. According to tradition, Satan was the King of the Angels at the time Allah created Adam. But he became jealous of Adam, and refused to serve mankind as Allah had commanded. *Surah* 18 reports: 'And when We said to the angels: Make obeisance to Adam; they made obeisance but Satan [did not].' Then Satan said: 'What! would you then take [Adam] and his offspring for friends rather than me, and they are your enemies?' (18:50).

After this argument Satan was banished from heaven and *Jibreel* replaced him as Archangel. Satan was bitter about this turn of events and decided to destroy mankind by leading it away from Allah towards paganism and eternal damnation.

Satan misleads men by whispering lies designed to make them believe that they are equal to Allah or can hide their thoughts and sins from Him. He attempts to lead Muslims into pagan ways and encourages them to break the Qur'anic law and corrupt Islam from within.

According to both the Qur'an and *hadith*, the only protection against the work of Satan is constant remembrance of Allah and the word of the Qur'an. The need to protect the mind against Satan is one reason why Muslims attempt to learn the Qur'an by heart and pray so frequently. A person is only really safe from Satanic misguidance when his mind is fully preoccupied with the worship of Allah.

ALLAH'S BOOKS (*KUTUBULLAH*)

In addition to the Qur'an, which Muslim scholars have 'proved' to be the infallible and literal word of Allah, the *shahada* requires Muslims to accept the basic truth of the Jewish Torah (*Tawrat*) given to Moses (*Musa*); the book of Psalms (*Zabur*) given to David (*Dawud*); and the Gospel (*Injil*) given to Jesus (*Isa*).

The Qur'an mentions these three books as being the authentic word of Allah, but warns that errors (either innocent mistakes or Satanic inventions) have been introduced into them. Muslims maintain that the Qur'an is the only authentic, unchanged and comprehensive version of Allah's word and that it supersedes all the others. They point out that the Bible was altered in translation from Hebrew or Aramaic to Greek, and that words authored by mortals were mixed with those of Allah, committing the sin of *shirk* and rendering most of the book worthless. Nevertheless, they accept the Biblical books of the Torah as authentic, though these too – especially the Book of Genesis – are said to contain errors.

According to Muslims, Genesis levels several minor gratuitous insults at various Prophets (Nuh, for example, is said to have been a drunkard) and contains one very serious error. This is Genesis' assertion that Ibrahim proposed to slaughter his son Ishaq (father of the Jewish nation) and not Isma'il (father of the Arab nation) until he was prevented from so doing by merciful Allah. This criticism, made in the Qur'an, underpins Islam's insistence that Allah is the God of all mankind and not just of the Jews.

Islam accepts most of the Christian Gospel as true but, as it was composed by Jesus' (*Isa*'s) followers long after his death, where the Gospel and the Qur'an disagree the Qur'an, as the literal word of Allah, must be taken before the Gospel. The main disagreement between the two books concerns Jesus' (*Isa*'s) resurrection, with the fourth *surah* of the Qur'an denying that the event took place.

THE DAY OF JUDGEMENT (*YAWMUDDIN*)

Just as Allah created the universe and everything within it with the simple command 'Be!', He will bring it to an end when He so desires. The end of the world is described in apocalyptic terms in *surahs* 81 and 82 of the Qur'an which tell how the sun and the stars are extinguished, the mountains crumble and great fires sweep the earth.

On the Day of Judgement the graves will be opened. Those who were sinful on earth will already have been suffering in the fires of hell, but they may now be saved if they are prepared to sincerely repent. But those who have committed the sin of *shirk* will remain beyond salvation because they have refused to recognise the existence of Allah and His mercy.

Surah 82 says: 'And when the graves are laid open . . . Most surely the righteous are in bliss, And most surely the wicked are in burning fire, They shall enter it on the Day of Judgement. And they shall by no means be absent from it. And what will make you realise what the Day of Judgement is? . . . The day on which no soul shall control anything for [another] soul; and the command on that day shall be entirely Allah's' (82:4–19).

The timing of the Day of Judgement, or the signs indicating its imminent arrival, are not mentioned in the Qur'an. But there is a wealth of *hadith* on the subject, much of it attributed to Muhammad himself. And it seems very likely he believed the Day of Judgement would follow relatively shortly after his death. This follows from his belief that he was Shiloh, the first and last non-Jewish Prophet in the line of Ibrahim, whose coming is foretold in the book of Genesis as one of the signs that the world is about to end.

Muhammad probably also shared the view, prevalent amongst Christian and Jewish scholars during his time, that the world was about 5,500 years old and would end before the 6,000th year – about AD 1100. Even if he himself did not believe this, many of the earliest Muslim scholars – such as ibn Ishaq, a learned former Christian monk and his first 'official' biographer – certainly did.

The *hadith* describe the events immediately prior to the end of the world in stirring and enormous detail. The first sign will be the splintering of Islam in a great many rival sects. Qur'anic law (the *shari'ah*) will be ignored or overthrown. Brutal civil wars will rage throughout the world and the degree of savagery and torture will be so great the living will envy the dead.

Allah will send not a Prophet but the *Mahdi* (the 'chosen one', a Messiah or political ruler) to restore order. *Hadith* attributed to Muhammad describe the *Mahdi* as 'one of my stock and he will be of broad forehead and aquiline of nose'. The *Mahdi* will proclaim himself at Mecca and then lead an army of the faithful to Jerusalem, where he will establish himself as ruler of the world and restore order, peace, justice and Qur'anic law.

The *Mahdi*'s rule, however, will last for less than a decade before the people desert him for the anti-Christ (impostor-Messiah), a figure clearly identifiable as he will have only one eye.

The anti-Christ will be enormously popular because he will legalise sin, provide food and material comfort, heal the sick and perform other pseudo-miracles to convince the people they have no need of Allah. Islam will be reduced to a rump of core believers – 'a body of my people will not cease to fight for the Truth', says Muhammad, 'Islam began in exile and it shall end in exile.'

But, just as the anti-Christ is about to destroy this last group of True Believers, the resurrected Jesus (*Isa*) will descend to earth in armour and kill the anti-Christ in battle at the town of Armageddon in Palestine. *Isa* will then rule Earth gloriously. There will be peace and plenty for all. Amongst his edicts *Isa* will order the removal of crosses from the Christian churches.

But this golden age will eventually give way to the physical destruction of the Earth, as described in *surah* 81, the opening of the graves and the Day of Judgement.

Early Muslim scholars confidently expected this sequence of events to begin around the year AD 1100 (the 6,000th year of creation according to tradition). As a result the preceding century was marked by fanaticism, redoubled *jihad* and proclamation of *Mahdi* status by rival Muslim rulers.

When the world did not end Islam was thrown into a theological crisis which speeded up the division of the formerly united Islamic Empire into rival sects and states, many of them led by rulers claiming to be the *Mahdi*.

Throughout the subsequent history of Islam various rulers and scholars have continued to do this and Muslims still believe that the sequence of events will take place. They believe in it literally, but at the same time know it will be modified for the modern context. Jesus in armour, for example, could be a tank division.

Muhammad Ahmad ibn 'Abd Allah (died 1885), the Sudanese leader who defeated the British General Gordon at Khartoum, is probably the best-known self-proclaimed *Mahdi* in recent history. It is also clear that post-war Muslim leaders such as Abdul Nasser of Egypt, Ayatollah Khomeini of Iran and Colonel al-Qaddafi of Libya have often been regarded as *Mahdi* by more fanatical followers and, in general, have done little to dispel this myth.

Because of the importance of Jerusalem in the story of the end of the world the current Arab–Israeli conflict over control of the city has, in the eyes of many Muslims, apocalyptic significance. It explains, to a very large degree, the bitter intransigence of Muslim states towards Israel.

LIFE AFTER DEATH (*AKHIRAH*)

The Muslim Paradise and Muslim hell are tangible domains, described at length throughout the Qur'an. Paradise is a state of bliss, peace and tranquillity where men are free from earthly concerns and where longed-for comforts – possibly intended to mean sacrifices made whilst on earth such as not drinking alcohol – may be enjoyed at last. Hell is full of fire and the torture of facing eternity without the knowledge of Allah and His mercy.

Those pious Muslims who die as martyrs in the defence of Islam are especially blessed. According to *surah* 2 of the Qur'an Islamic martyrs do not die. Instead, their souls remain alive in a state of bliss until the Day of Judgement when they will be admitted to Paradise without difficulty.

PREDESTINATION (*AL-QADR*)

Muslims must accept that Allah has already decided their fate in advance. There is nothing they can do to alter it. Islam teaches that Allah created the universe with a single command – 'Be!' His creation is not chaotic, but it has an inner

order and purpose beyond human understanding or questioning. All nature is under the command of Allah, as is every
aspect of human life. A Muslim attempts to live his life as
ordered by Allah, accepting His control of everything he does
at every moment of his life.

At the same time Allah has given men free will and the
ability to disobey Him if they choose to. The Qur'an is quite
clear that Allah expects many people to disobey Him or to be
led astray by Satan into false religions.

The Qur'an is equally clear that no Muslim can convert an
unbeliever to Islam by force. So, if a person chooses to ignore
the word of Allah and face eternal damnation, that is their
right.

Predestination is the last of seven articles of the *shahada*
together forming the first of the 'Five Pillars'. Everything else
in the Qur'an relates to the laws (the *shari'ah*) which Muslims
must follow in order to enjoy a successful, happy and holy life
leading to salvation after the Day of Judgement.

The most important of these laws – the four obligations of
the *ibadah* – form the remaining four of the Five Pillars.

OBLIGATORY PRAYER (*SALAT*)

According to the rules of *ibadah*, *salat* prayers must be offered
five times each day, every day – before sunrise (*as-subh*), noon
(*az-zuhr*), mid-afternoon (*al-asr*), immediately after sunset
(*al-maghreb*), and before midnight (*al-isha*).

Whenever possible a Muslim must offer prayers in congregation at the mosque, where women and men pray separately,
but these congregational prayers are only obligatory on
Friday at noon. Otherwise Muslims may pray on their own,
always facing in the direction of Mecca, on any clean
surface.

In Sunni Islam congregational prayers are led by any
member of the congregation well versed in the Qur'an and
beyond moral reproach. What is preached will be decided by
the mosque's own Imam (resident Qur'anic scholar) except in
Islamic monarchies such as Saudi Arabia and Morocco where
the lesson may be decided centrally by state officials.

In Shi'ite Islam prayers are led by either the Imam (who has a broader political and leadership function than a Sunni Imam) or a mullah – a Shi'ite priest-teacher.

THE *MASJID* AND MOSQUE

The word 'mosque' is derived from the Arabic term *masjid* ('place of prostration') where *salat* is offered to Allah in congregation.

The simplest *masjid*s are desert prayer grounds (*musalla*) consisting of a small square marked off by pegs with stones indicating the direction of the *Ka'bah* of Mecca. This is perfectly adequate for offering *salat* so long as it is maintained in a state of ritual purity with all traces of dirt – especially blood, urine, excrement, wine or animal fat – painstakingly removed.

Any structure or space may be used as long as the rules of ritual purity are observed. In Britain the first *masjid*s used by immigrant Muslims from the Indian sub-continent were often in disused cinemas, warehouses or large Victorian houses.

The magnificent mosque architecture surrounding *masjid*s in many Muslim countries is entirely optional in strictly theological terms. No building regulations appear in the Qur'an. Mosque architecture is nevertheless sacred in origin because it follows the pattern of the first mosque built by Muhammad and his companions around their *masjid* in Medina.

Mosques built according to the Muhammadan pattern enclose the *masjid* within either a large hall or open courtyard depending on weather conditions. The central piece of architecture is the *mihrab*, an arch which indicates the direction of the *Ka'bah* of Mecca. Usually the *mihrab* is protected by a dome originally copied from the Orthodox Christian Church architecture of Byzantium.

The stunningly beautiful early Arabian mosques, dating from the Golden Age of Baghdad, follow this simple design of courtyard and dome. The best example of early mosque architecture is the astonishing seventh-century AD Dome of the Rock mosque in Jerusalem which marks the site of the desecrated Temple of Solomon and Muhammad's miraculous Night Journey to the gates of Paradise.

The distinctive minarets – tall, thin towers used to call the faithful to prayer – are a later, Ottoman Turkish invention. The Ottomans also began the tradition of placing crescents on the tops of domes and minarets to indicate the direction of Mecca.

The crescent is a symbolic reminder that mortal life, like the phases of the moon, comes and goes within an allotted time. It usually appears above three or five spheres representing descending levels of reality. At the top is Allah, the absolute reality, whilst the bottom sphere represents the lowest level of reality – the physical world as experienced by humans.

The great mosques of Arabia and Persia are decorated with quotations from the Qur'an in Arabic or Persian with the flowing calligraphy woven into delicate and repetitive patterns often lavishly adorned with gold and bright-blue lapis tiles. In other parts of the world mosques incorporate local architectural traditions. The great Djenna mosque of Mali, central Africa, is square and made from dried mud and tree trunks. The mosques and Islamic architecture of Mogul India, including the Taj Mahal, reflect Hindu influences.

However the mosque is decorated, its design is dominated by the need for cleansing and purification before prayer. All mosques, however humble, have a plentiful supply of clean, drinkable water and this can make them important social institutions in many parts of the Third World.

The more splendid mosques often have fountains and streams running through beautiful gardens adjacent to the *masjid*. Muhammad himself said that the mosque should be a beautiful place: 'between my house and my pulpit is a garden of the gardens of Paradise'.

CALL TO PRAYERS (*ADHAN*)

Before each prayer session a mosque official known as the Muezzin (caller) chants the call to prayer (*adhan*) from the tallest point of the mosque, usually the minaret. The *adhan* is made with a series of rhythmic Arabic phrases devised by Muhammad himself. These days the *adhan* is often a tape recording broadcast through loud-speakers.

The *adhan* begins with the phrase 'Allah is the greatest' ('*Allah akbar*') which is repeated four times. This is followed by four more phrases – 'I bear witness that there is no god but Allah; I bear witness that Muhammad is Allah's messenger; rush to prayer; rush to success; Allah is the greatest' – each of which is repeated twice.

The *adhan* ends with the phrase: 'There is no god but Allah' – the *tawheed* or central dogma of the faith. *Adhan* for the dawn prayer session includes the phrase: 'Prayer is better than sleep' between 'rush to success' and 'Allah is the greatest'.

RITUAL WASHING (*WUDU*)

Elaborate ritual washing (*wudu*) must take place before prayers, and most mosques are equipped with baths and clean, drinkable water which must, according to custom, be given free to all comers. The Qur'an specifies the way in which a Muslim must wash to remove all sacrilegious uncleanliness. Any traces of urine, excrement, blood or unclean substances such as wine or the blood or fat of animals must be removed from the body and clothes.

Before using the water the Muslim must first sniff it three times to ensure it contains none of the unclean substances. He must then wash his arms up to his elbows and his feet up to his ankles, rinse out his mouth, wash his ears and pass wet fingers three times through his hair and across the back of his neck. If the Muslim has had sex he or she must wash the entire body before the next prayer session.

Wudu becomes invalid if the Muslim visits the toilet, passes wind, burps, falls asleep or bleeds from a wound between the act of washing and praying. If any of these things happen the process must be repeated.

Then, facing the *Ka'bah* in Mecca, he assumes the *qiyan* (standing) position, with head bowed and hands folded in front of him. At the direction of the prayer leader he bows forward in an L-shape, the *ruku*, keeping the legs and back straight.

He then resumes *qiyan* before prostrating himself (*sajda*) with his legs tucked under his body and his forehead on the ground. (Shi'ite Muslims rest their foreheads on small cakes of

dried mud gathered during pilgrimage to Karbala, the site of
the martyrdom of Husayn – the second Shi'ite Imam – in Iraq.)

Each cycle of standing, bowing and prostration is known as
a *ra'kah* and the number of *ra'kahs* varies between two and
four according to the time of day.

POOR TAX (*ZAKAT*)

The Qur'an specifies that all Muslims who live above subsis-
tence level must pay *zakat*, the poor tax for the relief of poorer
Muslims. *Zakat* is not charity, but the rightful and legal claim
of the poor against the rich. Charity, which is also an
obligation placed on the rich by Islam, must be paid in
addition, according to conscience.

As *zakat* is an annual wealth tax, rather than income tax, it
is not payable unless a Muslim has amassed some capital. The
scale of payments, fixed by *hadith*, varies according to the type
of property held, starting with a basic rate of one fortieth (2.5
per cent) of the individual's total capital, including savings,
jewels and land.

In oil-rich Muslim countries like Saudi Arabia individual
liability for *zakat* can in theory be enormous. But the actual
amount paid may be purely nominal as the Qur'an specifically
forbids the establishment of a bureaucracy to collect the tax.
Instead the money must be paid out of a sense of duty, on pain
of punishment in the afterlife. Even in oil-rich Brunei – where
zakat is the only tax – there is no system of accounting.

Although rampant inequality exists in many Islamic nations,
in theory the religion is wedded to egalitarianism – a commitment that began with Muhammad's warnings to the rich and
worldly merchants of Mecca. The basic teaching of the Qur'an
is that all worldly wealth is unclean unless it is used in the
service of Allah and Islam and the Book is full of warnings of
the terrible fate awaiting those becoming rich through 'usury'
or failing to share their wealth with other Muslims. One
passage tells of a rich man in hell being burned by white-hot
coinage.

The rich man may only 'purify' his wealth, which he is then
free to enjoy with the blessing of Allah, by paying *zakat*.

FASTING (*SAWM*)

To show obedience to Allah and willingness to forgo the pleasures of this life, every Muslim must fast each year for the whole thirty days of *Ramadan*, the ninth month of the Islamic calendar. This is the month, according to tradition, when Muhammad received the first *surah* of the Qur'an from Allah after being called by the Archangel Gabriel at Hira.

From dawn to dusk Muslims may not eat, drink, smoke or have sex. *Ramadan* builds up to the 'Night of Power' (*Laylat al-qadr*), generally on the 27th day but dependent on the arrival of the new moon. This commemorates the actual day the revelation began. The most devout Muslims spend the last ten days of *Ramadan* in continuous prayer, ending with the Feast of Breaking the Fast ('*Id al-Fitr*), one of the few occasions when Muslims may celebrate and take part in festivities.

Every Muslim who has reached puberty must take part in *sawm* (fasting). There are exemptions at the time for the sick and women nursing newly born babies, but they must make up for any days missed by fasting at other periods throughout the year.

The Qur'an permits all Muslims to rise one hour before dawn and eat a special large breakfast called *suhur* to help them through the day. Some Muslims, especially in Muslim-minority countries like Britain, practise only a limited form of fasting by giving up something like smoking or eating rich foods.

The spread of Islam to lands far north and south of Arabia has caused many practical difficulties for observance of *sawm*. In far northern or southern latitudes it often falls, according to the Muslim lunar calendar, in the summer when the time between dawn (first glow of sunlight) and sunset (last glow of the sun) can be as much as 20 hours. This applies to Britain, and there is much inconclusive debate amongst British Muslims on how to deal with the problem. In the past the requirements of *salat* and *sawm* have been one reason why Islam has been restricted to tropical latitudes, where the times of prayer and fasting do not vary considerably. A Muslim community could not exist within the Arctic Circle without breaking the laws of *salat* and *sawm*.

PILGRIMAGE TO MECCA (HAJJ)

Hajj translates from Arabic as 'visitation of Holy Places' (of Mecca). All Muslims must attempt it at least once during their lifetime. The focus of *hajj* is not Mecca as such, but the Great Mosque which encloses Islam's holiest shrine, the Holy *Ka'bah* (Arabic for 'House of Allah').

The *Ka'bah* is a cube-shaped stone building, believed to have been built at the beginning of time by Adam for the exclusive worship of Allah. The fate of the shrine is symbolically linked to Islam's battle against mankind's repeated reversion from the true religion of Allah-worship into paganism.

In the centuries after Adam's death his offspring became pagan, allowed the *Ka'bah* to fall into disrepair and filled the remains with pagan idols. About 3,500 years ago the Prophet Ibrahim smashed the pagan idols and rebuilt the temple. But by the time of Muhammad's Prophethood the *Ka'bah* had once again degenerated into a pagan shrine. This time Muhammad cleared out the idols and defeated the pagans. And it was here that he first preached Islam, gaining converts from the pagan tribes worshipping there.

To take part in *hajj* Muslim men must be sane, free from serious physical infirmity and – most importantly – able to provide for their dependants whilst they are away. This is one of the main reasons why Muslims fear getting into debt.

Muslim women may take part in *hajj*, subject to various restrictions. During it each must be accompanied by a male chaperon (*mahram*), who must be a man she is legally unable to marry – for example her father or brother. Preparations for *hajj* start in the last days of *Ramadan*, especially after the night of *Laylat al-qadr* (Night of Power), with the process of entering the state of cleanliness and physical and spiritual consecration known as *ihram*.

Before leaving for Mecca pilgrims (*hajji*) pray almost continuously and perform extended versions of elaborate washing rituals (*wudu*) required before prayer. *Hajji* also shave, and cut their hair and nails.

They then don the special *ihram* costume consisting of two unsewn pieces of clean white cloth, one tucked around the waist covering the legs down to the knees and the other wrapped around the shoulders. Both men and women wear sandals rather than shoes, and women in addition wear extra garments entirely covering their legs and face.

Once *hajji* have entered the state of *ihram* they are not allowed to remove their ritual dress, even when sleeping. No Muslim in a state of *ihram* may wear tailored clothes, jewellery or perfume. A male pilgrim may not shave or cut his hair, and no pilgrim is allowed to harvest crops, hunt animals, arrange to be married or have sex even if they are married already.

The pilgrims then make their way to Mecca by any transport or method they choose. Some make epic journeys on foot from faraway Muslim countries like Indonesia and central Africa, but today most fly. Once at Mecca they cannot enter the precincts of the Great Mosque surrounding the *Ka'bah* until the first day of the month of *Dhu al-Hijjah*, two months after *Ramadan*.

On entering the Great Mosque the *hajji* performs a ceremony known as *tawf* – the core ritual of *hajj* – which involves circling the *Ka'bah* seven times anti-clockwise. Most attempt to touch or kiss the 'black stone', about a metre square, which Muhammad himself placed in the wall of the shrine. Numbers are often too great to allow contact with the stone and *hajji* may instead raise their right arm in its direction, keeping it raised.

Men make the first three laps at a jogging pace and walk the last four. After each lap there are ritual declarations of faith and prayers. Women must walk slowly for all seven laps.

Once the *tawf* is completed most *hajji* drink from the *Zamzam* stream which flows through the basement of the Great Mosque, though this is not obligatory. The stream has religious significance, according to *hadith*, as Hagar, the first wife of Ibrahim and her son Isma'il were wandering in Mecca unable to find water. Just as they were about to die of thirst Hagar dug her heel into the ground and Allah caused a spring to come to life. The water gushed so quickly she had to shout '*zam*! *zam*!' the Arabic for 'stop! stop!' – hence the stream's name of *Zamzam*.

The significance of this story for Muslims is that it shows Allah's mercy towards Isma'il, the founder of the Arab nation and direct ancestor of Muhammad. If Allah had allowed Isma'il to die, Muhammad would not have lived and mankind would never have received the final prophecy.

The salvation of Hagar and Isma'il is commemorated by drinking from the *Zamzam* and by *sa'yee*, the second obligatory ritual of the day, during which *hajji* believe they are following the exact path taken by the pair as they searched for water. The *hajji* passes seven times between the nearby peaks of as-Safa and Marwa at an increasing pace, quoting whatever passages they have memorised from the Qur'an.

The Saudi Arabian royal family, which has taken upon itself responsibility for the upkeep of the Holy Places, has considerably modernised the setting for today's age, with a wide, air-conditioned, marble-lined corridor between the two peaks to accommodate the huge numbers of people performing *sa'yee* at any given time.

After *sa'yee* the *hajji* returns to the campsites (*mawaqueets*) outside the precincts of the Great Mosque – which these days includes several five-star hotels as well as the more traditional tents – where they must remain in a state of *ihram* until sunset on the 8th day of the month. How long this is depends on which day they choose to begin *tawf* and *sa'yee*.

They then move to Mina, about eight kilometres east of Mecca, and spend the night at prayer. At sunrise the next day they travel en masse to Mount Arafat, in the hot desert fifteen kilometres east of Mina, for the climax of *hajj*. Most people now travel in buses or private cars along the new ten-lane motorways.

After arriving at Arafat pilgrims spend the afternoon standing in prayer. Up to two million pilgrims of all races and classes can be seen on the slopes of the mountain on this day, rendered anonymous by their *ihram* costume and chanting – truly one of the most remarkable sights in the world.

At sundown the pilgrims return along the motorways and flyovers to Mina to prepare for the feast of sacrifice ('Id al-Adha) on the following day, the most important in the Muslim calendar.

'Id al-Adha celebrates Ibrahim's willingness to sacrifice his own son Isma'il to show obedience to Allah, and Allah's mercy in allowing Ibrahim to substitute a ram thus allowing Isma'il and his offspring (including Muhammad) to live. During *'Id al-Adha* Muslims are required to slaughter a live animal in commemoration and at Mina *hajji* slaughter hundreds of thousands of sheep, camels and cattle in the culmination of their pilgrimage.

At the same time every Muslim in the world, whether taking part in *hajj* or not, is called upon to slaughter an animal in his home for the feast. Sometimes, especially in countries where Muslims are a minority, liberal-minded mosque officials will accept money as a substitute for the ritual slaughter, but this is rare even amongst Muslims in Britain. It is common, however, for British Muslims to preside over the sacrifice at an *halal* (lawful) butcher's shop rather than in the kitchen of their own home.

In India and Indonesia the slaughter of cows is sometimes a cause of strife between Muslims and Hindus, who worship the cow as sacred. And in Mina and Mecca the disposal of the hundreds of thousands of sacrificed carcasses has created a growing public health problem as the number of pilgrims has increased and the number of poor Arabians who used to live off the sacrifices has declined.

Following the feast in Mina, *hajj* ends with the ritual of *ramyee*. Pilgrims throw stones (a ritual form of Muslim execution) at three pillars symbolising Satan which they pass on their way back to Mecca. *Hajji* throw seven stones at each, chanting: 'Allah is the greatest!' (*Allah akbar!*).

In practice these days sheer numbers prevent many *hajji* from getting near enough to take accurate aim, and serious injuries have been caused by overenthusiastic *hajji*, too far away to hit the pillars, throwing stones which land on those closer to the front.

In an attempt to solve overcrowding problems the Saudi Arabian royal family has employed Western architects to build tiered walkways, ten-lane highways and stadiums to ease movement between the various Holy Sites.

This has brought widespread complaints that the Holy Places have now been turned into a nightmare landscape of motorways, flyovers and towering Western-style hotels on the sacred campsites overlooking the *Ka'bah*. This has been coupled with complaints about high prices charged by *hajj* tour operators, sponsored by the Saudi government.

The government is also accused of having too tolerant an attitude to rich Muslims, who perform *hajj* from the comfort of air-conditioned limousines and five-star hotel rooms, paying poorer Muslims to stand in the queues for them.

But, despite these complaints, most *hajji* are profoundly moved by the experience and often return to their communities as truly changed people.

During *hajj* they may also have joined one of the bewildering array of Islamic sects and sub-sects which use it, in the tradition of Muhammad, to preach their version of the true faith. The Shi'ite Muslims (as found in Iran) have been particularly active in this missionary work in recent years and have also attempted to politicise the event by turning *hajji* against the Saudi royal family, whom they regard as usurpers.

DEFENCE OF ISLAM (*JIHAD*)

Shahada, *salat*, *zakat*, *sawm* and *hajj* make up the Five Pillars of Islam. But these obligations are the absolute minimum a Muslim can do in order to serve Allah. The truly pious Muslim takes on many more obligations and, most important, the responsibility of responsibilities, is *jihad*, sometimes described as the 'sixth pillar' of Islam.

The literal translation of *jihad* is 'striving' (to serve Allah), but it is usually translated in the West as 'Holy War' which Muslims agree is a reasonable translation. All Muslims must constantly wage *jihad* to the best of their practical ability. In particular a fellow Muslim attacked for practising Islam must be defended by the rest of the Muslim community.

The duty to participate in *jihad* for the defence of Islam is, according to leading fundamentalist Muslim scholar Sayid Abdul Ala Mawdudi, 'just as much a primary duty of Muslims as daily prayers or fasting. One who *shirks* it is a sinner. His very claim to being a Muslim is doubtful. He is plainly a hypocrite who fails in the test of sincerity and all his *ibadah* (religious observance) and prayers are a sham, a worthless hollow show of devotion.'

5. ISLAMIC LAW – THE *SHARI'AH*

The Islamic concept of law and justice is entirely different from that of the secularised countries of the West. Muslims believe Allah, through the Qur'an, revealed the universal laws that govern not just the affairs of man, but also the very laws of nature.

Any man who disobeys these universal laws will find himself at odds not just with secular authority but also with his own nature and that of the rest of creation. And, since all Muslims must accept that their every action and thought is recorded by Allah's angels, there can be no escaping punishment for disobedience following the Day of Judgement.

The body of detailed Islamic law – the *shari'ah* (Arabic for 'what is prescribed') – is based on the later *surahs* of the Qur'an. The 5th, one of the last to be revealed, is also one of the most important sources of the *shari'ah*. It begins with the injunction: 'O you who believe! fulfil the obligations' (5:1) and ends with the words: 'Allah's is the kingdom of the heavens and the earth and what is in them; and he has power over all things' (5:120).

This *surah* also deals with dietary law and prohibits drinking and gambling, which are linked to pagan rites: 'Liquor and gambling, idols and divining arrows are only a filthy work of Satan; give them up so that you may prosper' (5:90). The same *surah* prescribes the punishment for theft: 'As for the thief, both man and woman, chop off their hands. It is the reward for their own deeds and exemplary punishment from Allah' (5:38).

The first part of the earlier *surah* 24 deals with sexual behaviour and prescribes punishments for adultery and false accusations of adultery: 'As for the fornicatress and the fornicator, flog each of them [giving] a hundred stripes . . . And those who accuse free women then do not bring four witnesses, flog them [giving] eighty stripes, and do not admit any evidence from them ever; and these it is that are the transgressors . . . Allah's curse will be on him if he is a liar' (24:1–7).

Muslims believe that legalistic later *surahs* such as these represent Allah's revelation of the law in its entirety. But it is also accepted that, in some cases, the laws thus revealed are lacking in detail. For example the Qur'an says that Muslims must pray frequently and wash themselves before so doing. But it does not say how often prayers should be offered or the way in which Muslims should wash.

To find these things out a Muslim must turn to *hadith*.

TRADITIONS AND SAYINGS OF THE PROPHET (*HADITH*)

The second source of *shari'ah* law is the collected deeds and sayings of Muhammad and his earliest followers known as *hadith* (Arabic for 'traditional reports or sayings').

The 33rd *surah* says: 'Certainly you have in the Messenger of Allah [Muhammad] an excellent exemplar . . .' (33:21). This is understood by Muslims as endorsement of the infallibility of Muhammad's *hadith*.

The rituals and obligations of the Five Pillars of Islam – including the *shahada* – as well as much of the criminal law originate from *hadith*.

LEGAL CONSENSUS (*IJMA*)

The process of *ijma* is a method of framing laws based on agreement between jurists. *Hadith* has Muhammad saying: 'My community shall never be in agreement in error'. It is a consensus decision which along with *hadith* and the Qur'an legitimises law.

A perfect *ijma* decision is possible, with everybody in agreement, but this position is often difficult to reach because of the lack of previous authorities. *Ijma* therefore usually means that consensus exists amongst the large majority.

ANALOGY (*QIYAS*)

Where legislation is required for social problems not dealt with in sufficient detail in either the Qur'an or *hadith*, Muslim rulers and law-makers must use analogy (*qiyas*) to frame legislation or new religious doctrines. This arises when situations which Muhammad or the Qur'an cannot have foreseen arrive and therefore cannot be dealt with by either the Book or *hadith*.

For example the Qur'an specifically prohibits the consumption of 'wine', but does not mention any other alcoholic drinks. By using *qiyas* Muslim jurists have extended the prohibition to other alcoholic drinks which cropped up later, such as whisky. When Islam was faced with the problem of drug-taking, *qiyas* dealt with it by making it analogous with drinking alcohol.

ISLAMIC JURISPRUDENCE (*FIQH*)

Fiqh is Islamic jurisprudence – the science of Islamic law. It is through *fiqh* that Islam demonstrates how it covers all aspects of life, by including those things which in the West would be considered private and beyond the scope of the legal system – such as style of dress.

Fiqh divides all human behaviour into five categories: forbidden (*haram*); discouraged (*makruh*); neutral (*mubah*); recommended (*mustahabb*) and obligatory (*fard*).

The obligatory (*fard*) category covers the Five Pillars of Islam including mandatory prayer, alms-giving, fasting and so on. These *fard* requirements are legally binding on all Muslims. Failure to carry out a *fard* obligation is both a sin and a crime punishable in *shari'ah* courts.

Forbidden (*haram*) behaviour is also both sinful and criminal. Anything mentioned as unlawful in the Qur'an and Old Testament falls within the *haram* category, including all the prohibitions of the Ten Commandments. In addition, the Qur'an explicitly prohibits the eating of certain food.

No Muslim may eat animals which have died from natural causes or which have not been ritually slaughtered. This ritual slaughter must be carried out by a clean knife cut to the throat and accompanied by a prayer said over the carcass. Only meat produced in this way is lawful (*halal*), everything else is *haram*.

Pig meat is *haram*, however it is produced, as is the meat of any carnivorous animal. A Muslim may not drink blood, eat dried blood, drink alcohol or eat any substance with even a drop of alcohol in it (2:168–173).

The discouraged (*makruh*), recommended (*mustahabb*) and neutral (*mubah*) categories deal mainly with such things as manners, charity, personal habits and social life. The law here is based mainly on the vast literature of *hadith*.

For example Muhammad once said: 'When a man drinks, he should not breathe into the beaker' and this now forms part of the *shari'ah* in the discouraged (*makruh*) category. He also said: 'Allah is polite and likes politeness' and so polite behaviour forms part of the *shari'ah* in the recommended (*mustahabb*) category. There are thousands of such sayings.

Discouraged (*makruh*) behaviour is not sinful but it is criminal and Muslims can be punished in a *shari'ah* court – especially if they deliberately persist with discouraged behaviour.

Much of what would be called civil law in the West is covered by the recommended (*mustahabb*) category of the *shari'ah*. Muslim courts will endeavour to reconcile the parties where there are disagreements but, if they fail, the party failing to follow *mustahabb* behaviour may be punished. Some of the most important *mustahabb*-based laws include those governing funeral rites, marriage and family life.

FUNERAL RITES

Islamic graves are anonymous because the erection of a headstone is seen as a form of idol worship. No coffins are permitted.

The corpse is washed according to the rules of *wudu* and simply wrapped in white sheets (three for a man, five for a woman) before being placed in the ground with feet facing towards the *Ka'bah* in Mecca. There is no elaborate ceremony and only a few short prayers are said over the grave. Islam does not encourage extended periods of mourning.

It is the duty of every Muslim to attempt to say the contracted form of the *shahada*: '*la ilaha illal lah; Muhammadon rasul Allah*' (there is no god but Allah; Muhammad is the prophet of Allah) as his last words on earth.

DUTY OF KEEP THE PEACE (*ALAYKUIM*)

Muslims have a general responsibility of civility and respect for other Muslims based on dozens of *hadith* and Qur'anic verses. The *hadith* requires a Muslim to greet another Muslim with the ritual salutation '*As-salamu Alaykuim*' (peace be on you). The other person replies: '*Wa-alaykuim as-salam*' (peace be on you also). If any of the Prophets are mentioned in conversation they should also say 'peace be upon them'.

The Qur'an says that slander, blasphemy, ridicule and the use of offensive names are crimes as serious as physical assault or murder and should be punished accordingly.

In the Middle Ages the punishment for false accusation – especially false accusation of rape on the part of women – was removal of the tongue by its root. This form of punishment may still take place in remote areas, though reports are rare.

The Qur'an and *hadith* also emphasise that Muslims should be fair and honest in commercial dealings and refuse to charge or accept the payment of interest on loans. Beyond this there are dozens of verses in the Qur'an and hundreds of *hadith* encouraging good manners, respect for elders, kindness to children and the like. Most of these further instructions have the *mustahabb* legal status which means they are recommended – and may be taken into consideration when weighing more serious legal matters – but are not obligatory.

DRESS

The Muslim rules of dress are also designed to prevent offence as well as making observance of *salat* (ritual prayers) easier. Men are required to cover their bodies from their navel to the knees and women must cover their entire bodies from the head to the ankles.

Other than this there is no prescribed form of dress, although *hadith* emphasises simplicity and avoidance of tight clothes which would make bending during *salat* difficult. No particular colours are recommended except white, which must be worn during *hajj*. The Shi'ites have a preference for black clothes symbolising their continual state of mourning for the martyrs. Other groups, such as the Bedouin Ibadites, prefer blue. These choices are cultural rather than Qur'anic.

Muslims tend to keep their heads covered at all times. This is a sign of respect for Allah's angels who symbolically reside in the skulls of men and women and must therefore be protected. Usually this takes the form of a small cap similar to the Jewish skull-cap.

Women, in addition, usually cover the cap with a shawl over the head. In some Muslim countries men wear additional headgear over the cap or instead of it. But no hat or turban may be worn which prevents the forehead touching the ground during *salat* and this accounts for the brimless hats, such as the fez, popular in some Muslim countries. Brimmed Western hats such as the trilby are often worn by secular Muslims in countries like Turkey (as are moustaches) as a deliberate sign of modernism.

WOMEN'S LEGAL STATUS

Muslim women are required to accept that they have different roles from men in most respects, and are expected to be obedient, firstly to their fathers and then to their husbands – unless they ask her to do something which would break other parts of the *shari'ah*.

The fourth *surah* of the Qur'an describes a woman's father or husband as her 'master', with the right to beat her if she does not obey. The same *surah* says: 'Men are the maintainers of women . . . the good women are therefore obedient [to their masters]' (4:34). And the second *surah*, whilst revealing the laws of divorce in great detail, says of women: 'And the men are a degree above them' (2:228).

The *shari'ah* requires both men and women to take part in the obligations of the Five Pillars, but communal prayers at the mosque on Fridays are optional for women and tend to be predominantly male affairs. No woman is allowed to lead prayers.

Islam has a strong menstruation taboo and no woman may attend the mosque during her period. In some Muslim countries – especially amongst the Shi'ites – it is the practice to confine women until their period is over (*purdah*). The taboo is understandable given the great emphasis placed on avoidance of blood, especially during the frequent prayer sessions, but is still basically cultural and not Qur'anic.

In some Muslim countries women are required to cover their entire bodies in the presence of men other than members of their immediate family. This law is based on passages of the Qur'an which instruct women not to wear jewellery (and, by analogy, make-up) and to cover their hair, breasts and 'private parts' in public (33:59 and 24:30–31).

The requirement for women to cover their entire bodies – as in much of Arabia and Iran – is again cultural rather than Qur'anic, as are many other examples of discrimination against, or maltreatment of, women throughout the Muslim world. These include the practice of removing parts of the female genitals, so-called 'female circumcision', which is widespread in Muslim Arabia and Africa.

Whilst the Qur'an does place restrictions on Muslim women, it also guarantees them the right to own and inherit property, to participate fully in political affairs and to sue for divorce – in short a complete, separate legal identity.

Muslims often point out that these rights, available in theory to Muslim women since the time of Muhammad, have only been introduced in Europe comparatively recently. And in the Third World – where Islam is mainly to be found – there is no doubt that the application of the *shari'ah* can improve the social position of women considerably.

MARRIAGE (*AN-NIKH*)

Muslim marriages are simple contracts specifying the obligations and duties of both the bride and the groom in advance. The *shari'ah* gives the bride the right to negotiate over the contract and specify such matters as the value of the dowry (*mahr*) to be paid by the bridegroom and, since Islam permits polygamy, whether he may or may not take further wives. The *mahr* need not be particularly valuable and, if the bride agrees, it may even be a token sum of money or a simple gift such as a new set of clothes.

In practice most Muslim marriages are arranged and the bride has little choice in the matter. This, however, is a cultural rather than a religious practice, and is common in peasant-based cultures throughout the world regardless of religion.

Nevertheless, the pressure on Muslim girls to accept the husband selected by their parents is intense, even in countries like Britain. But there are signs that increasing numbers exercise their legal right to repeatedly object to marriage contracts and therefore effectively turn down proposals.

Both the Shi'ite *shari'ah* and the most widespread version of the Sunni *shari'ah* grant women the right to contract for their own marriage. Only the minority versions of the *shari'ah*, found mostly in Indonesia, Malaysia, North Africa and Saudi Arabia, deny it.

All versions of the *shari'ah*, however, prevent a Muslim woman from marrying a non-Muslim male. A Muslim man, on the other hand, can marry any virginal women subscribing to a faith based on scriptures recognised in the Qur'an, such as Christianity or Judaism.

POLYGAMY

The Qur'an and *hadith* assume that large numbers of Muslim men will be killed waging *jihad* in the defence of Islam. Polygamy was legalised specifically to take care of the large number of widows likely to be left behind.

The relevant *surah*, number 4, was given to Muhammad shortly after the Quraysh inflicted a terrible defeat on his army at the Battle of Uhud. It says: 'And if you fear that you will not deal fairly by the orphans, marry the women who seem good to you, two or three or four; and if you fear that you cannot be fair to so many, then one only . . . (4:3).

This has been interpreted to mean that a Muslim man may take up to four wives, as long as he can provide for them and all their children. In practice the vast majority of Muslim men only take one wife these days and if they have a second the reason is usually that their first wife could not bear them children. And in many Muslim countries (for example Syria, Iraq and Pakistan) a polygamous marriage requires specific permission from the state. In Tunisia and Algeria they have been abolished, and even in conservative Morocco there is a law allowing divorce if a first wife objects to a polygamous second or subsequent marriage.

Throughout the Muslim world the *shari'ah* gives wives of polygamous husbands additional rights. They must, for example, be given a separate home of their own and they are entitled to an equal proportion of their husband's time, attention and estate.

The position is rather different for Muslim rulers and conquerors. The Qur'an says that military victors may take 'the captives that your right hand possess [as wives]' (4:3). Throughout Muslim history kings and generals have remarried the wives of their defeated opponents, usually to gain kinship with the aristocracy of newly conquered peoples.

The best-known recent example of this was Muhammad ibn Sa'ud, the founder of Saudi Arabia, who married the wives of the dozens of tribal rivals he killed whilst creating his state in the 1920s. The Ottoman Turkish sultans also took hundreds of wives for similar dynastic purposes and the practice of mass polygamy spread downwards through the aristocracy of their Empire creating, in the European mind, the legend of the rapacious, harem-keeping Muslim male.

DIVORCE (*TALAQ, KHUL* AND *FASKH*)

The customs preceding a divorce in an attempt to hold a failed marriage together vary enormously in the different Muslim nations. But once the position is irretrievable the *shari'ah* provides three types of divorce proceedings. The first, *talaq*, is simple unilateral renunciation of marriage by the husband. Under the rules of *talaq* a husband may divorce his wife, or wives, at will, provided he is not insane and has not made the declaration in jest or whilst drunk (drunkenness is a separate offence against *shari'ah* law).

No formalities are required other than his public declaration of the fact. The Shi'ite variant of the *shari'ah* requires four witnesses. The wife usually keeps her dowry and the husband has to provide for the children and give her additional maintenance for a short period.

Although *talaq* is still available in most Islamic nations, its practice is rare and it has been abolished outright in the former Soviet Muslim republics, Afghanistan, Algeria and Tunisia. Divorce by mutual consent (*khul*) is much more widespread and takes the form of a legal renunciation of the original marriage contract.

The *shari'ah* also provides for divorce at the request of the wife, usually on the grounds that the original contract has been broken. She can ask for this in exchange for repaying the dowry.

The availability of this form of female divorce, known as *faskh*, is granted to all Muslim women in theory but in practice availability varies from country to country. The most liberal conditions are found in Afghanistan, the former Soviet Muslim republics, Turkey and Egypt. The most restrictive, from the point of view of the wife, are found in Saudi Arabia, Iran and the Gulf.

The exceptional grounds of renunciation of Islam – apostophy – by either husband or wife leads to immediate judicial dissolution of the marriage.

INHERITANCE

The *shari'ah* laws governing inheritance are extremely complex, creating twelve separate categories of relatives entitled to fractions or multiples of one sixth of the estate remaining after funeral expenses. In general, at each stage, women are discriminated against by having exactly one half of the claim of any male in the same category.

PUNISHMENT (*QISAS* AND *HADD*)

Just as Islamic theology has no place for redemption of the individual mortal soul in the eyes of almighty Allah, the *shari'ah*'s penal code has no place for the rehabilitation of the individual offender in this world.

The code is extremely crude and severe and is based entirely on the doctrine of *qisas* – retaliation on behalf of the community as a whole. *Qisas* has its origins in the Old Testament doctrine of 'an eye for an eye; a tooth for a tooth' – the principle revealed by Allah to Moses (*Musa*) when He first revealed His law to the Israelites.

The punishment for murder or attempted murder is beheading; for theft, amputation of the right hand; for adultery and false accusation of adultery or blasphemy, stoning to death; and for drunkenness, severe flogging to the point of death.

Together these severe punishments are known as *hadd* – the Arabic word for the process of 'limitation' – and, like most things in Islam, can only be understood in the context of Muhammad's mission, the problems he faced and the revelations Allah gave in order to help him overcome those problems.

The society in which Muhammad lived was almost entirely lawless and disputes dragged on for generations, with rival tribes exacting endless revenge on each other in the form of blood feuds.

In the process of creating the Islamic state Muhammad brought the feuds to an end and replaced the endless quest for revenge with simple and inescapable 'retaliation' (*qisas*) against the guilty parties. This is why the severe *shari'ah* punishments are known as *hadd* – the Arabic for 'limitation' (of feuds).

The logic behind the punishments at the time was simple – it is better to mete out swift and severe punishment than to allow an incident like the theft of a camel, adultery or murder to become a tribal feud killing hundreds.

The Qur'an and *hadith* contain several warnings that these severe *hadd* punishments should be given sparingly and only when the offender has either been accused by four eyewitnesses of spotless moral character or, preferably, has confessed to the crime.

When the European powers established their rule in large parts of the Muslim world they found it was difficult to obtain a conviction in a *shari'ah* court, even when the circumstantial or forensic evidence was overwhelming. And because of the Qur'anic injunction to use the *hadd* sparingly, *shari'ah* courts had a reputation for arbitrary action.

It was entirely possible that two offenders convicted of identical crimes of theft on the same day would be treated entirely differently. One, who may even have committed the greater offence, would walk free with only the punishment of hell awaiting him, the other may have his hand chopped off.

It was mainly for these reasons that the *shari'ah* courts were superseded by more workable and efficient European-based systems of criminal law in the nineteenth and early twentieth centuries. Only in the Arabian peninsula, where tribal conditions have scarcely changed since Muhammad's time, did the complete *shari'ah* and *hadd* system remain unchallenged throughout the European colonial era.

The reintroduction of *hadd* punishments in countries such as Pakistan, Iran, Mauritania and Sudan after independence is part of a general desire to return to Islamic fundamentals. This reintroduction has visibly done little to curb crime and there are strong signs that the Qur'anic warning to use *hadd* punishments sparingly has been ignored in Sudan, Iran and Afghanistan.

6. THE MUSLIM YEAR

The Islamic calendar consists of twelve lunar months, totalling 364 days, and does not correspond with the Western calendar which is adjusted to ensure winter and summer solstices are always on the same date. Use of the lunar calendar ensures religious festivals and Holy Days do not coincide with pre-Islamic pagan seasonal festivals or fertility cults.

As a result important events such as the Muslim new year, the start of *hajj* and the *Ramadan* fast move steadily around the seasons and take place on different days of the Western calendar every year.

Islam has only two major 'official' Holy Days. The most important is the Feast of Sacrifice (*'Id al-Adha*) on the tenth day of *Dhu al-Hijjah*, the twelfth month of the Islamic year. The second, the Feast of Breaking the Fast (*'Id al-Fitr*) marks the end of the annual fast for the whole of the ninth month of *Ramadan*.

Classical Islam officially recognises only these two Holy Days, but in practice Muslims celebrate many more. Some of these additional festivals like *Mawlid an-Nabi* (Prophet's Birthday) resemble ceremonies from other religions Muslims have come into contact with – in this case – the Christian Christmas.

During periods of extreme orthodoxy Islamic authorities have attempted to ban 'pagan' festivals like this, but they persist.

MUHARRAM ('THE SACRED MONTH')

The year begins with the month of *Muharram* and the first festival, *Ashura*, takes place on its tenth day. *Ashura* began as the Jewish feast of Passover and still celebrates the Israelite flight from Egypt. According to Islamic tradition it is also the day on which Noah left the ark. To distinguish *Ashura* from Passover, Muslims fast for two days instead of one. Since the early Middle Ages *Ashura* has had a special importance for Shi'ite Muslims as the anniversary of the martyrdom of Muhammad's grandson (via his daughter Fatima) Hussein ibn 'Ali (see Part 3 – Islamic Sects, Shi'ite Islam).

SAFAR ('THE MONTH WHICH IS VOID')

By tradition *Safar* is the month in which Muhammad once suffered a serious illness and was unable to receive any further revelations from Allah – hence the title. Exceptionally devout Muslims spend most of it in mourning to commemorate the Prophet's illness. But the last Wednesday of the month is sometimes celebrated by a carnival day commemorating Muhammad's return to health.

RABI AL-AWAI ('THE SPRING')

The title of the third Muslim month is incongruous since, being lunar, it is not linked to the spring or any other season. The origin of the title is unknown. It may have been left over from the earlier pagan solstice-based Arabian calendar, or a mystical reference to its main event – Muhammad's birth-death day.

Most of the month is devoted to commemorating the birth and death of Muhammad, which, according to tradition, took place on the same day, the 12th of the month. The festival of *Id-Mawlid an-Nabi*, which marks the day, was first celebrated in 1207 in what is now Iraq and is associated with the growth of heretical Sufi teaching about the personal survival of the soul after death (for Sufi Islam see Chapter 14).

During *Id-Mawlid* Muslims give each other presents, dress in bright clothes and burn incense and candles. *Id-Mawlid*'s similarity to Christmas, with the doctrinal danger of worshipping Muhammad instead of Allah, has led to it being banned during periods of extreme Sunni orthodoxy.

RABI AL-THANI ('THE MONTH FOLLOWING SPRING')

The fourth month has no special significance for orthodox Sunni or Shi'ite Muslims but is celebrated by Sufis, especially in India and Pakistan. One of the largest Sufi monastic orders, the Qadiriyah, was founded during this month in the eleventh century AD.

Sufis dress in bright clothes and hold carnivals to celebrate the death of their 'saint' 'Abd al-Qadir, founder of the order. This activity is regarded as deeply heretical by Shi'ite and, especially, Sunni Muslims.

JUMADA AL-QULA ('THE FIRST MONTH OF DRYNESS') AND JUMADA-TH-THANIYYAH ('THE SECOND MONTH OF DRYNESS')

The fifth and sixth months are set aside for preparation of the intense series of festivals which begin halfway through the following month of Rajab. Any form of public religious devotion, except *salat* (prayer) is banned by Sunni Muslims during these months, though local Shi'ite martyr worship and Sufi saint worship does take place.

RAJAB ('THE REVERED MONTH')

Some Muslims mark the first day of Rajab with the minor festival of *Ragha'ib*, when it is believed that Muhammad was conceived by his mother Aminah. But the main preoccupation is increasing religious observance leading up to the 27th day, the most widely observed festival of the year even though it is not recognised by classical Islam – the festival of the Night of Ascent (*Laylat al-mi'raj*).

During *Laylat al-mi'raj* Muslims commemorate Muhammad's miraculous 'Night Journey' from Mecca to Jerusalem on the back of a winged beast. The site of the miracle where he was shown the gates of heaven and hell is now marked by the Dome of the Rock mosque in Jerusalem, to which many Muslims make a minor pilgrimage to celebrate the festival.

On the 13th day Shi'ite Muslims celebrate the martyrdom of 'Ali (son-in-law of Muhammad) the first Shi'ite Imam. As at the festival commemorating Husayn, the Shi'ites mark 13th Rajab with huge displays of public grief and declarations of willingness to die the death of the Muslim martyr.

SHA'BAN ('THE MONTH OF DIVISION')

The festival of *Laylat al-Bara'ah* ('Night of the Battle of Badr' or, popularly, 'Night of the Fates') takes place on the night of the full moon and formally commemorates Muhammad's conquest of Mecca.

Its real significance, however, is the superstition that this is the night on which Allah reviews all mankind and determines the fate of each believer (just as He determined that Muhammad should conquer Mecca).

Just as *Id-Mawlid* is the unofficial 'Muslim Christmas', *Laylat al-Bara'ah* is the unofficial Muslim version of *Diwali*, the Hindu 'festival of lights' when Hindus make pacts with their gods to ensure good luck for the coming year.

As such the festival is clearly pagan in origin and, although ferociously discouraged by Sunni Muslim authorities (especially in Pakistan), remains popular in countries with Hindu populations such as India, Bangladesh and Indonesia.

Believers often pray all night, presenting Allah with a type of confession of their sins over the past year before they beg forgiveness. This directly contradicts a central point of orthodox Muslim theology – that Allah cannot be addressed directly and has anyway already predestined believers' fates.

The day is also the key Shi'ite festival of *al-Mahdi* – the mystical birthday of the 'concealed' twelfth Imam descended from Muhammad, who will one day be resurrected or reborn and lead *jihad* to rid Islam of the Sunni 'usurpers'.

RAMADAN ('THE MONTH OF GREAT HEAT')

The ninth month, *Ramadan*, is the most demanding of the Islamic year. All Muslims must fast for its entire thirty days in accordance with the *ibadah* rules of *sawm*. Throughout the month all secular festivities are banned and in those countries where Qur'anic law is enforced, those breaking any part of the *ibadah* are severely punished. *Ramadan* climaxes with the festival of *Laylat al-qadr* ('Night of Power') on the 27th.

According to tradition this is the night on which Muhammad received the first *surah* of the Qur'an and he is thought to be at his most active in the world on this night. According to *hadith*, if a Muslim spends it at prayer this is believed to be more effective than 'a thousand months' of prayer during other times of the year.

Many Muslims – especially those preparing to take part in *hajj* in the following months – do pray all night, repeating a highly demanding routine (the *tarawih*) based on cycles of 20 and 23 repetitions of the *qiyam-ruku-sajada* (prostration) ritual of *salat* prayers.

SHAWWAL ('THE MONTH OF HUNTING') AND DHU AL-QA'DAH ('THE MONTH OF REST')

The first day of the tenth month begins with the festival of *'Id al-Fitr* (feast of breaking the fast) which ends the fast of *Ramadan* and is therefore a source of a huge officially sanctioned celebration. In Turkey it is known as the 'sugar festival' (*Seker Bayrami*) when large amounts of sweets are eaten. In stark contrast to *Ramadan*, Muslims tend to be in high spirits throughout the tenth and eleventh months.

DHU AL-HIJJAH ('THE MONTH OF HAJJ')

The tenth day of *Dhu al-Hijjah* is the holiest in the Islamic calendar and commemorates the willingness of the Prophet Ibrahim to sacrifice his son Isma'il to show submission to Allah.

It is on this day that every Muslim must ritually slaughter a *halal* (lawful) animal such as a sheep, goat, cow or camel. The focus of *Id al-Adha* is the valley of Mina, near Mecca, where pilgrims end their *hajj*.

The Shi'ites have one additional festival, *'Id al-Ghadir*, the day on which they believe Muhammad announced he should be succeeded by their first Imam, 'Ali. But apart from this *'Id al-Adha* brings the religious year to a climax, and there are no further festivals until the cycle begins again with *Ashura* on the tenth day of the first month of *Muharram*.

Part 2

ISLAMIC HISTORY

7. THE ISLAMIC EMPIRE (622–1258)

The Muslim calendar takes the year AD 622 as the start of the Islamic epoch. The date marks the *hiraj* (Holy Exile), when Muhammad and his followers were driven out of Mecca and settled in Medina, 480 kilometres to the north east, founding the first Islamic state and declaring war on the pagans.

Islam's choice of 'year zero' is highly significant. It shows how the religion, from the very beginning, was a political creed to establish the rule of Allah on earth. This mission has always been equal to and inseparable from Muhammad's purely religious and spiritual mission as a Prophet.

In the last ten years of his life Muhammad inflicted total defeat on his original enemies – the pagan Quraysh aristocracy of Mecca – and by doing so united all the Arabic tribes in submission to both his rule and that of Allah. The later Medinan *surahs* of the Qur'an, delivered to Muhammad after he became the ruler of Medina, Mecca and most of Arabia, are preoccupied with the laws under which the new state should be governed.

The Medinan *surahs* also address the immediate political problem Muhammad faced – holding together the fragile alliance of tribal leaders he had painstakingly constructed. Tribal alliances were not new in Arabia but they usually disintegrated after the short-term military objectives had been met and the spoils divided up.

Muhammad received help from revelations which stressed above all else the need for all believers to be united so they could carry out further expansion and avoid military defeat.

The third *surah*, for example, is addressed directly to the fractious tribal leaders: 'Be not disunited, and remember the favour of Allah on you when you were enemies, then He united your hearts so by His favour you became brethren; and you were on the brink of a pit of fire, then He saved you from it' (3:102).

The same *surah* also lays down detailed instructions for the care of the widows and orphans created by the battles in defence of Islam, and says how the booty should be shared between warriors and the new Islamic state.

But the Qur'an gave no guidance on the key question – how a successor was to be chosen after the Prophet's death. It was left to Muhammad himself to solve this tricky problem.

The traditional method of dynastic succession, probably acceptable to the tribes, was out of the question. Although Muhammad had a daughter – thus producing a Hashemite genealogical line meaning that various modern Arab rulers claim descent from Muhammad (and therefore Ibrahim) – he had no son. And as he had been proclaimed the last Prophet none of his subsequent followers could also claim leadership as a new Prophet.

THE SUCCESSION TO MUHAMMAD

In the event Muhammad nominated as his successor Abu Bakr, who had been his closest friend, was a fellow member of the Hashemite clan and had risen to be the leading general of the Islamic army. Abu Bakr himself stipulated he would have to face election and ratification by all the tribal leaders.

After Muhammad died in 632 Abu Bakr was duly elected Caliph (meaning something like Regent – a temporary ruler in place until the end of the world and the direct rule of Allah). Some of the tribes in Muhammad's confederacy immediately rebelled, supporting their own chiefs or others as the rightful successors to the 'Caliphate'. But Abu Bakr had enough support and military skill not only to put down the rebellion, but to go on to conquer northern Arabia and parts of Syria and western Persia before dying in battle just two years after his election.

Abu Bakr was succeeded by his nominee, 'Umar ibn al-Khattab, as the second Caliph amid a renewed political crisis and threats of revolts. The background was the firm expectation that the world was about to end. 'Umar, however, soon established his rule beyond question by sheer military skill and a stunning series of conquests throughout Arabia and well beyond which brought huge wealth back to Mecca.

'Umar not only conquered and rallied Arab tribesmen, but the army he thereby created came storming out of the Arabian peninsula and inflicted defeat after defeat on Christian Byzantium, the dominant power at the time. The capture of Jerusalem, the Holy City of all the Ibrahimic religions, was most significant to Muslims because of Muhammad's 'Night Journey' and the miraculous revelation of the gates of heaven and hell.

After 'Umar's death the Dome of Rock mosque, a magnificent architectural achievement, was constructed in Jerusalem on the site on Temple Mount and became a Muslim shrine equal in importance to all the Holy Places of Mecca except perhaps the *Ka'bah* itself.

'Umar's successes to the east of Arabia were even greater. The powerful Persian Empire was utterly destroyed and all of its territory as far as central Iran was incorporated into the Empire.

'Umar was undoubtedly a messianic figure who believed he could conquer the whole world. He conscripted the entire Arab nation and forbade any occupation other than warrior. As a result Arabs formed a military caste, doing no other work and effectively looting new territories. The Arab warrior class depended on conquered peoples, especially the highly literate Persians, to administer the Empire.

'Umar was stabbed to death by a resentful Persian administrator in Basra in 644. Unlike Muhammad and Abu Bakr, he had not nominated a successor but instead had appointed a six-man council (The Shura) to select a new Caliph. The two main candidates were 'Ali ibn Abi Talib, the husband of Muhammad's daughter Fatima and a member of Muhammad's Hashemite clan, and 'Uthman ibn 'Affan, a member of the more distantly related 'Umayyad clan.

The Shura offered the Caliphship to 'Ali on condition he did not proclaim a Hashemite dynasty. But 'Ali refused these conditions and so the position went instead to his rival 'Uthman of the 'Umayyad clan.

'Uthman's succession was controversial and contained the seeds of a civil war which was to threaten the very existence of the original Arab Islamic Empire and still divides Muslims into the two principal sects of Sunni and Shi'ites today. The Sunnis believe that 'Uthman was the right choice as Caliph, because he had the support of the majority of believers. The Shi'ites, in contrast, believe that 'Ali should have become Caliph, because of his direct descent from Muhammad.

For the first five years of his reign 'Uthman enjoyed the support of most of the clans opposed to 'Ali's Hashemite dynastic ambitions, as they were certain they would down-grade their own status. Continuing military success also made 'Uthman popular. But after 650 the pace of conquest slowed and taxes had to be introduced to replace the previous supply of fresh booty. 'Uthman was accused of misusing state funds, nepotism and plotting to establish a dynasty of 'Umayyad Caliphs to follow him.

THE KHARIJI REVOLT

Opposition to 'Uthman was strongest amongst Muhammad's original followers, known as the Khariji ('successionists'). They included many of his closest friends and relatives, and many Bedouin tribal leaders who had been the first converts outside Mecca and Medina. They were fanatical Muslims determined to uphold the traditions of Mecca at all costs.

The Khariji suspected that many of the tribes and peoples who had since joined the body of Islam and with whom they were now required to share the spoils were opportunists and fortune seekers. They even feared some might – as both the Qur'an and Muhammad had warned – actually be 'Satanic', working to destroy Islam from within.

Under the first two Caliphs Abu Bakr and 'Umar, conquered peoples had been allowed to convert to Islam by simply accepting the obligations of the Five Pillars. But in some cases they had only had to accept the *shahada*.

As a first step the Khariji insisted that acceptance and performance of all the duties of the Five Pillars were the bare minimum condition for conversion to Islam. They then categorised the people who had accepted the Five Pillars as 'Common Believers' (*Mu'minum*). But they said these converts could only be regarded as proper Muslims if they also led sin-free lives. It followed that any Muslim committing an act forbidden by the Qur'an, or failing to carry out additional 'good deeds' had renounced Islam and became a non-believer (*kafir*).

Khariji doctrine was rejected by 'Uthman as it would have been a serious brake on the Imperial expansion which was the source of his power. His answer was to sponsor a rival sect, the Murji'ah ('those who postpone judgement'), which taught that judgement of a Muslim's piety should be left to Allah – not the Khariji.

Those who broke the *shari'ah* were to be punished, but still regarded as Muslims. Non-believers could join Islam if they outwardly observed religious law and accepted the rule of the Caliph.

The establishment of the Murji'ah infuriated the Khariji. When 'Uthman was convincingly accused of breaking the *shari'ah* by stealing from state funds, the Khariji proclaimed him a Satanic anti-Muslim (*kafir*), demanded his overthrow and declared war on his 'Umayyad clan.

In 656 'Uthman was killed in Mecca by a rioting Khariji mob and the Shura immediately appointed 'Ali ibn Abi Talib as the fourth Caliph.

The Caliphship of 'Ali was welcomed by all but the most extreme Khariji groups. As a member of the Hashemite clan he was a much closer relative to Muhammad than 'Uthman and, most importantly, he was married to Muhammad's daughter

Fatima. Following her father's death Fatima had become prominent in Khariji circles, and 'Ali himself shared many Khariji ideas.

'Ali promised to root out 'Umayyad corruption and growing Syrian and Persian influence in the Imperial administration, but within a year was challenged by Mu'awiya, the 'Umayyad governor of Damascus and cousin of 'Uthman.

Mu'awiya pledged himself to avenge the death of 'Uthman, to destroy the Khariji and overthrow 'Ali's Khariji-backed Caliphship. Based amongst the newer converts of Damascus, he started an inconclusive and costly civil war against 'Ali and the traditionalists of Mecca.

'Ali's army was composed mainly of Bedouins, Kharijis and Meccan clansmen, while the Syrian and Persian forces supported Mu'awiya and the 'Umayyads. The result of the civil war was to halt external expansion of the Empire, and Byzantium was able to recapture important possessions such as Alexandria in Egypt.

After the costly Battle of Siffin in 658, 'Ali proposed arbitration. Mu'awiya accepted, but the Khariji were outraged, accusing 'Ali of breaking the *shari'ah* by failing to wage *jihad* against the 'Satanic' 'Umayyads.

The four thousand Kharijis in 'Ali's army, about one tenth of the total manpower, declared war on him, but 'Ali put down the revolt at the Battle of Nahrawan, killing all but a few hundred.

Mu'awiya and the 'Umayyads, meanwhile, broke off negotiations, resumed the civil war and over the next three years captured most of the Empire's territory. 'Ali's death, however, came not at their hands but through a vengeful Khariji survivor of the Battle of Nahrawan.

After his defeat of the Khariji 'Ali had declared his own dynasty, and was therefore succeeded by his eldest son Hassan but he lasted a mere six months before admitting defeat and accepting Mu'awiya 'Umayyad as Caliph. A year later he was murdered by the 'Umayyads and the Hashemite claim to the Caliphship passed to 'Ali's second son, Husayn.

THE SHI'ITES

Mu'awiya attempted to end the continuous crisis over the Caliphship by proclaiming an 'Umayyad dynasty based on simple patriarchal succession. Then, to reduce the influence of the Hashemite clan and Khariji-type traditionalists, he moved the capital of the Empire from Mecca to the 'Umayyad stronghold of Damascus.

These measures worked. The surviving Khariji repeatedly rebelled but, since they were using the old tactic of desert warfare, they were easily defeated by the larger and well-drilled army recruited and staffed by the 'Umayyads. By the end of the eighth century, after vicious persecution, the Khariji were effectively extinct. A remnant fled to remote regions of Oman, Yemen and North Africa where their descendants are known today as the Ibadites – living in small nomadic desert communities, observing a version of the *shari'ah* and lifestyle largely unchanged since the original Khariji revolt.

The remaining non-Khariji members of 'Ali's defeated army, now led by his son Husayn, became known as the *Shi'ah* (or the Shi'ites) from the Arabic word for 'partisans'.

The Shi'ites saw the 'Umayyads as Satanic usurpers who had stolen the Caliphate from the Hashemites in order to destroy it. Unlike the Khariji, whose puritanical tradition they largely inherited, the Shi'ites continued to present a serious military threat to 'Umayyads.

The first major Shi'ite rebellion came in AD 680 when Husayn took on the 'Umayyad army at the Battle of Karbala in Iraq. But he was hopelessly outnumbered, his army was destroyed and he was killed.

Thereafter Shi'ite Islam became predominantly a creed of rebellion and martyrdom and Husayn's death is still commemorated by the Shi'ites at Karbala in their most important religious festival of the year – *Ashura*.

The 'Umayyad Caliphs then gave free reign to the Murji'ah movement, established by 'Uthman to counter Khariji 'fundamentalism'. The Murji'ah ('those who suspend judgement') developed the relatively permissive theological and legal doctrines later to form the basis of Sunni Islam (from the Arabic word for followers of the 'smooth path').

Murji'ah doctrines were tailored to the political needs of the Caliph and designed to help Imperial expansion and government. They taught that subjugated peoples could convert to Islam, regardless of their actual commitment to the faith. All they had to do was accept 'Umayyad rule and carry out the duties of the Five Pillars, even if they did so uncomprehendingly. It did not matter if new subjects were insincere, as conversion would come later – perhaps even in generations – through constant practice of the Five Pillars.

The 'Umayyad Caliphs were efficient but tyrannical rulers. They introduced currency, regularised taxation and set up a crude system of justice. The new legal system was based on the Murji'ah principle that breaches of the *shari'ah* should be dealt with in 'Umayyad courts, but offenders still be allowed to profess Islam. The question of who was a sincere Muslim and who was a Satanic Muslim, which had caused the original civil war, was to be left to Allah on the Day of Judgement.

Although Shi'ite revolts continued in the east of the new empire – the Shi'ite heartland was in what is now Iraq and Iran – the 'Umayyads were extremely successful in their Imperial expansion, especially in the more fertile and agricultural west, capturing vast new territories including all of North Africa, Spain and southern France. The 'Umayyad capital of Damascus, so close to Jerusalem, became the capital of a great empire which was soon to encompass much of the classical (and by then Christian) Greek and Roman world.

In 732 the 'Umayyads began the conquest of northern Europe but were turned back when they were narrowly defeated at the Battle of Poitiers, less than a hundred miles from Paris, by a Christian army led by the Frankish General Charles Martel. In the east they gained the territory of modern Pakistan as far as the river Indus and mounted expeditions against Chinese armies in central Asia.

As more tribes and peoples were converted – from the Atlantic coast of Spain across to northern India and the borders of China – the number of religious practices and faiths held in the name of Islam multiplied enormously, which was just what the Khariji had feared. The 'Umayyads regarded their Empire first and foremost as Arab and had effectively turned Islam into a religiously decadent political tool for expanding (Syrian) Arab rule.

In the new territories 'Umayyad rule was based on granting generals the right to loot in return for a tribute of one fifth of their gain to the 'Umayyad treasury in Damascus. These local Arab rulers often became fabulously rich in their own right. Musa the Great, conqueror of North Africa and Spain, for example, personally owned 300,000 black slaves captured from the Vandal kingdom of Carthage based around modern Tunisia.

But non-Arab Muslims were not allowed to share in the spoils and Christian or Jewish Arabs were often given legal privileges over them. Arab Christians even became governors of non-Arab Muslims in parts of the Empire, which caused huge resentment amongst local Muslim populations.

The Persian Muslims, seeing themselves as more cultured than the Arabs, were particularly bitter about this doctrine of Arab superiority. In 749 a group of Shi'ite-influenced Persians led by Abu al-Abbas al-Saffah exploited a new successional wrangle within the 'Umayyad clan itself to attack in their heartlands of Syria and Egypt.

Al-Abbas struck when most of the Arab army was in Europe on another attempt to conquer France and the rest were demoralised by the repeated defeats at the hands of the Christians. In 750 Al-Abbas decisively defeated the 'Umayyads at the Battle of Zab in Egypt, captured Damascus and slaughtered almost the entire 'Umayyad aristocracy.

Those who managed to flee made their way to distant Spain where, in 755, the Abbasids allowed them to become Emirs (subject rulers) of their own independent Caliphate. Under them Muslim Spain developed as a great centre of European Islamic culture – one of the sources in fact of the European 'Enlightenment' and scientific revolution in the late Middle Ages.

THE GOLDEN AGE OF THE ABBASIDS

With the fall of the 'Umayyads the Shi'ites believed their time for revenge – their opportunity to purify Islam – had finally come. They had played a major part in al-Abbas's victory and now demanded their Imam (supreme religious and political leader) Ja'far as-Sidiq, great-grandson of the original Shi'ite martyr Husayn, should become Caliph in a position similar to that of Pope.

Al-Abbas was sympathetic, but he died in 754 to be replaced by his less accommodating son al-Mansur, who turned on the Shi'ites, murdered the Shi'ite Imam and within five years had crushed the Shi'ites as a coherent military force.

Al-Mansur declared himself Caliph and pronounced an Abbasid dynasty, and, although groups of Shi'ites revolted throughout the five hundred years of Abbasid rule, they were never successful. Al-Mansur's first act was to consolidate his clan's domination of the Empire by the construction of Baghdad as a purpose-built Imperial capital city, sited on the River Euphrates in the heart of the second major area of ancient Arab settlement, Iraq.

This massive project used up the greater part of the captured 'Umayyad treasury. Building work took forty years, employed 100,000 Persian architects and craftsmen, and claimed the lives of hundreds of thousands of exhausted slaves.

When it was completed Baghdad was by far the most advanced and civilised city in the world. It had amenities like a sewerage system, fountains and street lighting and was graced by hundreds of fine public buildings including mosques, law schools, universities and *madrasahs* (college-hospices and institutes of medical science).

Despite the brutal way in which their regime (and dynasty) began, the Abbasids emerged as enlightened rulers and great patrons of the arts and sciences. Learning flourished, especially after the conquest of parts of central Asia held by the Chinese, who introduced their science of paper making. Greek philosophical tracts, gathered from other conquered territories, were translated, published and made widely available. By 850 there were over seven hundred lending libraries in Baghdad.

In this atmosphere dozens of heterodox religious sects emerged, debating theology and law and trying to impose some order on the doctrinal chaos and legal arbitrariness inherited from the 'Umayyads and trying for the first time to get to grips

with the events and the significance of the Khariji revolt and
the civil war which followed the early years of Islam. The most
important of the new learned sects was the *Mu'tazilah*, a
rationalist group strongly influenced by the Greek philosophical texts, recently translated into Arabic for the first time.

The Mu'tazilah introduced into Islamic theology and legal
thinking the new concept of human free will over which Allah
had only a limited influence. According to the sect's teaching a
person was responsible for his own actions, regardless of his
knowledge of the Qur'an. This meant he could be judged for
his moral actions on earth, without reference to his status as a
Muslim. These doctrines led to the establishment of courts of
law with rules of evidence.

Judges were allowed to weigh the evidence without reference
to the Qur'an in all cases and the science of *fiqh* based on the
work of jurists in addition to the literal word of the Qur'an
and *hadith* was born.

These practices enraged traditionalists, especially Arabs and
the Shi'ites, who denounced the new rationalist doctrines as
Satanic. They demanded a return to the principle of predestination, where all matters were decided by Allah in advance,
with total reliance on the Qur'an and Muhammadan *hadith* to
settle legal disputes.

In the years that followed Muhammad's death vast numbers
of *hadith* attributed to him circulated throughout Arabia. Some
were clearly authentic, and others were clearly fabricated to
serve the political purposes of the various factions which
emerged amongst the Muslims immediately following his death.

The first major compilation of Muhammadan *hadith* was
made by the Abbasid lawyer Muhammad ibn Isma'il Bukhari
(died 870) and is known as the *Sahih al-Bukhari* ('authentic
according to Bukhari'). Bukhari examined a mass of *hadith*
and found the overwhelming majority to be the invention of
rival factions. Bukhari included only 7,000 *hadith* as authentic
after, according to tradition, examining 60,000.

Islam as it is practised today is largely based on the Sahih
al-Bukhari. The rituals and obligations of the Five Pillars of
Islam – including the *shahada* – as well as much of the criminal
law originate from Muhammadan *hadith* collected by Bukhari.

In addition to Bukhari's collection other Abbasid lawyers produced five more books of *hadith*, which are today regarded as entirely authentic. These six books of *hadith* are known as the 'smooth path customs' (Sunnah) from which Sunni Muslims take their name.

Once the *hadith* had been authenticated in this way the rationalists were prepared to compromise and reintroduce *hadith* as a vital part of the legal system. The basic shape of Sunni Muslim law was defined by the great Abbasid lawyer 'Ali ibn Isma'il al-Ash'ari (died 935) in his book *The Elucidation of the Foundations of Religion*.

Al-Ash'ari shaped Sunni'ism as a combination of rationalist judicial reasoning (*fiqh*, *qiyas* and *ijma*) and traditionalist reliance on the legal verses of the Qur'an and *hadith*. And the four main legal schools founded by the Abbasids during al-Ash'ari's lifetime – the *Maliki*, *Hanfai*, *Shafi* and *Hanbali* – remain the four sources of modern Sunni law.

Al-Ash'ari's legalism brought great stability and led to the rapid development of political and legal institutions. The first two hundred years of Abbasid rule became a Golden Age for the Islamic Empire with subjects guaranteed a large measure of peace, protection and access to rationalist courts with rules of evidence and well-defined procedures.

The economy boomed and Baghdad became the centre of a thriving network of trade routes. The sciences of mathematics, astronomy, architecture, chemistry, medicine and navigation all flourished. A vast collection of art treasures was created and amassed. The Qur'an was translated into Persian and other languages, and the foundations of national literatures were laid in many parts of the Empire – not least Persia itself, where many works of superb poetry and fiction were written.

The army was reformed and Turkic horsemen recruited from the territories in central Asia steadily replaced Arabian tribesmen as its cutting edge. The ferocious Turks, backed up by the Persian scientific discoveries gave back the momentum of the early 'Umayyad days and there were spectacular new military successes in central Asia and India.

THE EMIRATE SYSTEM

The Abbasids continued the 'Umayyad policy of allowing local rulers to run outlying areas of the Empire with little interference from central government. But the old 'Umayyad anarchy, when local conquerors were free to do as they pleased, was progressively phased out with the introduction of the Emirate system.

The first Abbasid Emirate was established in Spain by surviving members of the 'Umayyad aristocracy who had fled there following the fall of Damascus. Rather than pursuing the civil war the Abbasids allowed the 'Umayyads to rule Spain in return for payment of tribute and acceptance of their overlordship. The 'Umayyad rulers were given the title of *Emir* (subject Caliph) and their state was known as an Emirate.

The system was developed by succeeding Abbasid Caliphs and widely applied throughout the Empire to prevent it disintegrating into rival national states. The duties of the Emirs varied according to the strength and financial circumstances of the Abbasids.

In periods of Abbasid strength Emirs were little more than local governors and tax collectors but when central government was weak – especially in the latter part of the dynasty – Emirs effectively became independent sovereign rulers. From the eleventh century onwards an increasing number of Emirates declared themselves fully independent Caliphates.

In general the rival Caliphs restricted their ambitions to their own states, except for the pro-Shi'ite Fatimid Emirs (and, after 1022, 'Anti-Caliphs') of Egypt, who repeatedly staked a claim to rule the entire Empire.

The Fatimids sponsored a fanatical Shi'ite sect called the Assassins who terrorised the Abbasid lands for two centuries from their base in Syria. But they never managed to muster an army strong enough to seriously challenge Baghdad.

The Abbasid Caliphs, secure in their palaces, steadily began sinking into decadence, and the Caliphs became distant, semi-divine figures, inhabiting a Chinese-style 'forbidden city' in the centre of Baghdad. But as early as the ninth century the Caliphship had already become a largely ceremonial institution, only one part of an increasingly complex legal and constitutional system.

The actual administration of the state, justice and religion passed to the plurality of law schools and government departments, whilst control of the army passed to shifting alliances of Seljuk Turkish generals and Persian lawyers. Plots and conspiracies were rife and groups resembling political parties emerged to lobby for the interests of various factions, with the Turks beginning to emerge as the most powerful force.

Meanwhile, the fabulous wealth and growing decadence of the Abbasid court became legendary throughout the world. Caliph al-Mutawakkil, who ruled from 847 until 861, had four thousand concubines whilst his successor, Caliph al-Mustain, owned a carpet 400 metres square, sewn from gold, silver and silk thread and studded with diamonds and rubies representing the eyes in figures of birds. From the tenth century onwards it was normal for Caliphs to appear in solid gold armour during court ceremonies.

The Caliphs were to live in powerless splendour for another four hundred years, attempting to keep alive the myth that they were rulers of a united Islamic Empire destined one day to rule all the world. But, in reality, by the end of the twelfth century the Abbasid Empire had degenerated into a loose federation of autonomous Emirates. Baghdad, still enormously wealthy as a trading centre, was under day-to-day control by a group of Seljuk Turks with a large force of military slaves, many black, and known as the Mameluks.

The most serious secessions of the late twelfth and early thirteenth centuries were by the Turkic Ghaznevid Emirates in northern India and Afghanistan. The Ghaznevids declared themselves to be fully independent Sultans (the Turkish word for Caliph) and in so doing opened up a split in the Empire.

The growing pagan Mongol Empire founded by Ghengis Khan was quick to exploit it and the Abbasids were able to put up little resistance when the Mongol armies of Halagu Ill-Khan (Khan of the West), the grandson of Ghengis Khan, swept into Persia in the 1250s.

In 1258 Halagu captured Baghdad itself and put the entire population of one million to the sword. Palaces were looted and libraries destroyed.

The events of 1258 were a calamity for Islam, the Persian nation and the whole of mankind. Human culture was set back at least a century by the destruction of centres of learning and the murder of hundreds of scholars and scientists.

The Mongol destruction of the Abbasid Empire also brought an end to the dream of maintaining a unified Islamic Empire. Islam would henceforth remain both divided and predominately Asiatic in outlook.

8. OTTOMAN SUPREMACY (1259–1650)

After the Mongol invasion and the sacking of Baghdad, the Islamic Empire split into three main parts which began to develop separately, diverging more and more as the centuries passed.

After converting en masse to Islam in about 1300, the Mongols turned their attention back to their central Asian homelands. The central area of the old 'Umayyad and Abbasid Empires, including Persia, Iraq and Arabia, became a backwater.

The centre of what remained of Arab culture moved west to Egypt and North Africa, where Arab rulers served the new Turkic and Mongol Emperors as Emirs. Although Arabic remained the sacred language of Islam, Turkish and Persian were to become the dominant languages for teaching, art, literature, politics and diplomacy. Contemporary Arab influence was almost completely extinguished at the centre of the new Turkish-dominated Empire. It could be said that at that point Arab history comes to an end – or goes into suspended animation – at least until modern times.

The Mongol Khan Tamberlaine moved his capital to Samarkand, in central Asia. From there he built a mighty Islamic Empire stretching from Kiev and Moscow in the West, to China in the East, which was also to form the basis of the great

Islamic Mogul Empire in northern India, and the brief but brilliant flowering of Islamic culture in central Asia.

In the west, power passed first to the Seljuk Turks and Mameluks whose greatest military achievement was the decisive defeat of the Christian Crusader states on the Palestinian and Syrian coasts. The Mameluks and Turks continued the anti-Crusader campaign north into the ancient Christian Byzantine heartland of Asia Minor (the territory of modern Turkey), a conquest almost completed by 1300.

Meanwhile, further afield, the distant Muslim lands south of the Sahara, where the first Negro Muslim communities had been established in the late Abbasid period, went their own way, ignored by both the Mongols and, later, the Ottomans.

THE OTTOMAN SULTANATE

The most important of the three independent centres of Islamic civilisation as far as the modern Western world is concerned was the Ottoman Empire. After an unpromising start, the Ottomans succeeded in bringing about what the 'Umayyads and Abbasids had fruitlessly attempted for almost six hundred years – the conquest of Christian Byzantium and the subjection of the Byzantine lands of Asia Minor and the Balkans.

The ground for this had been laid in the last century of the Abbasid Empire, when the Seljuks – the ferocious Turkic horseback warriors from central Asia – were being used as 'shock troops' in the centuries-long war against Byzantium.

After Baghdad fell to the Mongols, the Seljuks declared an independent Sultanate in eastern and central Asia Minor. There they were joined by wave upon wave of fellow Turkic warrior tribes fleeing from the Mongol expansion in central Asia. Just as the Abbasids had employed the Seljuks as 'shock troops', the Seljuk Sultans now used the newly arrived Uzbek Turkic tribes to strengthen their army and expand westwards. But again, like the Abbasids, the Seljuks became decadent and allowed actual power to pass to the Uzbek generals (pashas).

In 1301 Ozman, an Uzbek of the Ottoman clan, overthrew the Seljuk aristocracy and proclaimed himself Sultan of Asia

Minor. The Seljuks were relegated to becoming Emirs of the older, eastern part of the realm.

The new Ottoman state was religiously heterodox. The Sultans were Sunni, in the tradition of their former Seljuk-Abbasid masters, but many of their soldiers were Shi'ites and, steeped in the cult of Shi'ite martyrdom, vicious fighters.

The Ottomans inflicted a series of defeats on the declining Christian Byzantium Empire and the Ottomans quickly expanded westwards to threaten the capital of Constantinople, which was then by far the most important Christian city in the world.

Constantinople was conquered in 1453 by the Ottoman Sultan Mehmed II, who slaughtered much of the population and forced the rest into exile. Churches, including the great Cathedral of St Sophia, were converted into mosques and the city was renamed Istanbul ('city of Islam').

The effect of the fall of the Byzantine Empire on Christian Europe was enormous and the large numbers of scholars who fled to Italy were influential in the city states in sparking off the Renaissance and increasing trade with the east.

The centre of Christian Orthodoxy was forced north to Moscow, becoming the spur for consolidating the Russian nation. And, after the defeats and factional sectarianism which characterised the early Christian Crusades, Western or Roman Christianity was galvanised by the need to stop further westward Ottoman expansion.

At first the rule of the Ottoman Sultans was unstable and constantly threatened by the rebellious inclinations of Shi'ite soldiers. To counterbalance their influence the Sultans formed groups of fanatical fighters – the Orders of Janissaries (from the Turkish phrase Yeni Ceri – new soldiers), manned by the children of captured Christian Byzantine slaves who were raised as fanatical Sunni Muslims.

When Mehmed died in 1481 he nominated his eldest son Bayezid as the new Sultan and the Shi'ites promptly revolted in favour of Bayezid's brother, Jem. The Janissaries suppressed the revolt and from then on became the decisive force in Ottoman politics. After 1500 Bayezid attempted to reduce their power but they switched their support to his son Selim, who in 1512 defeated his father in battle and proclaimed himself Sultan.

With Janissary support Selim laid the foundations for a world Ottoman Empire based entirely on the despotism of the Sultan. The Shi'ites were ruthlessly suppressed and retreated to Persia, joining with local groups of Shi'ites and eventually forming their own state under the Safavid Shahs. Shi'ite Islam thereafter remained a largely Persian-Iranian (and to some extent Iraqi, or eastern Arabian) faith and the new state was in continual conflict with the Ottomans throughout the centuries that followed.

To end further successional disputes Selim confined his son Suleyman to the harem in the Imperial Palace and introduced the policy of fratricide (murder of brothers). Under this system whenever a new Sultan ascended to the throne his brothers would be locked into cells. As soon as the new Sultan had produced his first son the brothers would be slaughtered. The Sultan's sons would then be confined in the harem until their father's death and the cycle would begin again.

By the seventeenth century the system had grown to the point where Sultans had between 1,500 and 2,000 concubines and produced dozens of sons, only one of whom would become Sultan while all the others would be killed.

Although the Ottoman court retained many of the traditions of the Abbasids inherited through the Seljuks, their method of rule in their expanding domains was more similar to that of the earlier 'Umayyads, whom many Sultans conspicuously tried to emulate.

Ottoman rule also had the hallmark of the Sultan's nomadic Turkic ancestors. The idea of developing territory and investing in it for future gain was alien. Land and peoples were exploited to the point of exhaustion and then more or less abandoned in favour of new ground.

This short-term policy meant the Empire relied on continuous expansion for stability. Newly conquered lands became the property of the general (pasha) who had won them, who was left free to deal with the local population and resources as he saw fit. Usually this meant slavery, ruthless exploitation and brutal rule.

The Ottoman Empire reached the peak of its power during the rule of Selim's son, Suleyman the Magnificent (1520–66), and his grandson Selim II (1566–74). Its power was already in decline by 1683 when the second, and last, attempt was made to conquer Vienna. Victory would have opened up central and western Europe but, without the conquest of these lands, and no new significant wealth to distribute to the pashas, the Empire lost momentum and went into slow decline.

SAFAVID PERSIA

The first people to benefit from Ottoman decline were the Shi'ite Safavid Shahs of eastern Persia.

The Safavid dynasty had been founded much earlier by a Sufi, Safi al-Din (died 1334), who converted to Shi'ism and turned it into a revolutionary Persian nationalist movement. The guerrilla army of the Safavid Shahs – known as the Red Heads because they wore bright-orange turbans – had first fought the Mongols in 1250 and then continued their battle against the Ottomans. But in 1501 they declared independence when the Ottomans outlawed Shi'ite Islam in their territory, strengthened by important Shi'ite elements from the Ottoman army who had fled from persecution.

Under Safavid rule eastern Persia once again became a great cultural centre, with a flowering of the arts and sciences. The influence of the monastic-type Sufi orders, founded in Persia during the Golden Age of the early Abbasids, was all-important in enabling Abbasid culture and learning to survive the Mongol holocaust. And with the rise of the Ottomans the Safavid benefited from their geographical position at the centre of the trade routes of the ancient world and became rich on the growing trade between Europe and the new Islamic civilisations of central Asia and India.

Safavid art was particularly fine, and survives in collections of Persian carpets dating from the period. The Safavid Shahs also encouraged portrait painting, especially of miniatures. Islamic portrait painting is almost unknown outside Safavid Persia because of the danger of presenting images of Allah. But as Shi'ites the Safavids were religiously heterodox, and the existence of portraiture says much about the prevailing liberal religious climate.

As the Ottoman military threat receded in the seventeenth century the Safavid Shahs became increasingly decadent. Power passed to the Shi'ite *ulama* (religious council of wise men), which eventually deposed the Shahs and proclaimed the world's first 'Islamic republic' in the late eighteenth century. But the republic lasted only for a few years before eastern Persia was once again conquered, this time by the Turkic Sunni rulers of neighbouring Afghanistan.

After the conquest a division of powers was agreed between the new Afghan Shahs and the Shi'ite *ulama*. The Shahs controlled the state and foreign policy, and could levy taxes and make secular laws. The *ulama* retained control of religious practice, and enforced the Shi'ite version of the *shari'ah* in personal and family matters. The *ulama* thus became an important and permanent theocratic institution in Persia, which it has remained.

The *ulama* continued to tolerate non-religious Shahs right up until the 1970s but finally overthrew the monarchy in 1979, claiming total power exercised through its highest officials, the Ayatollahs. From the time of the Safavids the *ulama* has believed that it rules as a 'caretaker' government on behalf of a mystical Twelfth Imam descended from 'Ali, the first Shi'ite martyr, who, as 'The Twelfth' will appear on earth shortly before the end of the world.

THE MOGUL EMPIRE

As the Ottoman Empire entered its long period of decline, the Turkic Islamic civilisation of the Mogul Emperors in India moved into the ascendant.

Al Babr, the first Mogul Emperor, was a direct descendant of Ghengis Khan. He captured the Turkic Ghur'iat Sultanate of Delhi in 1526, imposing his rule on most of northern India. The Empire he founded produced an astonishingly sophisticated civilisation based on religious toleration, a mixture of Persian, Mongol and Indian culture, and cross-fertilisation between Islam and Hinduism.

Ghur'iat rule in India had been based on Turkish racial and Islamic religious superiority. Hindu temples had been destroyed or crudely converted into mosques, and Hindu subjects forced to pay a punitive tax known as the *jiyaz*. The economy of the Sultanate was backward and, like that of the Ottoman Empire, based on slavery and looting newly conquered territories. The Ghur'iats were popularly known as the Slave Sultans.

Al Babr changed all this. Hinduism was tolerated and new temples were built with his permission. Trade with the rest of the Islamic world, especially Persia and through there to Europe, was encouraged. The importance of slavery diminished and peace was made with the Hindu kingdoms of southern India which had previously been subjected to looting expeditions.

The third Emperor, Abu Akbar, who was a Sufi, took the policy of religious toleration even further by breaking from Islam entirely. The Emperor proclaimed an entirely new state religion of 'God-ism' (*din-i-ilahi*) – a jumble of Islamic, Hindu, Christian and Buddhist teaching with himself as deity. It never spread beyond his court and perished with him.

His son, Emperor Jahangir, readopted Islam as the state religion and continued the policy of religious toleration. His court included large numbers of Indian Hindus, Persian Shi'ites and Sufis and members of local heterodox Islamic sects. He also began building the magnificent monuments and gardens by which the Moguls are chiefly remembered today, importing hundreds of Persian architects to build palaces and create magnificent gardens in cities such as Lahore, Agra and Delhi.

Jahangir's approach was typified by the development of Urdu as the official language of Empire. Urdu is a sort of 'Esperanto' of the Muslim east, using Arabic script, but with a predominantly Persian vocabulary and Hindi grammatical structure. Although it lacks precision, it has greater flexibility than any of the languages from which it is derived and allows great subtlety of expression. Under Mogul rule many great works of Urdu literature and poetry were written, inspired by a mixture of Muslim and Hindu cultures. Urdu is still widely spoken in India and is the official language of modern Pakistan.

The architectural achievements of the Moguls peaked during the reign of Jahangir's religiously heterodox successor, Jahan, between 1592 and 1666. Jahan commissioned the Taj Mahal, with its distinctively Persian dome, as his mausoleum and the Red Fort in Delhi as his palace.

The Gardens of the Red Fort are especially fine and the Islamic art of gardening – important because the Qur'an describes Paradise as a garden – reached new heights under the Moguls. The Persian inscription on the entrance to the Red Fort and its gardens reads: 'If there is Paradise on Earth, it is here! it is here! it is here!'

Jahan's son Aurangzeb, who was to be the last great Mogul Emperor, abruptly changed his father's policies and embarked on a determined campaign of Islamisation. Thousands of Hindu temples and shrines were torn down and the punitive Ghur'iat *jiyaz* tax was reimposed. In the last decades of the seventeenth century Aurangzeb invaded the Hindu kingdoms of central and southern India, conquering much territory and taking many slaves.

Under him the Mogul Empire reached the peak of its military power, but his rule was unstable. The Muslim governor of the newly conquered Mogul territory of Hyderabad in central India rebelled, establishing an independent Shi'ite state and reintroducing religious toleration of his overwhelmingly Hindu subjects. The Hindu kingdoms also fought back, often supported by the French and British, who used them to tighten their grip on the sub-continent.

The establishment of the Hindu Marathi Empire in central India as a direct response to Aurangzeb's expansionism cut off Mogul territories in the south and east such as Madras and Bengal, from Delhi. The great eastern Mogul city of Calcutta came under the control of the British East India Company in 1696 and in the decades that followed Europeans or European-backed Hindu princes conquered most of the Mogul territory, reducing the Empire to an impoverished rump around Delhi.

Aurangzeb's sectarianism caused Mogul creativity and enterprise to dry up and the Empire went into decline. He left a legacy of bitterness between Muslims and Hindus which continues to this day, whilst the Mogul Emperors who followed him effectively became British or French puppets. The last Emperor was deposed by the British in 1858.

9. THE RISE OF ISLAMIC 'FUNDAMENTALISM'

In the seventeenth and eighteenth centuries the Ottoman Empire became steadily more corrupt and was thrown into constant internal crisis by the failure to maintain momentum through military conquest.

In the east the martyrdom-seeking warrior bands of Shi'ite Safavid Persia wore away Ottoman numerical supremacy by attrition and finally won independence. Newly independent Persia blocked the only route for Ottoman expansion into India and the Far East and forced them to turn once again to Europe. But for the first time the Muslim world found Western expansion blocked by European powers reinvigorated by the Renaissance and able to match its scientific and military skill.

The germ of the European Renaissance had come, ironically, from the 'Umayyad Emirate of Cordoba. The Spanish Catholic civilisation which replaced the Emirate absorbed much of its tradition of learning, especially the science of navigation, making Spain the first great modern European power and laying the foundations for its conquest of the New World.

To the north, Ottoman expansion was prevented by the emerging power of Russia, whose rulers could be just as despotic and ruthless in battle as the Sultans. From the early

1600s settlements of Cossacks – Mongol warrior bands loyal to either the Orthodox Christian Tzars of Russia or the Catholic kings of Poland and Lithuania – began to encroach on the Ottoman territories in the Ukraine and western central Asia. The Ottomans were therefore hemmed in to the territory they had gained at the height of their power, yet still had a system of government entirely dependent on military expansion. The Sultans, confined within the warren-like harem of the Imperial Palace, proved to be incapable of reform, and the Empire stagnated and then started fragmenting.

Territory was lost both to straightforward annexation by the European powers, especially Russia, and local Pashas and Viziers (an Ottoman version of the Abbasid Emirs) who established autonomous rule supported by their European allies.

After the Ottomans' defeat in the first full-scale Russo-Turkish war in 1774, their decline accelerated and they lost naval control of the Black Sea and most of the Muslim lands bordering its north coast. As a condition of the peace settlement the Sultans were forced to accept the Russian Tzar as official protector of the Christians in the Balkans, with the right to intervene in Ottoman territory in their defence.

After this the Ottoman Empire became known as 'the sick man of Europe' – despotic, religiously degenerate and slowly and inevitably falling under European control. The last two centuries of decline are only significant for the Islamic reform movements which periodically erupted, a common theme of which was the demand for a return to a 'pristine' form of Islam, based on the fundamentals of Qur'anic law. The first and in many ways most important of these 'fundamentalist' revolts took place in Arabia under the Wahhabi movement in the last years of the eighteenth century.

THE WAHHABI REVOLT

The first modern 'fundamentalist' was, without doubt, Muhammad ibn-Abd Wahhab (died 1787), a camel trader from Uyaynad near Mecca in what was then the backward Ottoman province of Hejaz. After studying in Iraq and Persia, Wahhab settled in Mecca where he preached that the Ottomans and their local collaborators had 'usurped' the position of keepers of the *Ka'bah*. Like the Quraysh in Muhammad's time, the Ottomans had allowed the Holy Places to fall into disrepair (both actual and spiritual), flouted Qur'anic law and effectively become pagan.

Wahhab cast himself in a similar role to Muhammad, advocating purification of the religion and a return to the traditions of the Hanbali Sunni legal school – the most Arab-orientated and traditional of the four Abbasid schools – and rejection of the decadent Hanafi'ism of the Ottomans.

He then began preaching his austere version of the Qur'an to Arabian tribesmen as they arrived for *hajj* in Mecca, just as Muhammad had done, and soon gathered a small, dedicated band of followers known as the Wahhabi. In 1778 the Wahhabi declared *jihad* on the Ottomans and captured the governor's headquarters in Mecca, murdering him and smashing the jars of wine he kept in his cellars.

Wahhab then attempted to assemble an Arabian tribal confederation along Muhammadan lines, starting with an important alliance with Muhammad ibn Sa'ud, the Ottoman Emir of the Najd desert region of central Arabia. The alliance was consolidated in traditional Arab manner by Wahhab's marriage to ibn Sa'ud's daughter shortly before his death in 1787. Thereafter leadership of the Wahhabi movement passed to ibn Sa'ud and his clan.

In 1802 ibn Sa'ud launched a full-scale war on the Ottomans and rival tribes continuing to support them in the name of the Wahhabi cause. Ibn Sa'ud captured Mecca, Medina and Karbala – the Holy City of the Shi'ites in Iraq – but was defeated by the Ottoman rulers of Egypt, who recaptured the Hejaz in 1813. But the Wahhabis were not crushed and managed to retreat to the Sa'udi tribal lands where they remained in a state of open rebellion against the Ottomans (and later the British and their tribal allies) until they finally conquered almost the whole Arabian peninsula and proclaimed the Kingdom of Saudi Arabia within its present borders in 1934. The Saudi state enforced the strict Hanbali version of the *shari'ah* and became the first modern 'fundamentalist' Muslim state.

IJITIHADI'YAH (SUNNI MODERNISERS)

The Wahhabi revolt inspired Muslims throughout the world to question the tangle of arcane practices, mysticism and authority-worshipping cults which had grown up in the name of Islam under the rule of the Ottomans, swamping its basic, simple message.

This intellectual movement became known as the *Ijitihadi'yah* (those who question tradition) and gained strength throughout the Muslim world in the nineteenth century. Although the Ijitihadi'yah began as a movement for return to Qur'anic fundamentals, by the middle of the century it had gone much further by questioning traditional literal interpretations of the Qur'an in a way not seen since the days of the rationalist Mu'tazilah in ninth-century Baghdad.

This trend was most developed in Egypt, where in the 1880s Muhammad 'Abduh, the Grand *Mufti* (chief legal officer), produced a greatly simplified 'fundamentalist' version of the *shari'ah*. 'Abduh encouraged total devotion to Islam and scrupulous practice of the Five Pillars but at the same time denied that the Qur'an in its entirety was the inspired word of Allah. He denied the literal accuracy of the Qur'anic and Biblical creation story claiming, like many modern Christians, that it was allegorical. He also demanded full legal equality for women and an end to polygamy, and preached the equality of all religions and peoples.

'Abduh was accused of apostophy (reversion from Islam) by Egyptian traditionalists and forced into exile. In Paris he formed a nationalist political association, *Urwah al-Wuthaq* (Unbreakable Bond), and began agitating for a full-scale revision of Islam to make it a rational and modernising creed capable of leading the Muslim nations to independence and equality with the West.

The Ijitihadi'yah movement quickly gained followers throughout the Muslim world and, in addition to Egypt, became an influential force in many nationalist movements, including the Indian nationalist movement, where it was led by Ameer 'Ali and, above all, Muhammad Iqbal (died 1938), founder of the Muslim League. Like 'Abduh, Iqbal attempted to introduce Western rationalism and scientific thinking into Islam. He baldly proclaimed, for example, that the appearance of man on earth had 'absolutely nothing' to do with the creation story contained in the Qur'an. He also said that the Qur'an was capable of human interpretation and joined in Western scholastic attempts to reform its apparently illogical structure.

Iqbal argued that Islam, freed from European influence and internal decay, could flourish into a civilisation far superior to Europe, which he saw as dominated by a Godless worship of technology, mindless industrial growth, devastating warfare, colonial exploitation and racialism. To him Islam was the religion most able to enshrine the common spirituality of all mankind.

Many of these principles were upheld by nationalist movements which secured independence for their countries immediately after the Second World War, but the reality of independence did not bring with it the rationalist spiritual revival thinkers such as 'Abduh and Iqbal had hoped for and Sunni modernism has found itself increasingly on the defensive.

Today, more than half a century after the Ijitihadi'yah achieved their aim of secularising most of the Muslim world, 'modernised' Islamic rationalism is steadily being pushed aside by a revival of Wahhabi-type fundamentalism.

THE MUSLIM BROTHERHOOD

The Wahhabi revolt, with its call for a return to Qur'anic fundamentals and the overthrow of 'Imperialist' and 'pagan' rulers, shone like a beacon in a world where Muslim states had fallen under the control of European powers. Throughout the Muslim world small groups of intellectuals began to preach versions of the Wahhabi creed, saying domination by the 'pagan' European colonialists was Allah's punishment for straying from the true path.

A Wahhabi-type movement calling itself Islamic Jihad developed in India in the middle of the nineteenth century. But like similar movements elsewhere (for example, a Sufi-inspired rebel movement in the Muslim lands of the Russian Empire) it lacked mass support throughout the nineteenth century and was easily suppressed.

The first effective Islamic fundamentalist movement within the British Empire began in 1929, when a Sufi called Hasan al-Banna founded the Muslim Brotherhood (*al-Ikhwan al-Muslimum*) in Egypt. Al-Banna's aim was the destruction of the British-inspired secular constitution which had been imposed on Egypt in 1923 and its replacement with a Saudi Arabian-type Islamic constitution. He modelled the Brotherhood on the lines of a militant Sufi monastic order, combining evangelism for fundamentalist Islam with underground revolutionary activity against the British-backed government of King Farouk. Members came from all walks of life and pledged to put Qur'anic law into action within their own families. The Brothers adopted religious dress, strictly practised the *ibadah*, and violently attacked nominal Muslims who drank alcohol, gambled, fornicated or adopted other types of Western behaviour.

Throughout the 1930s and 1940s the Brothers carried out military training in the desert, established arms dumps and mounted occasional terrorist attacks on both political opponents and establishments such as casinos and drinking parlours, becoming a constant thorn in the flesh of the British and Egyptian secular authorities.

In 1948, after the defeat of Egypt and the other Arab nations in the war against Israel, the Brotherhood rose in open insurrection. At first the Brothers allied themselves with Gamal Abdul Nasser, a socialist and nationalist leader with strong support in the army. They played an important role in the 1952 revolution which deposed King Farouk and established Nasser as President of the new Egyptian Republic.

In the same year the Jordanian branch of the Brotherhood assassinated King Abdullah al-Hashim who, Arab nationalists believed, had gained the Jordanian throne from the British as a reward for helping create the state of Israel.

Nasser, however, emerged not as a 'fundamentalist', but an Arab nationalist committed to modernising Egypt along socialist and not Islamic lines. The Brotherhood turned against him and attempted to assassinate him in 1954. Nasser retaliated by hanging six leading Brothers, jailing dozens more and forcing thousands into exile – mainly in conservative Saudi Arabia and Pakistan.

Sayyid Qutb, one of the Brotherhood's jailed intellectuals, used his time in prison to clarify the movement's aims. He described it as no longer a simple movement for the introduction of *shari'ah* law in Egypt, but an international *jihad* against Western Imperialists, Russian and Chinese Communists and Muslim secularists. The Brotherhood's goal was nothing less than the purification and unification of the whole Muslim world into a single Islamic republic with Qur'anic law extended to every aspect of life and politics.

Qutb's work was published throughout the Muslim world but was especially popular in Pakistan where the immediate post-independence enthusiasm for Western-style secularism had turned into disillusionment.

Fundamentalist movements had been active on the Indian sub-continent since the Islamic Jihad group in the mid-nineteenth century but this was now boosted by the Brotherhood and growing support from increasingly wealthy and powerful fundamentalist Saudi Arabia.

In 1956 agitation by the Brotherhood's Pakistani allies, the Ja'mat-I-Islami Party (founded in 1932), led to the declaration of an Islamic Republic in Pakistan and the progressive replacement of secular with *shari'ah* law.

The Brotherhood remained illegal and severely repressed in Egypt and most other parts of the Arab world throughout the 1960s. The international leadership of the movement passed to the group of exiled conservative Brothers in Saudi Arabia who were encouraged by the government and increasingly became seen as its tool.

In 1970, when President Sadat ended Nasser's policy of reliance on Soviet aid in favour of the newly oil-rich Saudis, part of the price was acceptance of a degree of Saudi-style 'Islamisation' and the return of the Brothers to Egypt.

Although the Brotherhood is still technically illegal in Egypt, the organisation now acts as an intermediary between the Saudi and Egyptian governments and therefore wields great power and influence. The Egyptian Brotherhood's many 'front' organisations include the Egyptian Union of Islamic Students which constantly agitates for Saudi Arabian- and Pakistani-style 'Islamisation'. The Brotherhood also dominates the shell of the otherwise dead Wafd Party, which forms the tame official opposition in the Egyptian parliament.

Yet not all the Egyptian Brothers accepted the new and cosy relationship with the government imposed on the organisation by the Saudi Arabians. In the late 1970s a militant group split off to form an armed underground movement called *Takfir wa'al Hiraj* (The Excommunicated in Holy Flight). The name comes from the *Hiraj*, Muhammad's flight from Mecca to Medina. In 1981 the group was involved in the assassination of President Sadat.

The Brothers are also active in a number of other countries and during the 1980s were accused of sponsoring subversive fundamentalist agitation in Sudan, Algeria, Morocco and Tunisia, where the local branch uses the name Islamic Tendency. And in the early 1980s the Brothers were largely responsible for the adoption by Mauritania of Islamic Republic status.

Syria has been a particularly important target for the Brothers. In 1982 they gained control of the city of Hama and attempted a fundamentalist uprising against President Assad – a bitter enemy of their Saudi backers.

Today the Brotherhood is a mainly conservative force which agitates with varying degrees of violence for 'Islamisation'. It is especially popular with Arab businessmen and there is little doubt many of its middle-class members are chiefly there to curry favour with the Saudi government in the hope of acting as business as well as political agents.

THE IRANIAN REVOLUTION

In Islamic countries revolutionaries do not look to the future. Instead they look to the past. This is often a difficult concept for Westerners to grasp, but the fact is that the most radical Muslims are simultaneously the most conservative, believing the ideal society existed in the time of Muhammad.

In this sense the Shi'ites of Iran are the most fundamentalist. The roots of modern Iranian fundamentalism go back to the martyrdom of 'Ali and Husayn by the 'Umayyad 'usurper' Caliphs in the seventh century.

The 1979 Iranian revolution was carried out in the name of Shi'ite martyrs to recreate the perfect Muslim political state they died attempting to defend. Ayatollah Khomeini, in his book *Islam and Revolution* (1981), put it like this:

'Unfortunately, true Islam lasted only for a brief period after its inception. First the 'Umayyads and then the Abbasids inflicted all kinds of damage on Islam. Later the Shahs ruling Iran continued on the same path; they completely distorted Islam and established something quite different in its place . . . the Arabism of the Jahiliyya (pagan, pre-Islamic age of ignorance).'

'Sunni-populated countries', Khomeini continued, 'believe in obeying their rulers, whereas the Shi'ites have always believed in rebellion.' Shi'ite fundamentalism therefore not only involves introduction of the *shari'ah* but also demands the overthrow of Sunni rulers and monarchs. For this reason the 'fundamentalism' of Iran and that of a Sunni country such as Saudi Arabia or Pakistan are hostile to each other.

The practical, as opposed to ideological, roots of the Iranian revolution only stretch back to the seventeenth century – a relatively short time-scale for Muslim political rivalries – and the coming to power within the country by the *ulama*. Over the centuries the *ulama* developed into a body similar to the Roman Catholic conclave of cardinals and their Imam became, in effect, the Shi'ite 'Pope'. The priesthood they developed was a ramified, well-organised, hierarchical structure spreading its influence into every town and village. No other Muslim country has ever had anything as comprehensive.

At the bottom of the hierarchy are the common believers, organised into groups by thousands of *mullahs* (priest-teachers), with above them the *Hojjat-ul-Islam* (provincial judges), *Ayatollahs* (judges of appeal) and *Grand Ayatollahs* who form the *ulama*. Above them all is the *ulama*'s elected Imam.

By the middle of the eighteenth century force of circumstance meant that the *ulama* accepted rule by a Shah. But the Iranian Shahs (unlike the kings of Sunni Saudi Arabia or

Morocco) never became head of the religion. And the *ulama* system was so well established no Shah could rule without the Imam's support.

In effect a 'concordat' was reached by the *ulama* and the Shahs. The *ulama* controlled the religious and private lives of the population, and the Shahs controlled foreign policy and raised taxes. This system remained in force until the late 1970s when the last Shah, Reza, began to threaten the power of the Shi'ite clergy with modernising reforms. The Shi'ites at first supported secularising left-wing opposition to the Shah through the 'Red Mullah' movement led by Ayatollah Shariati.

The followers of Shariati fused the revolutionary rhetoric of Marxism with the traditional Shi'ite suspicion of monarchical rule. But the movement was based mainly amongst the foreign-educated middle classes and the small working class of the oil fields.

The more conservative Shi'ite landowners, peasants and, above all, bazaar merchants remained opposed to both the modernising capitalist reforms of the Shah and the proposed socialist policies of the 'Red Mullahs'. This more conservative opposition was ignored by the Shah and many of his advisers at first believed the conservative Shi'ites would support the regime against the 'Communist threat'.

The conservatives found a spokesman in Ayatollah Khomeini, a traditionalist critic of Shariati. Khomeini remained aloof and passive as the Shah crushed the 'Red Mullah' movement but, after Shariati's death in 1977, he stepped forward to lead the conservative or 'fundamentalist' opposition. Khomeini outlined his thoughts in a series of lectures entitled 'the Coming Rule of the Jurists' which resulted in his expulsion from Iraq and exile to Paris in 1978.

Typically, Khomeini's thinking about the political situation in 1970s Iran was dominated by the events of the seventh century. In his book *The Coming Rule of the Jurists* Khomeini compared the Shah to Yaziz 'Umayyad, the Satanic 'usurper' who martyred Husayn ibn 'Ali.

Khomeini called for *jihad* against the Shah and the establishment of an Islamic Republic run by the *ulama* as the divinely guided 'viceroy' of Allah. These teachings passed by word of mouth through the ramified network of *mullahs* and *Ayatollahs*.

The revolutionary message, no longer couched in the Marxist-influenced jargon of the educated middle classes, sparked a wave of religious revivalism. The rumour spread that Khomeini was the miraculously born and long-awaited 'Twelfth' Imam descended directly from Muhammad who, according to Shi'ite doctrine, would overthrow all unjust rulers and reunite Islam. His austere features and prophet-like religious dress deepened the impression that he was indeed some sort of messianic figure, even though he quietly denied it.

It was this wave of religious feeling that overthrew the Shah in 1978 and enabled Khomeini to outmanoeuvre his more radical and liberal rivals within the revolutionary movement.

The new revolutionary regime immediately introduced the Shi'ite version of the *shari'ah*, which has since formed the basic constitution of Iran.

Whether the Iranian model can serve as a model for Islamic fundamentalists elsewhere is another matter. No other Islamic country has a majority of Shi'ites, though Iraq, Syria, Saudi Arabia and some central Asian republics have sizeable minorities. But in none of these are the *ulama* and the Shi'ite clergy as well organised or autonomous from the state as they were in pre-revolutionary Iran.

By the year 2000 there were increasing demands for liberalisation of the country – and even for a full separation of religion and the state. These demands were repressed by the religious authorities, but it appeared that the authority and influence of the generation of clerics who had come to power in 1979 was declining and that the more numerous post-revolutionary generation increasingly desired modernisation in the sense of some sort of fusion between their country's Islamic identity and the benefits of democracy, freedom of speech and Western consumerism.

10. A CLASH OF CIVILISATIONS?

The idea that 'everything had changed' in the world of international relations after the 11 September 2001 terror attacks on the World Trade Center quickly became a cliché.

The far-reaching changes, of which the formation and activities of Osama Bin Laden's al-Qaeda network were a part, had in fact been taking place for almost two decades. Since the Iranian revolution, the start of the violent Palestinian *intifada* and, most of all, the destruction of the Communist system, the strategic position of the Third World had been transformed. And it just so happens that Islam is the biggest potentially unifying force in the Third World.

But even before the World Trade Center attacks, President Bush's announcement of 'war on terror' (including the ludicrously misjudged and ham-fisted announcement of a new 'crusade' against Muslim powers in the Middle East), many intellectuals on the influential neo-Conservative wing of American politics had decided that Islam represented complete anathema to the West and that, put simply, the West – whether it liked it or not – was locked into a life-and-death struggle with a more or less unified Islamic world.

This argument was most clearly put in a 1998 book by Harvard professor Samuel P. Huntington entitled *The Clash of Civilizations and the Remaking of World Order*. Professor

Huntington's argument was that the course of human history has always been marked by a struggle between forces of progress and 'forces of barbarism' – masked in recent times as Nazi Fascism, Japanese Imperialism, Soviet Communism and, now, militant Islam. The professor supports his case with comparative studies of many civilisations, the characteristics of each analysed, quantified and compared.

His main conclusion is that the future will be dominated by wars between civilisations, because the improvements in communications and increased economic activity known as 'globalisation' will mean there is no scope for them to live side by side, either in a state of 'cold war' or by ignoring each other and limiting contact as in the past. One further effect of 'globalisation' is that people (already in some cases, but increasingly so in the future) will no longer define themselves as members of nations (or classes) as in the nineteenth and twentieth centuries, but as members of a wider 'civilisation'. For people in the West this mainly means an identification with the European Enlightenment – with its dominant ideas of individualism and personal freedom. For people in much of the Third World the identifiable civilisation is either Asian Islam or Far Eastern and Chinese Confucianism – both of which are defined by submission of the individual to the will of the larger group.

In particular Professor Huntington took the more particular view that a war was shaping up between the US (representing 'the West') and 'Islamic civilisation' (represented in its most obvious form by Iran, and those 'Islamising' tendencies in a dozen or more countries which have followed the epoch-making Iranian revolution). Furthermore, the professor maintains, this 'Islamic civilisation' will be allied by what he calls the Sinic (meaning Chinese-Korean-Japanese) civilisation which he sees being characterised by such anti-individualistic and fatalistic cults and religions as Confucianism (Emperor worship) and Buddhism. Needless to say the professor views the fact that China is ruled by a Communist elite (and Communism being a Western doctrine with roots in the very same 'Enlightenment' as the rest of contemporary Western culture and politics) as a sort of illusion. Chinese Communism, he says, is nothing more than old-fashioned Confucian Emperor worship, just as the 'National Islamic Socialism' movements of the former Soviet Union represented only Islamic submission to authority.

In his predictions about the future, Professor Huntington is pessimistic. He is pleased that the Islamic world is relatively backward, especially in the field of computers and hi-tech weaponry. This fact – and only this fact – gives the West the decisive advantage in the coming struggle, but this advantage, the professor says, is temporary. He predicts that the more technologically adept Confucian civilisation of the Far East (which includes Japan) will finance the Islamic world and, in due course, supply it with all the high technology it could possibly require. Thus, at some unknown point in the near future, the West will face a deadly foe in the form of billions of fanatical Muslim fighters, financed and armed with high-tech weaponry by the latter-day space-age Chinese Emperor.

On one level the professor's theory seems to be little more than a paranoid conflation of the US's major preoccupations in the post-Communist world-Islamic insurgency (possibly threatening the smooth supply of Middle Eastern oil to the world economy it dominates) and the fear that China is a hugely populated 'sleeping giant' with the potential to outstrip the US economically (and militarily) within a few decades. On another level it ironically presents a sort of photographic negative of the views of the most extreme and totalitarian of the Islamists – such as the late Ayatollah Khomeini – who likewise spoke of an inevitable fight to the death between Islam and the West. Certainly the proclamation that Islam and Western secularism cannot co-exist is music to the ears of that tiny minority of living-breathing Muslims who would welcome the sort of apocalyptic nuclear-petrochemical conflagration Professor Huntington and his Islamic counterparts seem to envisage.

Still, in 2007, the prospects for peace between the West and many individual countries within the Muslim world (for it makes little sense to speak, as both the American professor and Osama Bin Laden would like, of a single, monolithic 'Muslim civilisation') look decidedly shaky in the wake of the US-led attacks on Afghanistan and Iraq, and amid threats of further possible attacks on Syria and Iran.

The reality is that only a tiny minority of the world's 1.3 billion Muslims are remotely interested in any sort of Holy War against the West. In contemporary Iran, for example, the younger generation sees no contradiction in enjoying the benefits of Western consumerism and, at the same time, maintaining an Islamic identity. The open sore of the Israel–Palestine conflict – so badly mishandled by American governments over the last half century – has the effect of radicalising some Muslims, and provoking what is still a small minority to engage in violent terrorist activities. Effective action to bring that conflict towards a conclusion would, at a stroke, reduce anti-Western feeling throughout the Muslim world.

Another destabilising factor in relations between the Muslim world and the West was the sudden collapse of the Soviet Union and Communist rule in Eastern Europe – particularly in the Balkans – and parts of Africa (such as Somalia). The collapse triggered a series of bitter, mainly ethnic (rather than purely religious) conflicts which led to the creation of large numbers of refugees. The refugee camps of Albania, Bosnia, Chechnya, Afghanistan and Somalia have provided fertile recruiting groups for violent Islamist movements, such as those loosely linked together in Bin Laden's al-Qaeda network.

But even in the case of Bin Laden, the target is not primarily the US or the West, but what are seen as the illegitimate Muslim leaders of Saudi Arabia and other regimes in the Islamic world which are seen as collaborating with the West or not doing enough to help the Palestinians in their struggle with Western-backed Israel. The attacks on the Twin Towers were not part of some abstract (impossible) plan for the forced conversion of the Western world to Islam. Rather they were an attempt to punish the US for its support for Israel and the regime in Saudi Arabia.

Bin Laden, himself a Saudi citizen, learned his terror tactics fighting with the Mujahideen against the Soviet-backed regime in Afghanistan. He only turned his fighters on Saudi Arabia and its military and economic backer, the US (the main purchaser of Saudi oil and therefore supplier of dollars to the

Saudi regime), when the Saudis, under US pressure, effectively recognised the right of Israel to exist. This was followed by the Saudis allowing the US to establish permanent bases in the country during and after the First Gulf War with Iraq. By allowing US troops effective control of the territory of Mecca and Medina the Saudi royal family had, in the view of Bin Laden and his followers, abandoned their Qur'anic role of protecting the Holy Places and therefore their right to rule. They had allowed 'pagans' to control the Holy Places and therefore had to be removed from power.

Bin Laden's problem was that Saudi Arabia is one of the most closed, authoritarian and security conscious countries on earth. There was little prospect of overthrowing the Saudi regime by force – at least so long as it was receiving Western oil money and American military support. Instead he gathered his followers in the 'collapsed state' of Afghanistan, where he was at least tolerated, and possibly welcomed by the Taliban regime which had established a sort of rough and ready, austere Bedouin-style form of *shari'ah* in the parts of the shattered country they controlled. There he gathered a steady stream of willing fighters and potential suicide bombers from the ranks of Islamists expelled from countries as far apart as Indonesia, Pakistan, Yemen, Chechnya, Somalia and Bosnia. These fighters did indeed represent the 'Muslim world' – but only a minuscule sample of it. The fighters were in due course joined by hotheads drawn from all over the world, including a handful from the Muslim communities of Western countries such as the UK and even the US itself. It was these people who carried out the bombing of the Twin Towers after warming up with attacks on US embassies in Africa and other symbolic targets around the world. Their aim was to force the US to withdraw from the Middle East, so that the attack on real targets – Israel and Saudi Arabia – could begin.

The US and its allies responded by attacking Bin Laden's bases in Afghanistan. The result was the scattering of his followers around the world – one faction infiltrated former Soviet Central Asia, others may have ended up as far east as the Muslim Chinese province of Xinijiang where, doubtless they are attempting to regroup. After US 'victory' in

Afghanistan, the troubled and ruined country received the latest in a long line of foreign-imposed governments which, at the time to writing, appeared to be on the brink of falling out over control of territory and the spoils of the production of heroin – the one industry that, under the protection of organised crime, thrives in the country.

Al-Qaeda-type attacks continued after American 'victory' in Afghanistan, though they were against softer targets such as Western financial interests in Morocco and against Western tourists in Bali, Indonesia. The American security establishment itself continued to warn that al-Qaeda was still active and would probably attempt further spectacular acts of terrorism against the US itself as soon as it was able.

11. CHRONOLOGY

MUHAMMAD AND THE FIRST CALIPHS

c570. Birth of the Prophet Muhammad, a Hashemite of the Meccan tribe of Quraysh.

610. Muhammad receives first revelations from Archangel Gabriel during meditation on Mount Hira.

622. The *Hiraj*. Muhammad and followers flee into exile in Medina.

622 (16 July). Muhammad and followers sign pledge of Aqaba with chieftains of Medina declaring Holy War (*jihad*) against Mecca. Signing of pledge regarded as the new year of the first year of the Islamic age (AH 1).

630. Islamic army of 10,000 Medinan Arabs and desert Bedouins directed by Muhammad and father-in-law Abu Bakr conquer Mecca with no resistance.

630–32. Muhammad leads military expeditions to Syria.

632 (8 June). Death of Muhammad. Abu Bakr (father-in-law of Muhammad) elected successor (Caliph) by congregation of leaders of converted tribes.

THE CIVIL WAR AND THE 'UMAYYAD EMPIRE

634. Death of Abu Bakr. Election of 'Umar as second Caliph.

634–45. 'Umar's conquests include Damascus, Jerusalem, Alexandria, Persia and Libya.

c640. Khariji sect establish religious courts to examine who amongst the newly converted tribesmen are true believers and who are not.

644. Death of 'Umar. Election of 'Uthman of the 'Umayyad tribe as third Caliph.

656. 'Uthman assassinated by Kharijis. Election of 'Ali ibn Abi-Talib (son-in-law of Muhammad) as fourth Caliph supported by Kharijis. Civil war between 'Umayyads and supporters of 'Ali – the Shi'ites or 'partisans of 'Ali'.

661. Mu'awiya 'Umayyad (cousin of 'Uthman and military governor of Damascus) becomes fifth Caliph after assassination of 'Ali. Resumes civil war against Shi'ites and Kharijis. 'Umayyad dynasty of Caliphs established (ruled until 750).

680. Shi'ite revolt peaks with the Battle of Karbala. Husayn, son of 'Ali, leads a force of only 100 warriors against a much larger force and is slaughtered by the sixth Caliph, Yazid 'Umayyad. Reconquest of Mecca by the 'Umayyads, dispersal of the Kharijis to increasingly remote areas.

685–705. Caliphship of Abdul Malik 'Umayyad, who unifies the Empire after civil war, founding a centralised state in Damascus. Flexible definition of Islamic faith adopted to ease mass conversion and growth of Empire. (Kharijis persecuted and effectively extinct after 750.)

698. Conquest of Carthage.

711–21. Peak of 'Umayyad power reached under Caliph Walid. Conquest of Kabul (Afghanistan), settlement of Transoxia and the Indus area. Renewed attacks on Constantinople, conquest of most of Spain and southern France including Toulouse. Islam, now the largest Empire the world had ever known, sets about the conquest of central and northern Europe.

732. Death of Zayd ibn 'Ali, founder of the Bedouin Zaydi Shi'ite sect as found in modern Yemen.

732. 'Umayyad armies defeated by Christian general Charles Martel at Battle of Poitiers, north-west France, loss of Toulouse, retreat to Spain.

732–50. Renewed unsuccessful Shi'ite and Khariji rebellions, fuelled by dissatisfaction amongst converts with high taxes needed for continuous war.

750. Army of Persian Islamic converts raised by Abu' al-Abbas of Ctesiphon – capital of ancient Babylon – defeats 'Umayyads at Battle of Zab. Entire leadership of the 'Umayyad clan killed to end any further doubt over the succession except for Abdur-Ahman 'Umayyad who escaped to the remotest part of the Empire – Spain.

THE ABBASIDS AND THE GOLDEN AGE

750. Abu' al-Abbas proclaims his own dynasty (The Abbasids) and renews persecution of the Shi'ites and Kharijis. Construction of Baghdad.

751. Defeat of the Chinese army in Transoxia opens the way for Islamic conversion of the Turkic tribes of central Asia.

875. The Samanid clan of Transoxania (Samarkand and Bukhara area) are given Emir status to rule on behalf of the Abbasids.

898. Death of Hakim al-Tirmidi, author of 'The Seal of the Saints' (*Khatm al-awliya*), first Sufi-type mystical tract.

c900. Hundred years' war with the Jewish Khazars of the Volga Valley. Conversion of the Bulgar Kings of Kazan. Foundation of Islamic power in Russia.

912. Abd ar-Rahman, an 'Umayyad, becomes Emir of Cordoba, introduces the first rationalist regime in Islamic Spain which becomes a centre of learning henceforth. In same year the Christian kingdom of Asturia is established in north-west Spain by Christian Norman invaders.

962. Ghaznevid clan, Turkic people, settle in Afghanistan and establish autonomous Sultanate within the Islamic Empire.

969. The pro-Shi'ite Fatimid clan conquer most of North Africa in the name of 'Ali (the first Shi'ite Imam) and descendants of his wife Fatima (daughter of Muhammad). City of Cairo founded as Fatimid capital.

c970. Foundation of neo-Khariji Qarmatarian (Qa'rmat'iyah) sub-sect of the Egyptian Ismaelites in Cairo.

992. Crucifixion in Baghdad of early Sufi thinker al-Hallaj for blasphemous teachings. Start of Sufi intellectual counter-reaction to al-Ash'ari's Sunni conservatism.

998. Mahmud the Great of the Ghurs, a Turkic tribe originally from central Asia, converts to Islam and declares himself the

semi-independent Abbasid Emir of Punjab and Afghanistan at the eastern fringe of the Empire.

999. Qarmatarians establish utopian communist state on east coast of Arabia. This is crushed by Abbasid military power within five years.

1001. The Ghurs begin a 200-year *jihad* against Hindu princes of northern India (the Rajputs) culminating in the establishment of the Sultanate of Delhi (founded 1206).

1008–28. Civil war over the succession to the 'Umayyad Emirate of Cordoba. Dissolution of the Emirate into rival smaller states is exploited by Christian forces who begin the 'Reconquista' in earnest.

1021. Al-Hakim, a prince of the pro-Shi'ite Fatimid dynasty in Egypt, is proclaimed the resurrected Isma'il (the repudiator prophet) who will overthrow Sunni Abbasid rule. His failure to do so causes the Ismaelites to split into many factions.

1037. Fall of Asturia, Spain, to Christian Reconquista forces.

1058. Death of Sunni Imam al-Mawardi, recorder of the Sunni statutes of Government (*Al-akham, al-sultaniyah*).

1082. First Islamic communities founded in Java (Indonesia) under the rule of the Hindu kings of Sumatra and Java. Growing spice trade with the Abbasid Empire.

1095. Pope Urban II declares the first Christian Crusade with the objective of reuniting the Eastern and Western Roman Empires and reconquering Jerusalem.

1099. Christian Crusader Kingdom of Jerusalem established by Godfrey of Bouillon 1144. Reconquest of Crusader territory in Asia Minor by the Emir of Mosul, a Seljuk Turk.

c1100. Expected date of the end of the world according to Muhammad's early followers. Wave of religious fanaticism sweeps Islam and many sects formed.

1147. Launch of Second Christian Crusade under the leadership of King Louis VII of France.

c1150. Al-Ghazali, a Sunni jurist and scholar at the Abbasid court, reforms Sunni and Sufi theology along rationalist lines.

1150–71. Further splits amongst the Ismaelites leads to foundation of the mystical Tayyibiyah sect and the warlike Assassin sect, which establishes a fortress-kingdom in the Alamut Valley in Iran.

1157. Fall of northern Spanish provinces of Leon, Portugal, Castile, Navarre, Aragon and Catalonia to the Christian Reconquista.

1166. Foundation of the first Sufi monastic-type order (the Qadiriyah) by Sufi 'Abn al-Qadir al-Jilani of Baghdad. Rapid development of Sufi *zawiyah* college-hospices throughout the Islamic world. Henceforth the Sufi orders dominate the intellectual life of Islam.

1171. Saladin of the Kurdish Ayyubid clan overthrows and replaces the Fatimid dynasty of Cairo in the name of the Sunni faith and loyalty to the nominal Abbasid rulers of the Empire. Ayyubid dynasty makes Egypt the foremost Islamic military power of the Crusader period.

1187. Reconquest of Jerusalem from the Christian Crusaders by Saladin.

1189. Third Christian Crusade, led by Holy Roman Emperor Frederick Barbarossa (Redbeard), begins.

1191. Fall of Acre to Christian Crusaders. Peace treaty between the Crusaders and Saladin. Christians granted right of pilgrimage to Jerusalem as well as permanent administration of the coastal strip of Palestine from Tyre to Jaffa.

1192. Muhammad the Ghur, nominal Abbasid Emir of the Punjab, defeats the remains of the Hindu Rajput armies and occupies Delhi after the Battle of Taraori.

1202. Pope Innocent III announces 4th Crusade. Objective is reconquest of Jerusalem and the destruction of Ayyubid Egypt and the Remains of the Christian Byzantine Empire. In the event Crusaders do not get beyond Constantinople, the capital of Byzantium, which they successfully subjugate.

1206. Muhammad the Ghur proclaims himself Sultan (supreme ruler) of Delhi and independent from the Abbasids. Proclaims his own dynasty – the Ghur'iat 'Slave' Sultans.

1219. Western territories of the Ghur'iat Sultans of Delhi occupied by Mongol Khan. Start of Mongol destruction of the original Islamic Empire.

1221. Advance of Genghis Khan into the Punjab. He makes peace with the Ghur'iat in return for tribute.

1227. Death of Genghis Khan. Partition of pagan Mongol world Empire into four parts. Genghis Khan's son Halagu declares himself *Ill-Khan* (ruler of the west) and begins making raids into Abbasid territory in eastern Persia and northern India.

1228. Fifth Christian Crusade begun by Frederick II, Holy Roman Emperor. Conquers Acre and obtains Jerusalem by means of a treaty with the Ayyubid Emir of Egypt, El'kamil.

1236. Christian Reconquista forces occupy Cordoba, seat of the Arab 'Umayyad Emirs of Spain.

1240. Death of Iban al-'Arabi, grandmaster of the Sufi order in Granada, southern Spain and first formulator of the humanist Sufi creed 'Unity of Being'. Sufi influence in Islamic Spain leads to great period of scientific discovery – the Alhambra (age of brilliance).

1243. Muslim Ottoman Turks begin arriving in Asia Minor in a westward movement before waves of invading Ill-Khan pagan Mongols. Ottomans place themselves at the service of the Seljuks (fellow Turks and administrators of the late Abbasid Empire) as a caste of warriors and palace guards in the continuing war with the fading Christian Byzantine Empire.

c1240. Decadent Ayyubid Sultanate of Egypt revived by Turkic administrator-warriors.

1244. Reconquest of Jerusalem by the Mameluke Turks. Crusaders never again possess Jerusalem.

1248. King Louis IX of France begins the 6th and penultimate Christian Crusade. Captures Damietta, near Suez but is defeated at the Battle of Mansura and taken prisoner by the Mameluke-Ayyubids.

c1250. Foundation of Alawite (Alawiyan) Isma'ilite sub-sect in Syria. They refuse to recognise the Assassin (Nizariyah) Imams.

1251. The pagan Ill-Khans conquer most of Islamic Persia.

1254. Louis IX returns to France after payment of heavy ransom and increasing the fortifications of Acre, the last Christian stronghold in the Holy Land.

1258. Catastrophe for Islam. The Mongol Ill-Khans led by Halagu Khan destroy Baghdad, a city of one million people. Fall of the Abbasids and end of the unified Islamic Empire and suspension of the Sunni Imamate.

THE MONGOLS AND THE OTTOMANS

1257–9. Sufi order founded by the Shi'ite Safi al-ha'din secretly in Baghdad with the aim of preserving Persian Islamic culture and converting or overthrowing the Ill-Khans.

1259. Ill-Khan conquest of Syria (Damascus and Aleppo put to the sword).

1260. The Mameluke Caliphs of Jerusalem defeat the seemingly invincible Ill-Khans at the Battle of Ain-Jalut (spring of Goliath) near Cairo.

1270. Seventh and final Christian Crusade launched by Louis IX of France, but comes to an end in Tunis where Christian forces are wiped out by plague.

1291. Acre, the last Crusader fortress, falls to the Mamelukes and Christian Crusades are never repeated. Henceforth the Holy Land is in Turkish possession until the end of the First World War.

c1300. The Ill-Khans convert to Islam, possibly because of contact with the impressive and persuasive Sufi tradition of Baghdad. After their conversion the Ill-Khans continue to rule the land conquered from the Abbasids.

1301. Ozman of the Ottomans usurps the Rum Seljuk Sultans (independent Islamic rulers) of Asia Minor and proclaims himself Sultan of the Ottoman Empire. Rum Seljuks become minor Emirs of Ottoman territories.

1316. Alah'din Khalji, Ghur'iat Sultan of Delhi, repulses the Mongol Ill-Khans from north-west India and frees the Sultanate from Mongol tribute and overlordship.

1325. Muhammad ibn Tughluk becomes Sultan of Delhi and conquers the whole of the Indian sub-continent (except for Ceylon). Serious rebellion, however, begins amongst Hindu subjects within five years.

1326. Death of Ozman the Ottoman. His son Orkhan Ozmani becomes Sultan and rules small area in what is now central Turkey.

1327. Orkhan Ozmani conquers Byzantine city of Brussa, 160 kilometres south of Constantinople on other side of Bosphorus, and declares it capital of the newly founded Empire of the Ottomans. Turkic clans were therefore in control of both the eastern and western extremities of the Empire – the Ottoman Turks in Asia Minor and the Ghur'ati Turks in India.

1328. Civil war in declining Christian Byzantium. John Cantacuzene challenges Emperor Andronicus II and allies himself with Orkhan's Ottoman state.

1337. Orkhan Ozmani subjugates ancient Byzantine province of Nicomedia (renamed Ismid in Turkish) and establishes ramified state with own currency and institutions.

1347. John Cantacuzene overthrows Byzantine Emperor Andronicus II using Orkhan Ozmani's Ottoman troops. As Emperor, gives the Ottomans a base at Gallipoli, just south of Constantinople, their first territory on the European continent.

1349. Ottoman conquest of Epirus expands their control to the whole of Asia Minor (territory of modern Turkey).

c1350. Hindu subjects of the Sultanate of Delhi begin rebellion culminating in the independent Hindu state of Vijayangar in south-central India. The Hindu success is followed by rebel Muslim groups who establish themselves as semi-autonomous Emirs in the various regions of the sub-continent.

c1350. Ottoman Empire adopts and sponsors the Sunni Hanafi legal school which serves to legitimise their rule and spread their influence against the Persians and Seljuks who sponsor the rival Shafi school.

1354. The Ottomans occupy the Gallipoli base granted to them by Byzantine Emperor John VIII (John Cantacuzene).

1359. Death of Orkhan of the Ottomans, succeeded by Murad Ozmani, who invades the Balkan territories of European Byzantium.

1361. Conquest of Adrianople by Murad Ozmani. Foundation of Ottoman Balkan Empire. Reduction of Byzantium to Constantinople alone and John IV to the status of 'Christian Emir'.

1370. The Mongol Khan Tamberlaine gains control of territory of the Mongol Golden Horde (ruled by his blood relatives since the death of Genghis Khan and the division of his Empire into four parts) for Islam. Territory included Moscow and Kiev, the Crimea, Caucasus, northern Asia

Minor and southern Ukraine which become the Islamic Khanates of Crimea, Kazan and Astrakhan.

1389. Ottomans destroy all effective resistance in the south Balkans at the Battle of Kosovo on Serbia–Albania border.

1398–9. Tamberlaine's advance into India. Destruction of Delhi, looting of the Punjab, destruction of Turkic Ghur'iat Empire and restriction of Sultanate to Delhi and its immediate surroundings. The Punjab is ravaged and looted but not annexed.

1402. Tamberlaine defeats the Ottomans at the Battle of Angora (near site of modern Turkish capital of Ankara) and checks Ottoman expansion for fifty years.

1404. Tamberlaine's followers, the Timurids, capture Afghanistan and establish a capital at Herat which becomes one of the largest and most prosperous cities of Islam.

1405. Death of Tamberlaine, the Mongol ruler responsible for most of present-day Islam's following in central Asia, the Volga-Tartar region and northern Black Sea areas such as Crimea.

1405–50. Ottomans steadily regain territory from the Ill-Khans following the death of Tamberlaine. Difficulties over the succession.

c1450. Small but thriving Islamic Sultanates established on the north coast of Java (Indonesia) to control spice trade.

1453 (29 May). Fall of Constantinople to Muhammad Ozmani, Ottoman Emperor. Constantinople's name changed to Istanbul ('city of Islam') and thereafter serves as the capital of the Ottoman Empire. Decree of fratricide to prevent successional disputes.

1459–63. Ottoman conquest of southern Balkans – Greece, Bulgaria, Serbia and Bosnia.

1461–75. Ottoman conquest of the Mongol Khanate of Crimea and last isolated bastions of Byzantium in eastern Asia Minor – Caramon ('little Armenia') and Trapezus (in what is now the extreme north-eastern corner of modern Turkey, on the Black Sea coast).

OTTOMAN SUPREMACY

1481. Death of Muhammad the Conqueror, Ottoman Sultan who had conquered two hundred cities and twelve kingdoms during his thirty-year reign. Muhammad proclaims himself 'ruler of all the faithful' and *al-Mahdi* – the 'chosen one' – who would unite the Islamic world in the name of Sunni Islam.

1492. Conquest of Granada by Queen Isabella of Spain. Reconquista complete. End of brilliant Sufi-inspired Spanish Arab Islamic civilisation. Sufi sciences of navigation, medicine and mathematics absorbed by the Spanish monarchy.

1501. Isma'il Safavid, a Shi'ite of the Sufi Safavid dynasty, is declared Shah (Persian word for ruler) of Persia after successful uprising against Sunni Ill-Khans.

1507. Al-Babr, a Muslim Ill-Khan expelled from Baghdad by the Safavids, captures Afghanistan from the Timurids and establishes an independent principality. Allies with the Ottomans for a two-front war against Shi'ite Persia.

1511. The Christian Portuguese capture Malacca, the leading Hindu Malay city state. The Malay and Javanese (Indonesian) Hindu princes ally with Islam in a failed attempt to expel them. Thus Islam becomes a military force in Indonesia and Malaya for the first time.

1516. Assassin-led Shi'ite Syrian army defeated by the Ottomans (Sunnis of the Hanafi school) at the Battle of Dabik, near Damascus. Rapid decline of Assassins as autonomous military force.

1500–50. (Ottoman conquests in the reign of Sultan Suleyman the Magnificent 1520–66):

1512 Moldavia (Eastern Rumania)
1516 Syria and the Holy Land
1517 Egypt (forcing exile of Shi'ites Ismaelites)
1521 Belgrade (capital of Serbian Empire)
1522 Rhodes (defeat of Knights of St John, Crusader state)
1526 Jedisan (southern Ukraine – final defeat of Mongol Khans)
1529 First siege of Vienna (trade monopolies secured)
1529 Acceptance of vassal status by Ayyubid Emirs of Algiers

1534 Western Persia and Baghdad (remains of Abbasid culture)

1538 Sultan proclaimed guardian of Mecca and Medina

1541 Transylvania (Central Rumania)

1541 South and Eastern Hungary (partitioned Austrian Empire)

1550 Acceptance of vassal status by Libyan Ayyubid Emirs (also Tunis 1574).

1526. Al-Babr, the Mongol Khan Sultan of Kabul, invades India founding the Islamic Mogul Empire of north and central India.

1530. Al-Babr dies in Kabul. Afghanistan partitioned between al-Babr's Mogul Empire in the east and the Safavid Shi'ite Shahdom of Persia in the west.

c1550. The largest Indonesian harbour-state, Ahceh, converts to Islam and becomes an independent Muslim Sultanate. Islamic influence grows rapidly in Java with military support from the Mogul Empire.

1583. Mogul Emperors enact Edict of Toleration of other religions. Sufi'ism becomes widespread throughout India.

OTTOMAN DECLINE AND THE RISE OF PERSIA

1606. Ottomans defeated in renewed attempt to conquer Vienna. The way to further expansion in Europe remains blocked by growing Austrian military and Venetian-Spanish naval power. Whilst the Ottomans are preoccupied with Vienna the Shi'ite Shah Abbas ('Abbas the great') of Persia defeats an Ottoman Uzbek (Mongol) army in Azerbaijan and threatens the Anatolian heartlands of Ottoman Asia Minor.

1624. Death in India of Ahmad Sirhindi, formulator of modern orthodox Sufi theology. Growth of Sufi movement both within and beyond the Ottoman Empire independent of Sunni establishment.

1639. Ottomans grant peace treaty to Safavids in return for recognition of their rule in Iraq, including Baghdad which henceforth declined into a provincial town. The Ottoman–Persian border remains in force until 1918.

1640. Safavids move the capital of Persia to Isfahan which becomes one of the leading cities of contemporary world culture (128 mosques, 48 Sufi colleges, 273 public baths, many public buildings, fountains, monuments, etc.). Arts and sciences flourish, especially portrait painting.

1648. Shi'ite *ulama* of Persia challenges divinity of the Shi'ite Safavid Shahs. Ayatollah Ahmad Ardabili defines modern Shi'ite creed that rule of 'the Twelfth' is vested in the *ulama* which should be composed of the wisest and most learned Qur'anic scholars to be found in the realm.

1652–94. Reign of the powerless 'Four Drunken Shahs' in Shi'ite Persia. Institution of monarchy discredited by degenerate court. Riots against un-Islamic morality – e.g. smashing of jars of wine found in the royal cellars, etc. Growing power of the Shi'ite *ulama*.

1659. Day-to-day control of the Ottoman Empire passes from the Sultans to the Albanian Grand Vizier Muhammad Kuprulu who organises a final, futile Ottoman push against Vienna. The events marking Ottoman decline in the late seventeenth century are as follows:

1664 Peace of Vasvar. Austrians gain southern Hungary

1671 Hungarian peasant uprising against the Ottomans

1683 Second siege of Vienna. Ottomans defeated by Polish army

1684 Liberation of all Hungary by Papal army

1688 Liberation of Belgrade (Russia joins Papal Alliance)

1691 Liberation of Transylvania (central Rumania)

1696 Tzar Peter I conquers parts of Crimea

1697 Liberation of Sarajevo and parts of Serbia.

1690s. Uprisings of Christian peoples of Ottoman Balkans

1691. Islamic Mogul Empire in India reaches peak of power under Aurangzeb.

1694. Ayatollah Muhammad Majlisi deposes last Safavid Shah, Sultan-Husayn 'the drunkard', and rules Shi'ite Iran on behalf of the *ulama* (exactly the position in Iran today). Majlisi weakens the state by persecuting monarchists, Sufis and the Sunni minority.

1696. The Mogul city of Calcutta comes under the jurisdiction of the British East India Company.

1709. Mir Veys Khan leads a successful rising of the Afghan tribes against Persian Shi'ite Safavid rule. By 1720 all Afghanistan is independent under the rule of the Asaduallah Khans.

1722. The Asaduallah Khans capture the Persian capital of Isfahan and overthrow the Safavid dynasty. Persia again comes under Sunni rule. The Asaduallahs repulse a Russian attack from the north and an Ottoman attack from the west.

1726. While the Asaduallahs are preoccupied with subjugating Persia, reforming its institutions and limiting the power of the Shi'ite *ulama*, their Afghan homeland is conquered by Nadar Qajar, a Mongol-Uzbek tribesman from central Asia.

1729. Nadar Qajar subjugates Afghanistan and captures Persia from the Asaduallahs after the Battle of Damghan.

1732. The Asaduallahs rise against Nadar Qajar and re-establish their rule in Afghanistan.

1736. Nadar Qajar, a Sunni, elected Shah of Persia by gathering of his tribes and with consent of the Shi'ite *ulama* and founds Qajari dynasty of Persian Shahs.

1737. Shah Nadar recaptures Afghanistan and threatens the western borders of the Mogul Empire.

1740s. Shah Nadar raids the western Mogul empire looting Delhi, but not establishing rule. The fabulous booty taken from the Mogul treasury includes the Peacock Throne, used in subsequent coronations of Persian Shahs.

1747. Death of Shah Nadar. His descendants become the Qajari dynasty of Sunni Persian Shahs, but Afghanistan again rebels. Ahmad Khan Abdali elected King of Afghanistan by tribal assembly and founds Durrani dynasty of Afghan Kings.

1768–74. During the first Russo–Turkish war, 'infidel' Russia becomes the official protector of the Christians of the Balkans, conquers parts of Crimea and the north coast of the Black Sea, and gains naval superiority in the Black Sea.

1793. Death of ibn al-Wahhab a fanatical Sunni Hanbali revivalist from Mecca, which is under decadent Turkish Ottoman rule. (Al-Wahhab was the originator of modern Sunni conservative 'cleansing' fundamentalism.)

c1800. Al-Wahhab's follower Shah Wali-Allah of Delhi founds Islamic Jihad, a powerful modernising fundamentalist movement in British Indian Raj.

EUROPEAN COLONIALISM

1803–15. Revolt against the Turks by fundamentalist followers of al-Wahhab (Wahhabis) in Arabia leads to establishment of a shortlived traditionalist Hanbali Sunni state with its capital at Ridyah. The Wahhabis seek British help, but this is not to come until a century later during the 1914–18 war, and the Wahhabi state is temporarily crushed by Ottoman army.

1803. British General Lake conquers Delhi. Mogul Empire becomes a British protectorate.

1805. Muhammad 'Ali, the modernising Ottoman Vizier of Egypt, declares effective independence from the Ottoman Sultan.

1809. The British grant protection to the Durrani Kings of Afghanistan who are under pressure from Russian expansion in the north and Indian Sikh expansion in the east.

1818. Barakazi tribe rebels against the British-supported King of Afghanistan and take Kabul and Peshawar. The Barakazi divide the country into small fiefdoms (*sardars*) allowing Sikhs to capture eastern provinces and granting independence to southern provinces. Muhammad Barakazi establishes the much-weakened kingdom of Afghanistan under the rule of his dynasty the Muhammadazi-Barakazi.

1820. British pact with Arab *shayhks* of the Gulf brings support for revolts against the Ottomans and effective British control of the area.

1831–40. Muhammad 'Ali, ruler of independent Islamic state of Egypt, annexes Ottoman provinces of Sinai, Gaza, Palestine and Syria.

1839. The Qajari Shah of Persia attacks the weakened kingdom of Afghanistan with Russian support. British General Burns repulses the attack and Afghanistan becomes an effective protectorate of the British Indian Empire.

1844. Baha'i sect founded during a wave of anti-clerical feeling in Persia.

c1850s. Continuous rebellions and uprisings in Afghanistan against the British-supported Kings until Amanollah Shah installs himself as King and is granted 'complete independence' by the British.

1861. Lebanon established as an independent state under French protection with Egyptian–Syrian toleration.

1875. Ottoman Empire declares public bankruptcy. Urgent reform movement (including the abolition of torture) culminates in the first Ottoman 'constitution' which, in theory gives rights to subjects and recognises the equality of religions within the Empire. The constitution, however, is regarded as an heretical Western imposition and the Sultans pointedly ignore it.

1880s. Modernising Egyptians encourage Sufi orders of Tijani, Sanusi, in missionary work in Sudan and the western sub-Sahara.

1880. Death of Jamal al-Din al-Afghani, leader of early and effective modern fundamentalist movement in Egypt.

1880. Ghulam Ahmad founds theologically degenerate pantheistic Sunni Ahmadiyah sect in East Punjab.

1882. Direct British rule in Egypt and the introduction of Anglo-Muhammadan law with the consent of Egyptian Sunni elites. Chief Egyptian legal officer (Grand Mufti) Shayk Muhammad Abduh (1849–1905) founds a modernist legal reform movement.

1888. Death of Namik Kemal, leader of the 'Young Turk' secularising reform movement in Ottoman Turkey. Leadership passes to the pro-European secularist Kemal Ataturk.

1890. Shi'ite agitation against the granting of trade monopolies to British companies as part of the division of Persia into Russian and British spheres of influence with the acceptance of the hereditary Persian Sunni monarchs, the Shahs.

c1900. Islamic Jihad Movement founded in northern India (now Pakistan) by followers of Wali-Allah. Aim is purification of Islam in preparation for Qur'anic law after British have been defeated as colonial power.

1900. Influential Egyptian nationalist Qasim Amin publishes *Women's Emancipation* arguing that women should simultaneously return to the role prescribed for them by the *shari'ah*, but at the same time play a prominent and militant role in national liberation movements.

1901. Muhammad ibn Sa'ud, a British-supported Wahhabi, captures Ottoman fortress of Masmak, near Riyadh in Arabia. Sa'ud clan are henceforth the de facto rulers of the area despite continuing nominal Ottoman rule.

1905. Formation of the Young Turk Party in Damascus as a secret association amongst reformist military officers of the Ottoman army.

THE RISE OF ARAB NATIONALISM AND ISLAMIC 'FUNDAMENTALISM'

1906. Constitutional revolution in Iran forces the Shahs to establish a national assembly on European parliamentary lines.

1906. Muslim League, a group of Egyptian-style modernists and reformers, formed in Delhi.

1908. Military uprising against the despotic Ottoman Sultan Abdul Hamid II led by Enva Pasha and the garrison of Salonika. Abdul Hamid II is overthrown and replaced by Sultan Muhammad V who promises to abide by the 1876 constitution and support the reforming efforts of the Young Turk Party.

1914–18 War. Ottomans allied with Germany and Austria. British and French support Arab nationalist and Islamic fundamentalists such as the Wahhabis of Saudi Arabia against the Ottomans.

1921. Egypt becomes a sovereign nation under rule of British-type constitutional monarch King Farouk who continues the Anglo-Muhammadan legal tradition in the teeth of opposition from traditionalists and modernists demanding a return to the primacy of Islamic *shari'ah* law.

1922. Formal abolition of the Ottoman Sultanate and formation of the modern secular state of Turkey by Kemal Ataturk.

1925. Reza Shah Pahlavi gains power in Persia from the last of the hereditary Sunni Shahs of the Qajar dynasty in a military coup. An admirer of Hitler, he renames the country Iran (land of Ayran race) in 1935. (Later the Shah allied Iran with Germany during the Second World War claiming Azerbaijan and much other territory in Soviet central Asia.)

1928. Muslim Brotherhood founded in Egypt.

1932. Wahhabi-Sa'ud clan proclaim themselves monarchs of the new kingdom of Saudi Arabia.

1933. Constitution adopted in Afghanistan limiting absolute power of the king, establishing a tribal parliament with limited powers and enshrining the *shari'ah* as the country's fundamental law.

1940. Ali Jinnah's Muslim League declares aim of establishing Pakistan as a homeland for Indian Muslims after end of British rule. Wartime links with the Japanese.

1941. Muhammad Reza Pavlavi becomes Shah of Iran and follows firstly pro-German and then pro-Western foreign policy combined with Western-type modernisation and repression of the majority Shi'ite population.

1945. Independent republic of Kurdistan briefly proclaimed before being crushed by the combined armed forces of Iran, Iraq and Turkey between whom the Sunni Muslim Kurds, with much justice, claim their country was divided by the Ottoman and, later, European Imperialists.

1945. Arab League founded (result of Saudi–British diplomacy).

1946. Britain recognises Transjordan as a Monarchy under King Abdullah, a Hashemite (direct descendant from Muhammad), who seeks Sunni leadership with British support. British military aid including creation of Jordanian army under British General Glubb 'Glubb Pasha'.

1947. Pakistan becomes independent.

1948. End of British Mandate in Palestine leads to division of territory between British 'puppet' King Abdullah of Jordan and the new state of Israel. Abdullah is ostracised for his involvement in the plan and forced to join war of all Arab states against Israel.

1948. The Muslim Brotherhood assassinates Egyptian Prime Minister Nuqurashi Pasha following Egypt's defeat in the war against the new state of Israel.

1951. British and French install King Idris as Sunni ruler of Libya.

1952. Yasser Arafat becomes a member of the Muslim Brotherhood whilst a student at Cairo University.

1952. King Abdullah of Jordan assassinated by pro-Nasser Sunni fundamentalists because of his co-operation in creation of the state of Israel.

1953. Muslim Brotherhood instrumental in the overthrow of British-backed King Farouk of Egypt and establishment of Egyptian Arab Republic.

1954. Nasser becomes President of Egypt and expels British and German military advisers.

1954. Guerrilla forces of the Algerian National Liberation Front declare all-out war on their French colonial masters.

1954. An attempt on Egyptian President Nasser's life provides the pretext for hanging six leaders of the Muslim Brotherhood and driving hundreds of others into exile in Sudan, Saudi Arabia and Pakistan. Whilst in prison Brotherhood leader Sayyid Qutab formulates the post-war version of modern Sunni fundamentalism which amounts to nothing less than a united Islamic republic based on the *shari'ah*.

1956. Sudan, Tunisia and Morocco become independent.

1956. Pakistan declared the modern world's first Islamic Republic.

1958. Nasser proposes federation of Egypt, Syria and Iraq. Only Syria agrees and forms the United Arab Republic with Egypt.

1960s. 'Black Muslim' movement founded by Elijah Muhammad in the US.

c1960. Yasser Arafat begins recruiting militant young Palestinians who are willing to take up arms against Israel for his organisation al-Fatah. (By 1965 he was in effective political control of the Palestinian refugee camps in Jordan and Lebanon.)

1961. Nasser's United Arab Republic plan collapses when Syria withdraws. Egypt retains the title until 1970.

1962. Independent Algerian Republic recognised by France after a bitter eight-year guerrilla war.

1964. Formation of the Palestine Liberation Organisation (PLO) as an umbrella organisation for Palestinian refugee welfare and guerrilla organisations, chief amongst them the

al-Fatah guerrilla movement started in the Palestinian refugee camps by Yasser Arafat. The organisation's formation is
sponsored by President Nasser of Egypt.

1965. First Indo-Pakistani war.

1965. Indonesian coup brings General Suharto to power with
the active support of the *santri* councils of *shari'ah* jurists.
After the coup 500,000 Communists are executed over a
period of years.

1966. Military coup in Syria brings Alawite (militant Shi'ite
sub-sect) General Salah Jedid to power. In keeping with
Alawite tradition Jedid appointed the leader of the strongest Alawite clan. Hafez al-Assad elected President of the
country.

1967. Six Day War of Arab nations against Israel.

1967. Communist government of Albania closes all mosques in
an anti-religion drive (about 70 per cent of Albanians are
Muslims).

1967. Mu'mammar al-Qaddafi overthrows the pro-British
King Idris of Libya in favour of his own 'divinely guided'
dictatorship.

1969. President Numiery of Sudan introduces *shari'ah* law.

1969. Saudi Arabians found the World Muslim League Secretariat to finance Muslim causes with newfound oil wealth
and assert their claim to leadership of the Sunni Muslim
nations.

1970. Under the leadership of Yasser Arafat the Palestine
Liberation Organisation, with Arafat's al-Fatah guerrillas at
its core, attempts a military coup to establish a Palestinian
state in Jordan.

1971. Pakistan defeated in second Indo-Pakistani war over
possession of the Muslim majority state of Kashmir.
Bangladesh breaks away from West Pakistan citing discrimination against East Pakistanis, corruption and abuse of the
shari'ah law for political purposes. New republic declares
itself secular and socialist.

1971. Bahrain given independence by Britain.

1972. Islamic constitution adopted in Morocco, allowing King
Hassan II to dissolve parliament and rule by decree at any
time.

1973. Death of Elijah Muhammad, founder of the Black Muslims of America and Nation of Islam movements.

1973. Republic declared in Afghanistan after overthrow of King Zahir Shah, a Sunni Monarch. Muhammad Doud, the King's cousin, takes over as President.

1973. *Ramadan* war of Arab nations against Israel. Arabs use 'oil weapon' against West.

1974. Ahmadiyah sect officially declared non-Islamic by Pakistan government.

1974. PLO leader Yasser Arafat addresses the United Nations General Assembly, speaking as a 'head of state'.

1975. King Faisal of Saudi Arabia assassinated.

1977. Coup in Bangladesh brings the military to power and a new constitution which abolishes secularism and enshrines elements of *shari'ah* law.

1977. Military coup in Pakistan brings General Zia ul-Haq to power. Introduction of full *shari'ah* legal code and start of Islamisation campaign.

1977. President Sadat of Egypt signs treaty of mutual recognition and peace with Israel causing consternation in the entire Arab and Muslim world.

1977. Mu'ammar al-Qaddafi of Libya pronounces his 'third universal theory' including the theoretical abolition of the Libyan state in favour of a *Jamahirya* ('state of the people') where, according to the slogans, 'the people are the Caliph' and 'parliaments are now defunct'.

1977. The small Muslim state of Djibouti in the horn of Africa is granted independence by France.

1978. President Daoud of Afghanistan is overthrown by a coup. His rule is replaced by the pro-Soviet People's Democratic Party of Afghanistan which embarks on a radical programme of land reform and modernisation.

1979. Islamic revolution in Iran.

1979. Iranian Shi'ite fundamentalists attack the great Mosque in Mecca during *hajj*. Saudi Arabian government executes 73 conspirators. In keeping with the *shari'ah* they are beheaded in public.

1980. New 'basic law' is added to the Israeli constitution

stating that Jerusalem will remain Israel's capital 'eternally'. The Saudi Arabians officially rededicate *jihad* in response.

1980. Start of Iran–Iraq war.

1980. Military coup in Turkey.

1980. Mauritania declared an Islamic republic.

1981. Louis Farrakhan becomes leader of US Nation of Islam Movement (in 1985 confirms receipt of $5 million from Colonel al-Qaddafi).

1981. President Sadat of Egypt assassinated by a Muslim Brotherhood splinter group after recognising Israel and signing a peace treaty.

1981. Egypt expelled from Arab League.

1982. Serious fundamentalist rioting in all Algerian towns and cities leads to the fall of President Hourai Boumedienne and the emergence of President Chadli who embarks on a policy of limited Islamisation of the law and government.

1982. Polissario guerrillas proclaim the independent Saharan Arab Democratic Republic (SADR) in Moroccan-occupied territory of Western Sahara. SADR supported by Algeria and recognised by the Organisation of African Unity and most Third World governments.

1982. President Assad of Syria puts down an attempted Muslim Brotherhood uprising with the death of 10,000 people in the city of Hama.

1982. Fundamentalist riots in Asyut, Egypt, put down by the army.

1983. General Ershad becomes President of Bangladesh following military coup. Islam enshrined in previously secular constitution.

1983. In just five weeks the Islamic authorities of Iran announce over three hundred public executions for heresy and crimes against *shari'ah* law.

1983. Right-wing Motherland Party wins Turkish elections. Pledges to take secular Turkey into the EEC.

1983. Palestinians expelled from Lebanon. Start of Lebanese civil war.

1983. *Shari'ah* law imposed in Sudan, sparking a civil war with the mainly Christian and animist black African population in the south of the country.

1984. Libya and France come to the point of war over the Chadian civil war.

1984. Fundamentalist riots against secularising policies in Indonesia.

1984. Serious drought and famine hit parts of Chad, Sudan, Mali, Niger and Mauritania.

1985. Sultanate of Brunei becomes independent from Britain.

1986. President Zia of Pakistan dies in mystery plane crash.

1986. Martial law lifted in Pakistan.

1986. Algeria adopts new Political Charter to guide the future development of 'Islamic Socialism' which introduces *shura* (religiously guided councils) in the running of the state and the nationalised industries.

1987. Benizir Bhutto's Pakistan People's Party wins first elections after end of military rule. Bhutto maintains Pakistan's status as an Islamic Republic based on *shari'ah* law.

1988. Start of serious rioting between Muslims and Christians in Armenia.

1989. Chinese Muslims demonstrate in Beijing for greater religious freedom.

1989. Hojatoleslam Hashemi-Rafsanjani announces sentence of death on Salman Rushdie, British author of *The Satanic Verses*.

1989. 600th Anniversary of the Battle of the Field of Blackbirds (establishing Ottoman rule in the Balkans) causes Muslim–Christian riots in Yugoslavia.

1989. Death of Ayatollah Khomeini. Hojatoleslam Hashemi-Rafsanjani becomes President of Iran.

1989. Saudi Arabians behead sixteen pro-Iranian Kuwaitis after an attempt to plant bombs in the Great Mosque during *hajj*.

1989. Defeat of Communism in East Europe and central Asia leads to eventual independence for a number of formerly Ottoman Turkish Muslim-majority countries and territories stretching for thousands of kilometres from Bosnia in Europe to Tajikistan on the borders of China.

1989. Soviet troops withdraw from Afghanistan, leaving secularist, modernising regime of Najibullah exposed to attack by US-backed 'Mujahideen' regional-tribal narcoterrorist warlords.

ISLAM AND THE CONTEMPORARY WORLD

1990. Civil war in Lebanon comes to an end.

1990. Unification of North and South Yemen. Ensuing civil war resolved by the effective conquest of the former South Yemen by the North in 1994.

1990–91. The First Gulf War – Iraqi invasion of Kuwait; American-led coalition leads to ejection of Iraqi army from Kuwait, but leaves the Ba'ath Party regime of Saddam Hussein in power. The US increases its military presence in the Gulf region, including the basing of large forces in Saudi Arabia (including, controversially, women soldiers).

1991. War between the newly independent ex-Soviet nations of Muslim Azerbaijan and Christian Armenia over possession of disputed territory.

1991. Pakistani Prime Minister Nawaz Sharif liberalises his country's economy while, at the same time incorporating *shari'ah* law in the constitution.

1991. Madrid conference starts new Israeli–Palestinian peace process. Yasser Arafat recognises the right of Israel to exist and calls for two states – one Palestinian and one Israeli – to occupy the territory of historic Palestine.

1991. The state of Somalia disintegrates in civil war between rival warlords who divide territory on Sufi–tribal lines.

1991. Chechnya declares itself to be independent of Russia – more than a decade of war between Russian forces and Chechen insurgents leads to the complete destruction of the capital Grozny, terrible human rights abuses, the declaration of an Islamic republic and the launch of *jihad* against the Russians and the creation of huge numbers of refugees.

1992. Civil war between Islamist and secularists in newly independent Tajikistan lasts for two years, leaving Tajikistan the central Asian state most threatened by Islamic insurgency. Islamic militants establish bases in neighbouring Afghanistan, where there are many ethnically Tajik tribes in the north.

1992. Civil war breaks out in Bosnia – 'ethnic cleansing' of Muslim minorities in Serb- and Croatian-controlled territory of the former Yugoslav republic.

1992. Temporary federation of regional narco-terrorist and tribal leaders topples the government of Afghanistan. Afghan leader Najibullah is tortured and murdered and power is taken by a succession of gang leaders fighting for control of the country's heroin production industry.

1992. The military take power in Algeria to preserve secular constitution after the 'fundamentalist' Islamic Salvation Front (FIS) wins landslide in country's first relatively free elections. A decade of war between FIS and the state follows, leaving at least 100,000 dead.

1993. Conservative secularist Tansu Ciller becomes first female prime minister of Turkey.

1993. Start of the 'secret' Oslo Peace Process talks between Israel and the Palestinians, designed to overcome deadlocked official peace talks.

1994. Osama Bin Laden is expelled from his native Saudi Arabia after agitating for the removal of 'pagan' American troops whose presence gives them effective military control over the Holy Palaces of Mecca and Medina.

1994. Yasser Arafat and the PLO return to the Gaza Strip after the withdrawal of Israeli troops. As part of the 'peace process' a new Palestinian Authority is established, and in return Jordan signs peace treaty with Israel, ending 46 years in which the two countries were in a state of war.

1994. Israeli settler in Hebron machine guns Muslims at prayer, killing 29 and threatening to derail Palestinian–Israeli peace talks. Israeli Prime Minister Yitzhak Rabin assassinated by Israeli extremist who accused him of giving away 'Jewish land'.

1995. Slaughter of thousands of Muslim refugees by Serbian forces in the UN 'safe zone' of Srebrenica. NATO air strikes against Serbian targets follow.

1996. Yasser Arafat elected President of the new Palestinian Authority in the Gaza Strip. But Arafat's position and the entire 'peace process' is undermined by a new suicide-bombing campaign unleashed by the Palestinian Islamist group Hamas.

1996. Terrorist bomb attack on US base at Dhahran in Saudi Arabia kills nineteen and injures three hundred.

1996. The satellite TV station Al-Jazeera starts broadcasting from Qatar – the first major and basically free TV news presence in the world media to be produced by independent journalists in an Arab and Muslim country.

1996. In Operation Grapes of Wrath Israeli forces bomb Hezbollah bases in southern Lebanon.

1996. Taliban movement seizes power from the narco-terrorist regime in Afghanistan and imposes an austere version of the *shari'ah* on the country. Osama Bin Laden and the al-Qaeda network form an alliance with the Taliban and set up bases in the south of the country and in the borderland with Pakistan.

1996. Ethnic Tajik Afghan Islamic militants capture town in the neighbouring ex-Soviet republic of Tajikistan, rekindling that country's civil war.

1997. Israel hands over 80 per cent of the occupied Palestinian West Bank province of Hebron and holds out the possibility of complete withdrawal from the West Bank in return for peace, security and anti-terrorist undertakings by the Palestinians and surrounding Arab countries.

1998. US forces launch missile attacks on al-Qaeda bases in southern Afghanistan.

1998. Israel signs the Wye River Agreement, setting out a plan for withdrawal from the occupied Palestinian West Bank.

1999. Serb attacks on ethnic Albanian Muslims in Kosovo led to mass exodus of Yugoslav Muslims to Albania and NATO air strikes against Serbia.

1999. Pakistan and Indian forces exchange fire in Kashmir. Months later the Pakistani military depose Prime Minister Nawaz Sharif and install General Pervez Musharraf.

1999. Terrorist bombings carried out by the fundamentalist Islamic Movement of Uzbekistan kill twelve in the Uzbek capital Tashkent and prompt anti-Islamist clamp-down by the secular, ex-Communist government.

2000. Several states in the Muslim north of Nigeria adopt *shari'ah* law, causing friction with the country's large non-Muslim minorities.

2000. US navy warship USS *Cole* severely damaged by suicide attack in Aden harbour during visit to Yemen. Later that year Yemeni extremists blow up British embassy.

2000. Liberal reformers win general election in Iran, but Islamist 'hard-liners' hang on to power.

2000. Israeli forces withdraw from southern Lebanon as part of the Middle East peace process. The Iranian-backed Shi'ite Lebanese Hezbollah militia claims victory and is openly praised by Saudi Arabia and other Arab states. The Palestinian *intifada* (uprising) including suicide bombings intensifies, adding pressure to demands that Israel should withdraw entirely from the occupied Palestinian West Bank. The *intifada* has an increasing Islamist character, pushing the secular Palestinian leadership of Yasser Arafat more and more to the margins.

2001. Muslim Brotherhood legalised in Syria as new leader Bashar al-Assad softens his secular regime's anti-Israeli and anti-Western stance.

2001. Seventy suspected terrorists arrested in Uzbekistan after claims that the Taliban-al-Qaeda regime in neighbouring Afghanistan had been infiltrating Islamic militants into the country.

2001. The governments of China, Russia and five secular ex-Soviet central Asian states form the Shanghai Co-operation Organisation, designed to co-ordinate anti-terrorist activity throughout central Asia.

2001. Taliban blow up giant ancient Buddha statues at Bamiyan in Afghanistan.

2001. 11 September. Terrorist aeroplane attacks on the World Trade Center, New York, attributed to Osama Bin Laden's al-Qaeda network.

2001. October. US-led forces bomb, attack and occupy Afghanistan placing elements of the narco-terrorist rulers back in charge. Within twelve months record quantities of Afghan heroin reach Western cities.

2002. Tension increases between Muslims and non-Muslims in Nigeria after a *shari'ah* court in the north of the country sentences a woman to be stoned to death after being found guilty of adultery. The sentence is later quashed by Nigeria's federal court. Later in the year two hundred people die in riots which flare after Muslim opinion is outraged by a decision to hold the Miss World beauty contest in a Muslim-majority city in the north of the country.

2002. Yemen expels more than one hundred foreign Islamic 'scholars' believed to be linked to al-Qaeda.

2002. US President Bush says Iraq, Syria and Iran form part of an 'axis of evil' sponsoring terrorism around the world.

2002. Pakistan's military dictatorship bans a number of Taliban-type political groups, alleging links to the al-Qaeda network.

2002. Tajikistan asks for US help to prevent al-Qaeda and ethnic Tajik Taliban supporters 'invading' as they flee from neighbouring Afghanistan.

2002. Government of Azerbaijan accuse Iranian-backed Islamic militants of leading anti-government riots near the capital Baku.

2002. Renewed bombing campaign by Islamic militants in the Philippines. Al-Qaeda blamed for bombing a synagogue in Tunisia, killing nineteen people including eleven German tourists.

2002. Indonesia grants independence to East Timor.

2002. Chechen Islamic rebels seize a Moscow theatre and take 800 hostages. Action by Russian forces kills all rebels and 120 civilians. The Chechens step up a campaign of suicide bombing against Russian targets in Moscow, Grozny and elsewhere.

2002. Israel reoccupies much of the Palestinian West Bank, saying that its security has been undermined by Islamic Palestinian militant groups such as Hamas and Islamic Jihad, operating from autonomous Palestinian territory recently surrendered as part of the peace process. As part of the reoccupation process, the Israeli army kills 52 Palestinian civilians in the West Bank refugee camp at Jenin.

2003. Mass demonstrations in Tehran, Iran, demand liberalisation of the Islamic regime.

2003. Second Gulf War – American-led forces easily overwhelm the Iraqi army and depose Saddam Hussein's secularist Ba'ath Party regime. Sensitive to the dangers of further inflaming supporters of al-Qaeda and Islamic opinion generally, Saudi Arabia refuses the US the right to use its bases in the country to attack Iraq.

2003. Three Saudi members of al-Qaeda sent to jail in Morocco after planning to blow up British warships in the

Straits of Gibraltar. Later that year terrorists set off a bomb in Casablanca, killing 41 and injuring more than 100.

2003. Eleven Islamic militants sentenced to death in Tajikistan. Later that year the leader of the legal-parliamentary Islamic opposition party is also charged with murder and executed after he attracts growing popular support.

2004. Saudi forces kill al-Qaeda leader Abdul Aziz al-Muqrin and offer amnesty for militants who renounce violence.

2004. Libya normalises relations with the West.

2004. US Secretary of State Colin Powell describes Islamist Janjaweed campaign against non-Muslim population of Sudan's Darfur region as 'genocide'.

2004. Millions of Muslims affected by the South Asian Tsunami.

2004. Three hundred Muslims massacred by Christian paramilitaries in city of Yelwa, Nigeria. Widespread sectarian fighting between Muslims and Christians follows.

2004. More than 330 people, many children, killed by Chechen terrorists during school siege in Beslan, North Ossetia. This is the culmination of attacks by Russian forces and terrorist outrages committed by forces aiming at establishing an Islamic Republic in Chechneya and, perhaps, throughout the southern part of the Russian federation.

2005. About half the Iraqi population votes in the first free election following the American-led invasion.

2005. Al-Qaeda-inspired British Muslims carry out extensive suicide bombing campaign on the London transport system as retaliation for British military action in Iraq and Afghanistan. The bombings took place on 7 July and '7/7' was said to be the British equivalent of the '9/11' attack on the World Trade Center in New York.

2005. Syrian troops withdraw from Lebanon during 'Cedar Revolution'.

2005. Mahmoud Ahmadinejad elected President of Iran, promising anti-Western stance.

2005. Hamid Karzai elected President of Afghanistan.

2006. Militias loyal to the Union of Islamic Courts take control of Somalia after defeating clan warlords.

2006. More than three hundred people accidentally stoned to death during *hajj*.

2006. Hamas wins first free elections for the Palestinian
Authority.
2006. Israel raids Gaza and invades Lebanon following rocket
attacks by Hezbollah.

Part 3

ISLAMIC SECTS

12. SUNNI ISLAM

I slam can seem very baffling to outsiders because of its division into so many rival sects. Most people in the West know of the division between the dominant Sunni and the minority Shi'ite sects – the main sectarian divide. But beyond this there are dozens of sub-divisions which have shaped the development of the religion and continue to profoundly influence the politics of the Muslim world.

The vast majority of Muslims in the world today describe themselves as *Sunni* ('Followers of the Smooth Path'). The Sunnis take their name from the *Sunnah*, a collection of six 'authentic' (*sahih*) books of *hadith* attributed to Muhammad and his earliest followers, known as the Companions of the Prophet (*Sahabah Muhammadon*).

About 80 per cent of the Muslim world population is Sunni and every Muslim nation has a Sunni majority except Iran, Iraq, Azerbaijan, Yemen and some of the Gulf States. Almost all Muslims in the UK follow the Sunni version of Islam, though there are representatives of Shi'ite sects.

Sunni theology and law are based on the Qur'an, the Sunnah and, to a more limited extent, consensus of the community of believers (*ijma*). There are four main sub-divisions, all of which accept the Sunnah and vary only in the relative importance given to *ijma*. The most traditionalist, or 'fundamentalist', reject *ijma* completely but others accept a considerable degree of interpretation of Qur'anic law based on it.

Sunni law evolved during the Golden Age of the early Abbasid Empire with the first works of recognisably 'Sunni' theology produced by Abu-I-Hasan 'Ali ibn Isma'il al-Ash'ari (died 935). Above all else al-Ash'ari was concerned with supporting the political status quo and uniting all Muslims into one state to end the damaging civil wars over the succession to Muhammad. To do this he fused Arab traditionalism, demanding a legal regime based exclusively on the Qur'an and concept of predestination by Allah, with the wishes of 'rationalists' wanting a sophisticated legal regime more suited to governing an Empire and based on the principle of human free will.

According to Sunni teaching a potential Muslim ruler need not prove descent from Muhammad as long as he can gain the consent of the community of the faithful (the *intifada*). The ruler can either be elected, or be a tribal leader or hereditary Monarch – so long as he (or, sometimes, she) enjoys the support of the *intifada*. Once a ruler has proved his effectiveness – by upholding the Sunni version of the *shari'ah* – Sunni Muslims are obliged to follow him unquestioningly as 'viceregent of the prophecy' (khilafat al-nubu'n), regardless of whether he is just or oppressive, moral or immoral.

Sunni law does not recognise the right of the faithful to overthrow a bad or unjust ruler, as long as he nominally upholds the *shari'ah* and is prepared to wage *jihad* if Islam is attacked. Sunni'ism teaches that, as no man except Muhammad is free from sin, all rulers will be flawed and that this must be accepted by the faithful. The only exception is the *Mahdi*, a divinely guided political ruler Sunnis believe Allah will deliver to them shortly before the end of time.

Sunni Islam is a deeply conservative political creed. The early revolutionary tradition of Islam is only upheld today by various Shi'ite factions believing their leaders to be both divinely guided and 'mystically' descended from Muhammad. A central part of the mission of Shi'ite Islam is the overthrow of unjust Sunni rulers, and the two branches of the religion are therefore bitterly opposed.

SCHOOLS OF LAW: MALIKI, SHAFI, HANAFI AND HANBALI

All Sunni Muslims belong to one of four classical schools of Islamic law – the *Maliki*, *Shafi*, *Hanafi* and *Hanbali* – named after the lawyers commissioned by early Abbasid Emperors to clarify and set down the law.

According to Sunni law an Islamic ruler is free to select the school of his choice as the orthodoxy within his domain. But at the same time individual Sunnis have the right to be tried according to the school of their choice. The rulers generally adopt the same school as their father, which has led to fairly stable judicial regimes in various Sunni Muslim states.

The oldest Sunni legal school is the Maliki, founded by Malik ibn-Anas of Medina (died 795). Ibn-Anas successfully overturned the right claimed by the 'Umayyad Caliphs to make laws without reference to the Qur'an by re-emphasising the importance of *hadith*.

The Maliki school was based in Medina rather than the Abbasid capital of Baghdad, and was therefore highly Arab traditionalist. In addition Malik ibn-Anas possessed a great many *hadith* dating from the Prophet's time as ruler of Medina, when many of the more legalistic *surahs* of the Qur'an were revealed.

The largest and most important legal school during the Abbasid period was founded by his student Idris al-Shafi (died 820) who brought the Maliki doctrines from the backwater of Medina to Baghdad, where he founded his own Shafi school.

This attracted a great many Persian scholars who, in general were more sophisticated than the Maliki lawyers and gave more scope to the concept of free will and *ijma* (reasoning by jurists backed by the consensus of believers).

The great Abbasid jurist al-Ash'ari, for example, was a Shafi. The essentials of al-Ash'ari's teaching are accepted today by all four schools, which tend to define themselves by their degree of variation from Shafi law. In al-Ash'ari's time the Shafi legal school became the official law school of the late Abbasid Islamic Empire and remained the most important until Baghdad fell to the Mongols in the thirteenth century.

The Abbasid's successors as leaders of the Muslim world, the Ottomans, adopted the Hanafi school and both the Shafi and Maliki were pushed to the fringes of the Islamic world. Shafi became dominant amongst the merchant classes and the Maliki was re-established in Morocco.

Today the Shafi school is only dominant along the old trade routes and is the majority school only amongst Sunnis in the East Indies, East Africa and the islands of the Indian Ocean. The Maliki school is dominant throughout most of Muslim Africa.

The Hanafi school was founded in Baghdad by Abu al-Hanafah (died 767) to defend the more rationalist wing of legal thinking against the traditionalism of the Maliki Arabs. Al-Hanafah attached great importance to systematic consistency in application of the law, upheld the principle of the *ijma*, and used legal precedents other than those found in the *hadith* to expand the body of Islamic law and theology.

The Hanafi school greatly developed court procedure and rules of evidence and advised that extreme Qur'anic (*hadd*) punishments were to be used very rarely, and then only by way of example.

Hanafi doctrines were more suited to the smooth administration of the large and complex Abbasid Empire, and the Caliphs at first favoured them over the Shafi. But they were extremely unpopular with the traditionalist masses and sparked numerous revolts. In this unsteady political climate the Abbasids tried to remove the focus of Arab and Shi'ite unrest by switching their sponsorship to the al-Ash'ari's Shafi school, which took a middle course between the Hanafi and Maliki.

The Hanafi jurist Hasan al-Maturidi, a contemporary of al-Ash'ari, likewise modified Hanafi doctrines, accepting many of the traditionalists' demands for greater reliance on *hadith*. Al-Maturidi's legal compromises involved acceptance of additional *hadith*, especially the Sunnah, and less reliance on judicial independence and *ijma*.

After the fall of the Abbasid Empire the Arabs became politically powerless and their traditionalist creed was ignored by the new power in the Islamic world, the Ottoman Turks. The Ottomans, unable to claim legitimacy on even the most remote descent from Muhammad, were naturally hostile to the traditionalist Arab Maliki and Persian Shafi schools, and instead adopted Hanafi'ism. Ottoman sponsorship ensured that the Hanafi became the dominant Sunni law school throughout most of the Muslim world.

The Hanafi are the least 'fundamentalist' of the four Sunni schools and less inclined to accept legal regimes based entirely on the Qur'an and *hadith*. For this reason Hanafi Sunnis tend to be the most acceptable of all Muslims to the West, and during the colonial period Hanafi rulers in countries such as Egypt and India showed a marked affinity for Western customs and accepted hybrid Muslim–European legal codes.

Modern Turkey, the heartland of Ottoman Hanafi'ism, has adopted an entirely secular legal system, which would be out of the question in any country where one of the other legal schools was dominant.

The Hanbali Sunni law school is by far the most fundamentalist of the four. Today it is not found outside Saudi Arabia, where it is the official state creed. The school was founded by Ahmad ibn Hanbal (died 850), an extreme Arab traditionalist who broke away from the Maliki.

Hanbal entirely rejected the use of reasoning by jurists and *ijma*, and insisted that the *shari'ah* was to be based exclusively on the Qur'an. He was prepared to accept the use of *hadith*, but only reluctantly as he believed the collection which made up the Sunnah was not complete.

Hanbali'ism is thus the most puritanical version of Qur'anic law. It became virtually extinct during the Ottoman period, but was revived by the fundamentalist Arabian Wahhabi movement at the end of the eighteenth century.

MAHDI'IST MOVEMENTS

Sunni Islam is far less prone to schisms than Shi'ite Islam (which has dozens of sub-sects, some with extremely esoteric belief systems) and there have been no significant new Sunni sub-sects since the division into the four schools.

Splinter groups are usually short-lived and based around claims of '*Mahdi*' status by particular political leaders or religious scholars. The *Mahdi* ('chosen one'), according to Sunni theology, will be a divinely guided political leader whom

Allah will send to earth to unite all Muslims into a single political state shortly before the end of the world.

Over the centuries dozens of tiny *Mahdi* sects based around individual teachers, 'Holy Men', or tribal and village leaders have been proclaimed – only to disappear just as quickly when the *Mahdi* in question dies. The largest modern Mahdi'ist sect to both survive the death of its founder and gain some currency both in the Muslim and Western worlds is the Ahmadiyah, based in Pakistan. Founded by Mirza Ghulam Ahmad (died 1908) of Qadiyan in East Punjab in the 1880s, the sect now claims one million followers, mostly in Pakistan, West Africa and the US.

Ahmad claimed to be not only the Muslim *Mahdi* but the reincarnation of Jesus and an *avatar* (manifestation) of the Hindu god, Krishna. He proclaimed his mission as the unification of Islam and the incorporation of Christianity and Hinduism within it. After his death his followers formed themselves into an independent community within Islam, generally accepting Sunni teaching and law, and electing a Caliph in the manner of the four 'rightly guided' Caliphs who came after Muhammad.

When the first Ahmadiyah Caliph died in 1911 the sect split. The main group continued to teach that Ahmad was the *Mahdi*, whilst the smaller group, based in Lahore, claimed that, instead of being the reborn Prophet, he was simply a 'renovator' or 'cleanser' of Islam (*mujaddid*). Both groups developed some highly heterodox ideas, often tinged with anti-Semitism and casting the Jews in the role of murderers of Jesus and persecutors of Muhammad.

THE 'BLACK MUSLIM' MOVEMENT

Throughout the middle part of the twentieth century the Ahmadiyah carried out successful missionary activity especially in Muslim West Africa, with elaborate 'conversion rituals' similar to both Christian baptism and pagan tribal initiation rites. From the 1930s onwards, from their base in West Africa, the Ahmadiyah began missionary work in the West Indies and amongst black people in the US.

In the 1940s small communities of Ahmadiyah were established in the black ghettos of major American cities, and as they grew they slowly broke free of doctrinal guidance from Pakistan, developing a separate identity as the Black Muslims of America.

The growth of the American 'black consciousness' movement in the 1960s brought their message to a much wider audience. The group had considerable appeal to highly religious American blacks claiming, with some justification, that their traditional religion of Christianity was essentially a creed for whites.

The most important Black Muslim leader during the 1960s was Elijah Wallace of Chicago, who took the name Elijah Muhammad on conversion, and built a large mosque bearing his name. Elijah Muhammad's version of Islam was tinged with both anti-Semitism and anti-white racial doctrines. His more idiosyncratic theories included a claim that ancient Black Islamic scientists created the moon, and that an evil Arab scientist called Yakud had created the original race of white people as a disastrous experiment in the days before Muhammad.

Despite Elijah's eccentricity the movement attracted a considerable following amongst black political activists and celebrities. The best-known convert was the boxer Cassius Clay, who adopted the name Muhammad 'Ali on joining the movement. The leading civil rights activist Malcolm X also joined and took part in *hajj* to Mecca.

After Elijah's death in 1973 leadership passed to his son, Wallace Muhammad, who purged the more extreme racialist ideas and reformed the sect as a fairly orthodox Sunni community known as the Sunni American Muslim Mission. Today Wallace Muhammad is the resident Imam of the Chicago mosque built by his father.

While most of the original 'Black Muslims' followed Wallace Muhammad into Sunni orthodoxy, about 10,000 split from the movement to form the 'Nation of Islam', which retains much of Elijah's racialist outlook. It is led by Louis Farrakhan, a messianic figure who calls for the establishment of an entirely Black Muslim state within the US. In 1985

Farrakhan received a $5 million loan from Colonel al-Qaddafi of Libya. Part of this money has been used to establish a 'model Islamic community', named Dar al-Islam (Land of Islam), in the New Mexico desert.

Although Farrakhan's following is small it is growing, especially amongst poor young urban blacks, and his influence extends far beyond actual converts as the only black American leader prepared to openly express the anti-white and anti-Jewish feeling latent amongst some American blacks. Some of Farrakhan's followers form the 'bodyguard' of the Reverend Jesse Jackson, America's leading black politician, and there was controversy during the 1984 and 1988 presidential election campaigns over allegations of anti-Semitism in the Jackson campaign.

The original Ahmadiyah group in Pakistan was officially declared 'non-Muslim' in 1980 as part of the Government's Islamisation campaign and the imposition of Sunni orthodoxy on the country as a whole. The group remains active but its followers are targets for both Sunni and Isma'ilite Shi'ite missionary drives.

13. SHI'I (SHI'ITE) ISLAM

Modern Shi'ite Muslims, in their various sub-sects, make up about 20 per cent of the total population of the Muslim world, though the proportion rises to about 40 per cent in the Middle East (including Iran) where they are concentrated. The Shi'ites form the clear majority of the populations of Iran, Yemen and Azerbaijan, about half the population of Iraq and there are significant minorities throughout Arabia.

The 'Shi'i' title dates back to the first decades of the Islamic era when they formed the army, or 'partisans' of 'Ali ibn Abi Talib, the fourth and last 'rightly guided' Caliph to follow Muhammad. In AD 661 'Ali was murdered and the Caliphship passed to the 'Umayyads, who were not directly descended from the Prophet. The Shi'ites have since waged an intermittent 1,300-year war to overthrow the 'usurper' 'Umayyad dynasty and the Sunni rulers who followed them and place 'Ali's descendants back on the throne of a united Islamic Empire.

Shi'i Islam is therefore older in origin than Sunni'ism and modelled much more closely on the political practices of Muhammad and the original four Caliphs. It is also predominantly a creed of martyrdom and revolution, the result of centuries of uprisings and civil wars, and is therefore often seen in the West as typifying the unacceptable medieval and warlike aspect of Islam.

THE TWELVERS (ITHNA-'ASHARIYAH)

The 'Twelvers' (Ithna-'Ashariyah, usually shortened to Ithna) are by far the largest group of Shi'ites and their doctrines may be regarded as the 'orthodox' version of Shi'ite Islam. They form the vast majority of the population of Iran and about half the population of Iraq, where they are in the majority in the eastern provinces bordering Iran.

They also form the majority in the Soviet republic of Azerbaijan, which also borders Iran. There are large Twelver minorities in the eastern part of Saudi Arabia and the Gulf States, but they are only found in the rest of the Muslim world in small, scattered communities.

Like all Shi'ites the Twelvers believe that the direct descendants of the Prophet, via his daughter Fatima and son-in-law 'Ali, are the rightful rulers of the Muslim world. The line of 'Ali's offspring is held to be divinely guided, immune from sin and error, and is therefore accorded the same authority as the Prophet himself. Ignorance or disobedience to the word of any of the Shi'ite Imams is heresy.

The Twelvers take their name from Muhammad ibn al-'Askari, the twelfth Imam in the line of 'Ali. On the death of his father Hasan in 873, al-'Askari became Imam at the age of four. But within days he mysteriously disappeared in the cellar of his house in Samara, Iraq, and was never found. As he had no brothers the line became extinct.

The Shi'ites, however, refuse to accept that al-'Askari died. They believe he is still at large in the world in a miraculously 'concealed' form invisible to sinners (in practice, to all humans). One day he will make himself visible to sinners again as the al-Mahdi, the 'chosen one' mentioned in the Qur'an who will appear shortly before the end of the world. The mystical 'concealed' twelfth Imam therefore has the title al-Mahdi-I-Muntzar – 'the Awaited Mahdi'.

The early Muslims, including Muhammad, believed that the world was scheduled to come to an end by the year AD 1100 at the latest, and possibly earlier. The Shi'ites at the end of the ninth century almost certainly expected al-'Askari to reappear as *Mahdi* within the coming century.

When *al-Mahdi* failed to appear in the twelfth century, leadership of the Twelver sect passed to the *ulama* – the council of twelve Shi'ite elders selected on the basis of Qur'anic study and scholarship. The *ulama* claimed to be guided by the concealed 'Twelfth' Imam and elected a human Imam from among their number to rule on earth until the 'given time' (*gahybah*) of *al-Mahdi*'s return.

Over the centuries, as *al-Mahdi* failed to reveal himself, the *ulama* and the human Imams gained more authority. The *ulama* began to teach that its Imam was divinely guided, incapable of error, sin-free and able to converse directly with *al-Mahdi* in dreams. The *ulama* also became the central political and legal institution of the Shi'ites, during the period when Twelver Shi'ism was the official creed of the Persian Safavid state. At first its members tried all cases in person, but as their authority grew they devolved power to a ramified structure of clerics and judges under their control.

The leading *ulama*-appointed judges eventually became known as Ayatollahs and formed their own courts. The Ayatollahs (both those of the *ulama* and those lower down the hierarchy) were held to be divinely guided and were allowed to apply their own judgement without reference, in all cases, to the Qur'an.

In present-day Iran the *ulama* is the supreme governing body and court of appeal both for the Twelver faithful and for the state. It collectively fulfils all the duties of the Imam, from directing *jihad* to enforcing the *shari'ah* law and *hadd* punishments. It also appoints from within its number a mortal Imam to serve as *al-Mahdi*'s deputy on earth.

The *ulama*'s medieval belief that *al-Mahdi* intervenes directly to guide their choice of Imam is unchanged even today. The Twelver Imam is held to be the wisest and least sinful man on earth, immune from error and the only man to have a perfect understanding of both the inner (esoteric, religious) and outer (political, legal) meaning of the Qur'an.

In addition, Twelver Imams are given sole access to sacred books containing knowledge given by Allah to the twelve mortal Shi'ite Imams in the line of 'Ali. No other human is allowed to read these books which are believed to contain awesome and terrible guidance on interpretation of the Qur'an. They include the Sahifah, Jaf'r, Jami'ah, and the Mushaf, attributed to Fatima, the daughter of Muhammad and wife of 'Ali.

In the past, popular Twelver Imams were worshipped as godlike figures even though such ideas commit the unforgivable sin of *shirk*. Many individual Imams have encouraged the idea that they are the personification of the long-awaited *al-Mahdi*. It is certain that many contemporary Iranians – especially at the mass level of illiterate and superstitious villagers – believed that Imam Khomeini was *al-Mahdi*. Khomeini quietly denied *Mahdi* status, but did nothing to dispel the cult which grew up around him.

THE SEVENERS (*ISMA'ILIYAH* OR ISMA'ILITES)

The Isma'ilites are the second largest Shi'ite sect, spread thinly throughout the Muslim world with concentrations in Egypt, Syria, Pakistan, Bangladesh and India. There are about five million Seveners in the world, following their own line of hereditary rulers, the Aga Khans.

The Isma'ilites take their name from Isma'il, the eldest son of the sixth Shi'ite Imam Ja'far as-Sadiq. In 762 Isma'il died before his father, causing a succession crisis within Shi'ism. The main body of Shi'ites, the Twelvers, supported Isma'il's younger brother Musa-'l-Kazim, as the seventh Imam. But the Isma'ilites refused to recognise him, proclaimed the original line of Imams extinct, and adopted Isma'il's descendants as their new dynasty of Imams.

This dynastic dispute gave expression to a pre-Islamic cult of 'the sacred number seven' which had reasserted itself during the doctrinal chaos and confusion in Islam before the Abbasid Emperors laid down the doctrines of Sunni 'orthodoxy' in the ninth and tenth centuries AD.

The number seven had particular significance amongst early monotheists such as the Jews and Persian Zoroastrians as the number of days in which the world was created. A number of esoteric doctrines had developed around this article of faith, including the idea that Allah was the 'seventh dimension' of the universe holding the other six – left, right, forward, backwards, up and down – in balance. It was also believed there were seven degrees of both heaven and hell, that the earth rested on seven plates, the stars on seven veils and that the world would last for 'seven Divine days' (of one thousand years each).

Most importantly, the Shi'ites believed the Prophethood was also governed by the number seven. There would be seven major *rasul* Prophets before the end of the world, of which Muhammad was the sixth. Muhammad had completed the Prophecy, but also foretold of a 'seventh' – *al-Mahdi* – who would arrive on earth as a political leader shortly before the end of time, but would bring no further revelations.

The Isma'ilites began to teach that the Shi'ite Imamate also moved in cycles of seven. 'Ali had been the first, and Isma'il the seventh of the first cycle and therefore an entirely new cycle of Imams descended from Isma'il was about to begin.

The Isma'ilites took Isma'il's descendants as their Imams and named the dynasty Fatimid after 'Ali's wife Fatima, the daughter of the Prophet. They predicted that the last of the seven Fatimid Imams would be *al-Mahdi* or, failing this, would bring a new dynasty and a new cycle of seven Imams. The cycles would, in this way, continue until *al-Mahdi* finally arrived, possibly after seven cycles of seven or some other multiple of the number.

This highly metaphysical doctrine was codified in the *Rasa'il ikhwan al-safa* (Epistles of the Brethren of Purity), published by an Isma'ilite secret society in the middle of the ninth century. The Epistles are highly esoteric and densely packed with a bewildering array of philosophical and mystical ideas borrowed from Judaism, early Christian sects such as the Gnostics, ancient Babylonian astrology and Arabian pagan number cults. As a whole it is barely intelligible, but clearly owes much to Muslim contact with superior traditions of Greek learning encountered in the contemporary conquest of North Africa.

Despite the incoherence of The Epistles, the book neverthe-less marks the start of the impressive tradition of medieval

Islamic scholarship in which the Isma'ilites played a very large part. The sect was, however, ruthlessly repressed and persecuted by both the 'orthodox' Abbasid Caliphs and the main body of the Shi'ites.

In order to survive, the Isma'ilites formed an underground network of guerrilla fighters and missionaries (the *du'ad*) and at first hid their Imams in great secrecy. Members of the sect often posed as Christians or Jews in order to gain *dhimmi* (protected) status within the Empire. Recruits from amongst the orthodox Muslims and Shi'ites were encouraged to break the *shari'ah* (by for example drinking wine) partly as a method of disguise and partly to break down allegiance to Muslim orthodoxy in order to fully accept the developing Isma'ilite creed.

By the middle of the tenth century the sect had grown considerably and was able to mount a successful rebellion against the Abbasid Empire in Egypt. In 969 a Fatimid Isma'ilite Imam was established as the Anti-Caliph in Cairo and, after a brief civil war, gained recognition of an independent Egyptian state from Baghdad.

The Fatimid state, using the growing Isma'ilite mastery of the sciences and a trading and diplomatic network based on the widely dispersed network of *du'ad* underground cells, quickly prospered. Cairo, little more than a village at the start of the Fatimid epoch, grew into the greatest city of the Muslim world after Baghdad itself. The city's al-Azhar university became one of the great centres of learning, a position it maintains today.

The Fatimids pursued less hostile policies towards Christian Europe than Baghdad and sometimes effectively allied with Byzantium against Abbasid expansion. At the peak of their powers in the late eleventh century their state extended from Tunis in the west to Palestine in the east, controlling most of the territory of modern Egypt and Libya.

The Fatimid state was destroyed as an indirect result of the Christian Crusades. Fatimid rulers had sometimes co-operated with the Crusaders against the Abbasids, but in the twelfth century the Crusaders turned on them and inflicted several debilitating defeats. At the same time the Crusades had galvanised the military power of the Abbasids and in 1171 an Iraqi Abbasid force led by Sal'had-din (Saladin the Great) conquered Cairo and deposed the Fatimids. Thereafter the Isma'ilites resumed their underground guerrilla existence and became notorious as the ferocious Assassin warriors.

THE ASSASSINS (*ISMA'ILIYAH TAYYIBIYAH* AND *NIZARIYAH*)

After the destruction of the Fatimid dynasty the Isma'ilites split into two further sub-factions – the Nizariyah and the Tayyibiyah – both aiming to restore rival Fatimid princes to the Caliphship of Egypt.

The Tayyibiyah, the lesser of the two, supported the infant Fatimid prince al-Tayyib as the seventh Imam descended from Isma'il and therefore the awaited *Mahdi*. When the attempt to restore him to the throne failed the doctrine was discredited as, according to all schools of Islamic thought, *al-Mahdi* will be an invincible military leader.

The Tayyibiyah rationalised this problem by developing the doctrine of the Temple of Light of the Ten Intellects – a highly esoteric and metaphysical creed, even by Isma'ilite standards. According to the new doctrine al-Tayyib was indeed held to be *al-Mahdi*, but only one tenth of him. Nine other 'tenth-part' Imams would be born and, after their deaths, their spirits would stay in the world as an increasingly bright spiritual 'Temple of Light'.

This light, which is taken to mean greater knowledge and understanding, will illuminate all Muslims immediately prior to the end of the world, enabling them to recognise *al-Mahdi* when he arrives. The doctrine is thus similar to the Shi'ite Twelver idea that *al-Mahdi* ('the Twelfth Imam') is already in the world in concealed form invisible to sinners.

The larger Nizariyah faction supported the claim of al-Tayyib's older brother Nizar. Since Nizar was only the sixth Imam descended from Isma'il he could not, strictly speaking, be *al-Mahdi*. Instead the Nizariyah proclaimed him as the miraculous reincarnation (*qiyamah*) of Isma'il himself who, after an interval of four hundred years, had returned to earth to rule as the seventh Imam.

When Imam Nizar also failed to recapture his father's Caliphship, the Nizariyah proclaimed him not as *al-Mahdi* but as the founder of a new cycle of seven Nizariyah Imams. Unlike the Tayyibiyah, who had abandoned the human Imamate in favour of pure metaphysics, the Nizariyah had established a dynastic line of rulers whom they could follow and who thereafter became the dominant Isma'ilite sect.

They also taught that their cycle of Imams would be 'repudiators' – breaking the established laws of the *shari'ah* in preparation for the arrival of *al-Mahdi*, who would restore them. The Nizariyah were thus free to drink wine and smoke hashish and, more importantly, to kill other Muslims in the course of *jihad* (which is forbidden by the Qur'an). The orthodox authorities, unsurprisingly, denounced them as apostates (non-Muslims) who could also be killed at will, leading to a vicious guerrilla war.

The Nizariyah moved from Egypt into Syria, where they became known as the Assassins – the Arabic plural for hashish (marijuana) smokers. The Assassins revived the pre-Fatimid Isma'ilite *du'ad* system of underground cells and established a ramified network of agents and spies in all the cities of the Muslim world.

To try to overthrow the 'usurper' Sunni rulers they established a fortress headquarters in the Alamut valley in northern Persia, from where they mounted periodic attacks on Baghdad.

For over two hundred years the Assassins were the terror of the Eastern world and the Alamut fortress itself is now the subject of many legends. But it is certain that it was a quite extraordinary place. The most reliable accounts describe it as a monastic-type institution in which young men were constantly drilled in the black arts of murder, weaponry, poisoning and disguise.

The fortress itself was enclosed on three sides by steep valley walls, and according to legend – including accounts given by Marco Polo – it was an earthly paradise based on the descriptions of Paradise in the Qur'an. Waterways carried streams of wine (Muslims believe they will be allowed to drink wine in heaven as a reward for restraint on earth), water, milk and honey through perfumed gardens of flowers and fruit trees.

Hashish was in plentiful supply, and there were beautiful women, slaves and musicians.

According to legend Assassins would be called to perform a mission with the words: 'Where do you come from?' An Assassin would reply: 'From Paradise' and be told: 'Go then and slay a man I shall name. When you return you shall again dwell in Paradise. Fear not death because the Angels of Allah will transport you nevertheless to Paradise.'

The Assassins had similar fortresses to the Alamut in Syria and Palestine and they were well known to the later Crusaders as fanatical warriors who fought both the Crusader and Muslim armies. The Assassins of Syria intermingled extensively with the local Muslim and Christian populations, and the many modern heterodox Shi'ite sects and communities of the area, such as the Alawites and the mysterious Druze, all have Assassin origins.

In 1256 the Alamut fortress fell to the Mongols and the Assassins began to disintegrate as a military force. Their last strongholds in Syria were destroyed by the Ottomans in the early sixteenth century.

The Assassins nevertheless maintained a discreet identity within Islam even after their destruction as a military force, with dispersed communities in Syria, Egypt, northern Persia, Afghanistan and India. The dynasty of Nizari Isma'ilite Imams has continued, via various complications, right through into the present time. In 1818 the Nizari Imam Abu-l-Hasan was given the title Aga Khan by the Shah of Persia.

The present-day Isma'ilites have dropped the title Assassin and are now reconciled with the Tayyibiyah faction (now more commonly called the Musta'liyah and found mainly in the area around Bombay). The current Aga Khan, Karim II, is the 49th descended from Nizar and the seventh Imam of the seven cycles of Imams descended from 'Ali.

Despite this portentous arithmetic Karim II has made no claim to be *al-Mahdi*. He is a highly Westernised individual educated at Harvard and residing in some splendour in Paris. Karim II has modernised Isma'ilite doctrines, which he now describes as the *tariqah 'l-Islami* (spiritualist pathway of Islam).

Modern Isma'ilites have sincerely accepted the Qur'an's message of the equality of all races, and tend to be international-ist and charitable in outlook. Karim II administers several large charitable foundations established by his grandfather and is increasingly involved in the work of conservation organisations.

ALAWITES (ISMA'ILIYAH ALAWIYUN) AND DRUZE

Of the many Isma'ilite Assassin sub-sects which once existed in Syria, only two – the Alawites and Druze – have survived into the modern world in significant numbers. Both are concentrated in Syria and Lebanon where they function as the private religions of politically important tribes. Alawites are also found in large numbers in Turkey.

The Alawites (upholders of 'Ali) originated in the thirteenth century as a splinter group from the Syrian branch of the Assassins (Nizariyah Isma'ilites). Modern Alawites form about 10 per cent of Syria's population, but nevertheless dominate the state.

The origins of the split are shrouded in mystery and legend, but the basic issue appears to have been the Alawites' refusal to accept rule by the Nizari Assassin Imams and reversion to support for the extinct line of Twelver Imams descended from 'Ali. The Alawites are therefore much closer to the 'orthodox' Twelver Shi'ites of Iran than the rest of the Isma'ilites.

The main difference between the Alawites and other groups of Muslims is their open identification with aspects of Chris-tian theology – especially the doctrine of Christ's resurrection which is seen as paralleling Shi'ite faith in the 'second coming' of the 'concealed Twelfth Imam'. For this reason the Alawites celebrate the Christian festival of Easter.

But the sect's historical affinity with Christianity has not been so much of a moderating factor. Syrian Christianity (which is of an entirely different tradition to Western Christi-anity) is as theologically extreme as messianic Shi'ite Islam.

The Alawites are therefore one of the most extreme groups in modern Islam, effectively mixing the militant traditions of Isma'ilite Assassins with the fanaticism of fellow Iranian Twelver Shi'ites.

The Druze are a still more heterodox Assassin-derived group. In effect their religion is entirely separate from Islam, of which the Isma'iliyah branch merely provided the long-lost foundation. In the current Syrian–Lebanese conflict, however, they are usually counted as 'Muslims' and are closely allied with the Alawites in Syrian politics.

The sect was formed in 1021 in Cairo when a group of Isma'ilites declared the Fatimid Imam al-Hakim the reincarnation of 'Ali, the first Shi'ite Imam. They were driven from Cairo to Syria by the majority of the Isma'ilites who regarded the proclamation as premature and heretical. The original Druze leader was al-Dazari ('the cobbler'), who was a Turk.

At the beginning of the thirteenth century the Druze sect was declared 'closed' to anyone other than direct descendants of the original Druze faithful, who thus became a distinct tribe as well as a religious group. At the same time the Druze retreated to the mountains of Syria and Lebanon, where they have remained.

The theological content of the Druze religion was declared a secret at about the time of their emigration to the mountains and so virtually nothing is known of their beliefs other than their description of themselves as 'Unitarian'.

This probably means that, like orthodox Muslims, they worship the one god Allah, and accept much of the Qur'an. At the same time they have undoubtedly adopted the Jewish belief that Allah is the god of their tribe alone and, like the Alawites whom they most resemble, they probably also accept the doctrine of the reincarnation of Jesus. Beyond this the faith of the Druze will probably remain a mystery.

THE ZAYDIS (*SHI'I ZAYDIYAH*)

The Zaydis are the most conservative Shi'ite sect and closest to the Sunnis, particularly in application of *shari'ah*. They are mostly Bedouin Arabs and are only rarely found outside of the Yemen in southern Arabia, though there are small concentrations in northern Iran and Azerbaijan.

The sect was founded by the fifth Shi'ite Imam Zayd ibn 'Abidin (died 738), a rationalist who renounced his own

Divine status and that of the line of Shi'ite Imams descended
from 'Ali. After this renunciation Zayd was deposed by the
majority of the Shi'ites who proclaimed his brother Muhammad al-Baqir the fifth Imam. Because of these events the
Zaydis are sometimes known as the Fivers.

The Zaydi Imam is selected entirely on the basis of military
skill. According to their doctrines Allah chooses the true Imam
by ensuring his success in battle and by the death of all rival
claimants.

Unlike the Iranian Twelvers, the Zaydi Shi'ites do not
believe their Imams are either divinely guided or free from sin.
In this respect their version of the Imamate closely resembles
that of the Sunnis. But the Zaydis fiercely reject any attempt to
establish dynasties of rulers whereas, as in the cases of
Morocco, Jordan and Saudi Arabia, the Sunnis accept monarchical rule.

The result has been that Zaydi Imams have often been pious
'outsiders', often obscure desert Bedouin *shayks*, qualified by a
reputation for wise and rational settlements of legal disputes
and, above all, success in battle.

The Zaydi Imamate becomes binding on the pronouncement
of a simple declaration of allegiance (*da'wah*), usually on the
eve of war. After that no man may oppose the Imam on pain
of death until the war is concluded by either victory or defeat.

If two or more declare themselves Imam they are obliged to
fight to the death. In practice rival claims to the Zaydi Imamate
have often resulted in short-lived schisms with two or more
'partial Imams' being recognised until one emerges triumphant.
These 'partial' Imams are known as 'summoners' (*du'at*) and
have only limited jurisdiction.

14. OTHER ISLAMIC SECTS

In Islam there are dozens of sub-sects resulting from dynastic disputes and periodic attempts to cleanse and reunify the religion.

Within the Shi'ites there are estimated to be over seventy identifiable groups, some with only a few hundred followers, and all organised around rival proclamations of the arrival of the 'concealed Twelfth' Imam.

The 'Sevener' Isma'ilites are in general even more given to schism, with countless sects emerging around competing esoteric explanations of the non-appearance of *al-Mahdi* (now over nine hundred years overdue).

Contact with Christianity, often seen as the more effective religion of a superior colonising European culture, has influenced modern Islam far more than Islam has influenced modern Christianity. (In the Middle Ages the relationship was perhaps the opposite.) The result has been further schisms with Islamic sects adopting Christian-type beliefs, briefly flourishing, and then disappearing.

Isma'ilite Baktashis of Turkey, for example, have adopted the Christian doctrine of the Holy Trinity in the form of Allah (the Father), Muhammad (the Son) and the line of mystical Shi'ite Imams (the Holy Spirit).

Shi'ite Twelver sub-sects are also scattered throughout

remote tribal lands in Soviet central Asia and the North African desert. They often reflect the resurgence of tribal paganism and shamanism (worship of faith-healers) practised in desert areas for millennia before the sudden mass conversion to Islam. Dozens of other sub-sects are based on the worship of the shrines of individual Shi'ite martyrs who, despite strict Qur'anic injunctions to the contrary, have been granted effective sainthood.

THE IBADIYAH (IBADITES)

Only one group of Muslims, the Ibadites, have managed to preserve a faith strictly based on the original precepts outlined by Muhammad. They originated before the split between Sunni and Shi'ite Muslims, and date back to the first decades after Muhammad's death.

The Ibadites are direct descendants of the Khariji ('successionists') – a group of close companions of the Prophet himself, including his wife Khadijah, who is by tradition the first convert to Islam. They fought for the maintenance of strict Muhammadan principles but were defeated in Islam's first civil war and scattered to remote parts of Arabia.

Small numbers of Ibadites are found in the deserts of Arabia, Iraq and North Africa. They are almost entirely nomadic Bedouin Arabs, recognise no state or clerical authorities, and organise their own affairs in complete isolation from official Islam and modern Islamic states. 'Ibadite' translates from Arabic as 'upholders of the *ibadah*'. The Ibadites recognise no other laws and have no system of justice or permanent forms of state organisation.

Like their Khariji ancestors, they believe that it is not possible for sincere Muslims to sin or break the *ibadah* and that if they do so they commit apostophy. The Ibadites punish any crime not only with the draconian punishments prescribed in the Qur'an but also with expulsion from the religion and, therefore, also the tribe.

Unlike Shi'ite fundamentalists, Ibadites do not rebel against 'usurper' rulers but instead simply ignore them. Muslim rulers in turn have always left them to their nomadic desert existence.

Official Sunni Islam regards them as little better than the pagan tribes with whom they effectively form a halfway house and they are tolerated through force of circumstance as much as anything else.

THE SUFIS

Sufi'ism is the intellectual cutting edge of Islam, organised in a series of monastic orders which have both enriched Islamic theology and repeatedly saved the religion from doctrinal disintegration or destruction at the hands of pagan conquerors.

The essence of Sufi'ism is 'spiritual detachment' from the pleasures (*zudd*) of mortal life in preparation for death and 'obliteration' (*fana*) of the self into the mind of Allah. The earliest Islamic tract on this theme is 'The Seal of the Saints' (*Khatm al-awliya*) written by Hakim al-Tirmidhi (died 898), a Baghdad mystic who was clearly influenced by the vulgarised Greek philosophy popular during the time of the early Abbasid Caliphs.

About one hundred years later, Sufi tracts began to be marked by a belief in philosophical dualism – that there was a human self and a separate divine self. This doctrine contends that all humans are born with two souls, the human and divine. The human soul is at first dominant, as the 'midwife' of the divine soul. But it is the duty of Muslims to ensure their divine soul grows during their lifetime as the human soul steadily perishes.

This teaching meant that a Sufi had to follow a highly moral, preferably saintly, life on earth as his divine and human souls were in direct competition for spiritual nourishment. The more the human spirit was indulged through pleasures of this life, the more the divine soul would be weakened. If the divine soul was insufficiently nourished it would die and the entire person would be obliterated.

Sufi teaching went on to enumerate four separate states (*maqamat*) which had to be simultaneously attained to ensure the rebirth of the divine soul – detachment from worldly affairs, including politics (*zuhd*); patience (*sabr*); gratitude for whatever Allah does to one – including disease, disasters and

other misfortunes (*shukr*); and love (*hubb*), not merely acceptance of what Allah commands through the Prophets.

Various exercises were prescribed to help Sufis achieve the
maqamat. These included intense prayer, isolation in the
desert, prolonged fasting, self-inflicted pain and wearing un-
comfortable clothes. The actual origin of the term Sufi is
unknown, but the best explanation is a translation based on
the Arabic term for 'one who wears a hair shirt'.

Sufis also developed the concept that it was possible to
become one with Allah whilst still alive by inducing a
condition of 'holy intoxication'. In order to achieve 'intoxication' they developed extraordinary practices such as spinning
for hours on the same spot and ritual trance dancing which
earned the Mevlevi Order of Ottoman Sufis the title 'Whirling
Dervishes'.

Other Sufi groups, particularly in North Africa, developed
customs of walking on hot coals or lying on beds of nails. Still
others spent hours chanting ritual incantations to induce a type
of hypnotism. Qwaali, the repetitive popular folk music of
modern Pakistan, is directly derived from Sufi chanting, as are
some forms of traditional rhythmic African music.

Several early Sufis were crucified by the Abbasids for
proclaiming themselves to be 'Allah' whilst in a condition of
'intoxication', and in general Sufi'ism remained highly heterodox and subject to persecution until the middle years of the
Abbasid Golden Age.

The first attempt to integrate it into the emerging body of
'orthodox' Sunni theology was made by the great Abbasid
jurist of the Shafi school, Abu Hamid Muhammad al-Ghazali
(died 1111). Al-Ghazali's book *The Revivification of the
Science of the Faith* (*Ihya ulum al-din*) reconciles Sufi'ism and
Sunni'ism and remains one of the seminal works of Islamic
theology to this day.

Al-Ghazali injected self-denying Sufi morality into orthodox
Sunni teaching, rescuing it from the extreme permissiveness
and decadence of the late Abbasid period. At the same time he
simplified Sufi theology by pronouncing invalid the Prophet-
like pronouncements of the Sufi 'saints' made in an intoxicated
state. After being given a solid and coherent theological basis

by Al-Ghazali, the Sufis formed themselves into monastic orders to evangelise for Islam and develop its theology and related sciences.

These orders were circles of pious scholars, usually based around college-hospices (*zawiyahs*) for dying Sufis deemed to be in transition from the dominance of the human soul to the divine soul. The *zawiyah* became the basic unit of Sufi organisation and their growing mastery of medicine and related sciences was developed within them.

In the last two centuries of the Abbasid Empire the Sufis made outstanding progress in philosophy, medicine and sciences such as chemistry, and the Sufi orders became the engines of Islamic learning, culture and external influence. Eventually the larger *zawiyah* developed associated universities (*madrasahs*) where religious subjects such as the Islamic sciences of chemistry, astronomy and 'sacred arithmetic' – essentially mathematics and architecture – were taught to large numbers of students.

The leading *madrasah* in the early thirteenth century was at Granada in southern Spain, under the Grand Mastership of Iban al-'Arabi (died 1240). Building on the reforming al-Ghazali tradition, he helped to steer the Sufi away from pantheism (acceptance of the gods of other religions) and saint-worship, back to the original Islamic path of strict monotheism.

Al-Arabi's theory, the 'Unity of Being' (*wahdat al-wujud*), maintained the universe was ruled by Allah only in conjunction with mankind. Neither could exist without the other. This made him a radical humanist and rationalist almost three full centuries before similar advanced thinking was established in Europe during the peak of the Renaissance.

In Al-Arabi's time Spain became the centre of the Sufi Renaissance and the period between the twelfth and fourteenth century is now known as the *Alhambra* ('Age of Brilliance'). After the conquest of Granada in 1492 by the Catholic armies of Queen Isabella of Castille, Sufi learning was incorporated into Spanish culture by maintenance of the *madrasah*. Despite the loss of Spain, Al-Arabi's school of thought became the Sufi orthodoxy in the Muslim world and remained the dominant influence on Islamic intellectual life until the early seventeenth century.

MODERN SUFI'ISM

In the early seventeenth century Sufi'ism was again reformed, this time by the Indian Sufi Ahmad Sirhindi (died 1624). Sirhindi accepted most of al-Arabi's teachings but reverted to the earlier Sufi tradition of firm belief that the world and man were essentially evil, and that the force of goodness was unique to Allah.

This meant that Sufis could no longer simply retreat from the world, but brought them much more into line with all other Muslims in their obligation to wage *jihad* to overcome evil. Allah demanded struggle against evil – not merely saintly avoidance of it.

Sirhindi's 'activist' version of Sufi'ism was to provide the backbone for the eighteenth- and nineteenth-century Muslim modernising and reformist movements which began with the Ottoman Empire and spread to all the nations of the Muslim world in the form of Islamic fundamentalist and anti-colonialist movements.

Modern Sufi Orders are organised in *tariqah* ('pathways') which link the current members of the Order spiritually to the founder. The Orders are named after their founders and the current master of an Order is called *al-Qutb* ('the axis') which may or may not feature in his name as an honorary title according to circumstance.

The method of organisation is similar to Freemasonry in the Western world – combining public charitable and educational work with a type of secret society. Acceptance into a *tariqah* is usually by invitation and is accompanied by the swearing of oaths of brotherhood and the acceptance of the various items of esoteric wisdom peculiar to the particular order.

Sufi influence is greatest in those areas of the world where Islam has been threatened by outside forces. The Orders are very widespread in Africa, especially in the Negro countries such as Nigeria, where the Muslim community itself is in a minority. And in many countries admission to the *tariqah* of the ruling group is essential for commercial or political success.

There are dozens of Sufi Orders spread throughout all the Muslim countries. Some, such as the *Chistiyah* of India and the *Salihiyah* of West Africa, are purely local. The five main international Orders – in rough order of size and importance – are the *Qadiriyah*, *Naqshbandiyah*, *Daraqwiyah*, *Tijaniyah* and *Khalwatiyah*.

THE QADIRIYAH

The oldest, largest and most globally dispersed Order is the Qadiriyah, founded by 'Abd al-Qadir al-Jilani (died 1166) in Baghdad.

The Qadiriyah are particularly important in Muslim Africa where, by becoming advisers to the courts of local kings, they laid the foundation for the spread of Islam throughout the northern half of the continent. The Order is based in Egypt.

There are Qadiriyah *tariqah*s in most Muslim countries but they are particularly widespread in Pakistan, Egypt and North Africa. In the Maghreb desert (Libya, Algeria and Morocco), Qadiriyah are noted for trance dancing (hence Whirling Dervishes) and feats of endurance such as walking on hot coals.

THE NAQSHBANDIYAH

An Order founded by Muhammad ibn Muhammad Baha'as-Din Naqshband (died 1389), a noted philosopher and poet from Bukhara. The Naqshbandiyah are widespread throughout the Caucasus and central Asia where they have repeatedly organised guerrilla movements against Russian and Communist rule. The Order is based in Pakistan where it is closely associated with the movement for continuing Islamisation of the country and support for the rebels in Afghanistan.

The Naqshbandiyah Order is the most politically active of the global Orders with close ties to ruling Sunni establishments throughout the world.

THE DARAQWIYAH

An Order founded in the early nineteenth century by Mulay-I-'Arabi Daraqwi (died 1823) in Fez, Morocco. The Order promotes an extremely conservative version of Maliki Sunni'ism and was the driving force behind the Jihad Movement which secured mass conversions throughout the mixed Berber–Arab and Negro lands of sub-Saharan Africa.

Today the Order is influential in countries such as Mali, Niger and Chad where it works to maintain the purity of official Maliki Islam against the incursions of African paganism and European modernism. It is especially widespread in Morocco where the founder's birthday is celebrated as a national holiday.

THE TIJANIYAH

The Daraqwiyah are rivalled throughout Africa by the more moderate Tijaniyah *tariqah*s. The Order was founded by Abu-I-Abbas Ahmad at-Tijani (died 1815) and was, like the Daraqwiyah, important in the Jihad Movement. The Order took a more compromising attitude towards the French colonialists and often provided them with administrators and judges.

Co-operation with the French ensured the Order spread throughout North and Central Africa. Today it is associated with conservative businessmen in the region and membership often overlaps with the Muslim Brotherhood, a conservative pro-Saudi Arabian group.

THE KHALWATIYAH

The Khalwatiyah originated in the thirteenth century AD in Persia and Azerbaijan and quickly spread to the Caucasus and Turkey. The Khalwatiyah later became closely associated with the Ottoman Sultans, established headquarters in Istanbul and spread to Balkan Europe.

Although the Order was banned by the new secular government of Turkey in 1923 and its funds were confiscated, it has nevertheless survived and has *tariqah* as far apart as North America, Egypt and Indonesia.

The influence of the Sufi Orders within the Muslim nations remains enormous. It is rare to find a Sunni Muslim ruler who is not affiliated to one or other of them. In addition, education within many Muslim countries – both religious and secular – is carried out under Sufi auspices.

Ironically for a movement which played such a huge role in the advancement of human learning and culture, Sufi insistence on the unity of science and religion must now be regarded as one of the causes of the relative backwardness of the Muslim nations.

The great Sufi achievements were made within an entirely religious framework, based on the assumption that Allah existed and that the universe had a purpose. Therefore, great discoveries in mathematics – such as the use of the number zero – were based on investigation of such esoteric religious questions as the exact size of Allah and how He keeps the stars from colliding with each other.

Modern science makes no such assumptions and its achievements are instead based on the application of the questioning human intellect. Modern scientists may believe in God or Allah – and may even be practising Muslims. But, unlike Sufi'ism, modern science does not make the limited view of the universe given in the Qur'an its starting point.

Part 4

THE MUSLIM WORLD

The exact number of Muslims in the world today is difficult to estimate accurately. Statistics from vast countries such as Indonesia and Pakistan are unreliable. In some countries such as India, China, parts of Russia and the Balkans, the exact size of large Muslim minorities is politically sensitive, and estimates unreliable. Despite these difficulties it is clear that there are at least 1.2 billion Muslims in the world today and the religion is growing quickly both in size and influence, particularly in Africa and Asia. For the first time ever there are substantial and growing Muslim communities.

This vast community is concentrated in about fifty nations where Muslims form an overwhelming majority of the population. In theory all these nations form one vast and united political and religious entity – *Dar al-Islam* ('Land of Islam'). The non-Muslim world was designated *Dar al-Harb* ('Land of War') by Muhammad himself.

In reality, however, there are numerous identifiable 'Muslim Worlds', each corresponding to a phase in the religion's development and sectarian divisions. The original Muslim World was the Arabian peninsula, the birthplace of the Prophet and the land he ruled as Islam's supreme political and spiritual leader. Islam as practised here harks back to the days of the Prophet as though the intervening 1,300 years of history had not taken place.

The Islam of the Arabian peninsula is very different to the religion's second great heartland – northern Arabia – where it clashed with Christianity, became heterodox and founded a great world Empire administered from cities such as Damascus, Cairo and Baghdad, which were wonders of the medieval world.

After the collapse of the north Arabian Empire in the middle of the thirteenth century, Islam began to diverge into several separate 'worlds' – North Africa (and, for a time, Spain), the Muslim east (India and Indonesia), Iran and the Ottoman heartlands of Turkey, and the Balkans.

Still more divergence took place within the 'further lands' of Islam in distant sub-Saharan Africa, central Asia, China and the Philippines. Islam never spread to the far north or south partly because of the difficulty of observing the *Ramadan* fast in these regions, or to the Americas because of the extreme difficulty of conducting the *hajj* pilgrimage to Mecca before the invention of aeroplanes.

Islam as it is practised today within these 'worlds' remains united in adherence to the absolute doctrinal basics of the Five Pillars, belief in a strict One God monotheism and the literal divine truth of the Qur'an. Beyond this cultural and historical differences are considerable and defy the negative stereotype of a monolithic world Muslim community somehow engaged in a 'clash of civilisations' with the Western or non-Muslim world.

15. THE ARABIAN PENINSULA

SAUDI ARABIA, YEMEN AND THE GULF STATES: BAHRAIN, KUWAIT, OMAN, QATAR, UNITED ARAB EMIRATES
Total population: 57 million

Arabia is the cradle of Islam – the birthplace of the Prophet and the site of the holy cities of Mecca (Makkah in Arabic) and Medina. Arabic, the language of the Qur'an, remains the sacred language of Islam. The Arabs of the Arabian peninsula are Muslim almost without exception and have seen themselves throughout history as traditional protectors of the religion's purity.

But after the vigour and conquests of the original Arab Islamic state the Arabian peninsula including Mecca and Medina became a backwater under the political control of Northern Arabian, Persian and finally Ottoman Turkish Muslim empires.

In the early nineteenth century the Bedouin tribal leader Muhammad ibn Sa'ud brought together a confederation of desert tribesmen and began to fight the Ottoman rulers in the name of strict fundamentalist Sunni Islam.

For over one hundred years the rebels kept up a guerrilla war against first the Ottomans and then the British and their Arab allies, such as the Hashemite clan and the Sultan of Oman, before proclaiming the Kingdom of Saudi Arabia in 1932.

The new kingdom was the world's first Sunni 'fundamental-ist' state and had no constitution other than the Qur'an and the absolute power of the monarch to interpret it. Saudi Arabia at first claimed the British Emirates and the Shi'ite Zaydi majority lands of Yemen as part of its territory but, after a short war, recognised the existence of both the Emirates and Yemen within their current borders.

SAUDI ARABIA
Population: 25.6 million (UN 2005)

Saudi Arabia was never colonised by the Europeans though the country did fall under the nominal rule of the Turkish Ottoman Empire for three hundred years from the sixteenth to nineteenth centuries. The Turks did nothing to develop the region and left little mark. In the 1870s attempts by the Turks to directly occupy Mecca and Medina – in order to see off the growing influence of the British led to a ferocious revolt by Wahhabi desert tribesmen. Thirty years of guerrilla warfare led to the establishment of a Wahhabi kingdom in 1902 under the rule of 'Abd al-Aziz ibn Sa'ud who captured Riyadh at the head of a confederation of Wahhabi tribal chiefs.

As king, 'Abd al-Aziz ibn Sa'ud consolidated his power by marrying widows and daughters of defeated rival tribal leaders. He had approximately 300 wives and 45 sons, whose grandchildren and great-grandchildren, all princes, form the origins of the vast present Saudi Arabian royal family. The Kingdom of Saudi Arabia was proclaimed in 1932 after further wars with the Turks and the British who had wanted to put their allies, the Hashemite clan, in charge of a united conser-vative Arab monarchy encompassing all of what is now Jordan, Saudi Arabia, Yemen, the Gulf and Iraq.

The Kingdom of Saudi Arabia enforces the strict Hanbali Sunni legal regime, the most conservative and Arab tradition-alist of the four Sunni legal schools, also there is also a Shi'ite minority adhering to the Ja'fari school. The Qur'an and the authority of the king to interpret it form the sole constitution of the country. Family and ordinary criminal law is dispensed by *shari'ah* courts, but commercial law governing the raising of taxes, oil and gas prices, and immigration law, is regulated by Royal decrees and codes.

In the wake of the First Gulf War (1990–91) – which forced the Saudi Royal Family into greater reliance on American military power – there were essentially token moves towards 'liberalisation'.

A *Majlis al-Shura* (Consultative Council) was introduced in 1993. The strict *hadd* Qur'anic penal code is enforced, including hand amputation for theft, whipping to the point of death for drinking alcohol, and stoning to death for adultery. The size of the stones to be used in this form of ritual execution is strictly laid down by *hadith*. To ensure that death is slow and painful stones must be no smaller than a chickpea and no larger than a date stone.

Islam permeates every aspect of life. Saudi Arabia is the only major Muslim country where everything comes to an absolute halt five times a day for observance of *salat* – ritual prayers at the mosque. Business ethics, banking, clothing, food, methods of address and greeting and just about every human activity is governed by religious law.

Adherence to Islam is deeply felt and religious law is devoutly upheld by most of the Saudi population. At the same time the Committee for Encouraging Virtue and Preventing Vice (*Hay'at al-Amr bi'l-Ma'ruf wa'n-Nahi an al-Munkar*) and *Mutawaah* (religious police) exist to help prevent backsliders from straying from the true path. The *Mutawaah* roam the streets meting out instant punishment to anyone found smoking, drinking, gambling, dancing, singing, playing music in public or breaking the fast of *Ramadan*.

The Saudi's clan's guardianship of the Holy Places led the Saudi Royal Family to claim the title of 'Custodian of the Two Holy Mosques'. This, together with its massive oil wealth, has guaranteed the country a pivotal position in Islam and in the affairs of the world, generally. Yet the state's role in international relations is in many ways contradictory. The country is firmly in the Western camp, but at the same time remains hostile to Western support for Israel. At the same time, through sponsorship of groups such as the Muslim Brotherhood and the World Muslim League, it has used oil wealth to fund conservative 'fundamentalist' forces throughout the world. Saudi Arabia is a major provider of economic aid to poorer and more populous Islamic countries such as Egypt and Pakistan and exerts enormous and not always open influence in these countries. Critics of Saudi influence in the Muslim world have sometimes described Pakistan as a virtual economic colony of Saudi Arabia.

In 1990 King Fahd invited the US to establish military bases in the country when it became clear that Saudi Arabia – as well as Kuwait – was a possible target for conquest by Saddam Hussein's Iraq during the First Gulf War. The presence of US forces in the country became a serious cause of complaint for some fundamentalists as the Prophet had specifically warned against allowing non-believers to have military power over the Holy Places. US forces are seen as 'pagan' because they include women. There are many references in Muhammad's sayings to the fact that the pagan armies included women soldiers. This is quite apart from conservative Saudi ideas about the role of women generally.

The arrival of a permanent 'pagan' US military presence dominating the Fahd regime and therefore exercising effective military control over the Holy Places, led to dissent within the Saudi elite and, ultimately, to the expulsion of former Saudi subject Osama Bin Laden and his followers. One of the major objectives of Bin Laden's al-Qaeda network is the removal of the Saudi regime and US power from the Holy Places and the Middle East generally, rather than a wholesale conversion or destruction of the West, as is often suggested.

Prudently Fahd did not allow the US to use its bases in Saudi Arabia to attack Iraq during the Second Gulf War in 2003 and, instead, at the outbreak of the war announced it had persuaded the US to withdraw its forces.

Despite this, the number of terrorist attacks and suicide bombing aimed at the overthrow of the monarchy continued to grow, with al-Qaeda often claiming responsibility. Terror tactics included the new one of taking Western hostages, beheading them and then distributing videos of the horrific act via cable TV and the internet.

The regime responded with the twin strategy of savagely repressing suspected al-Qaeda while embarking on a programme of supposed democratic reform. Municipal elections which took place in 2005 were said to be the first ever free and democratic expression of Saudi public opinion – despite the fact that women were not allowed to vote. Later in the same year King Fahd died, to be succeeded by the former crown prince Abdullah. There were few signs that he was contemplating far-reaching reforms.

One problem for the new king was his adopted role as guardian of the Holy Places of Mecca and Medina. The number of pilgrims taking part in the annual *hajj* had become so large that stampedes and panic were becoming more frequent. In some years hundreds were simply trampled to death in the crush. In 2006 over three hundred *hajji* were accidentally stoned to death during a phase of *hajj* where pilgrims throw stones at pillars representing Satan. Numbers are so large that those closest to the pillar suffer a sometimes deadly hail of stones from those further away. At the same time the problem of disposing of the huge number of hoofed animals which had to be ritually sacrificed, along with the normal requirements to provide drinking water and sanitation for millions of people in the middle of one of the world's driest deserts, presented an enormous and growing public health problem.

In the meantime the conflict between an increasingly confidence al-Qaeda and Saudi security forces continued. In June 2004 Saudi forces killed al-Qaeda leader Abdul Aziz al-Muqrin and then offered an amnesty for militants who would renounce violence. The tactic appeared to have little immediate effect and violence continued almost undiminished. Large-scale attacks increasingly aimed at the regime's real bedrock – the infrastructure of the oil extraction and export industries.

YEMEN
Population: 21.5 million (UN 2005)

Yemen is a desert country with a small fertile coastal strip on the southern and south-western coastline of Arabia. The population is overwhelmingly Muslim, but divided between the largely nomadic Zaydi Shi'ite (Zaydis) majority and the more settled followers of the Sunni Shafi sect.

For six hundred years Yemen languished under the purely nominal rule of the Ottoman Emirs of Hejaz, who governed from Mecca. So slight was the contact that Yemeni Sunnis continued to practise Shafi'ism, an early form of Sunni'ism associated with traders and merchants and normally found only in the outlying lands of Islam such as Indonesia.

The country was ruled by the Zaydi dynasty of Sa'da, founded by Yahya ibn Husayn ibn Qasim ar-Rassi, from the ninth century until the twentieth century and the monarchs collaborated with the British who established the Aden Protectorate in Yemen in 1839. After more than seventy years of inconclusive war with tribal leaders and the nominal Ottoman rulers, the British planned to incorporate the territory into a single pro-Western Hashemite Arabian kingdom at the end of the First World War. The plan came to nothing when the Saudi clan conquered most of the peninsula. The British turned Yemen into a protectorate and used it as a buffer against Saud's forces' power in the centre of the Arabian peninsula.

The Saudis reacted by sponsoring a coup led by Sunni Colonels in the Yemeni army in 1962. After a civil war a conservative Sunni Yemeni Arab Republic was established in the north of the country. The British retreated to Aden and the south of the country became an Arab Socialist republic, The People's Democratic Republic of Yemen which had support from the Soviet Union and its then ally, Egypt.

Reunification of the country took place in 1990, when a new constitution declared the country to be an 'Arab Islamic State' with both the Shi'ite Zaydi and Sunni Shafi law schools forming 'the basis of all legislation'. The country has a mixed secular-Islamic court system. For example, polygamy is allowed, a man may divorce his wife by simply announcing the fact, and the minimum age of marriage is 15.

In 1994 northern and southern factions of the new unified Yemeni national army attacked each other, leading to a civil war and the triumph of the pro-Western and pro-Saudi north. Southern leaders and fighters were forced into exile, some almost certainly joining Osama Bin Laden's followers who were expelled from Saudi Arabia at the same time.

In 2000 the US warship USS *Cole* was attacked by suicide bombers in Aden harbour. Terrorist attacks on US, British and Saudi-linked targets continued, leading to the expulsion of a hundred 'Islamic Scholars', believed to be linked to al-Qaeda, in February 2002.

The expulsion achieved little – apart perhaps from replenishing the ranks of al-Qaeda's 'arab fighters' in Afghanistan. The civil war continued with the north of the country passing out of control of the central government, providing potential bases for terrorist and guerilla attacks on oil installations across the border in Saudi Arabia.

THE GULF STATES

KUWAIT, UNITED ARAB EMIRATES, OMAN, BAHRAIN, QATAR
Combined population:

The Arabian Gulf States on the eastern coast of Saudi Arabia owe their existence to nineteenth- century British attempts to dominate the Persian Gulf and block Russian advances into Persia itself and to prise Arabia away from Turkish control. From the 1860s onward the British agreed to support tribal rebellions against the Ottomans (and rival clans such as the Saudi confederacy) in return for naval bases and free access to areas liberated from Ottoman rule.

The states are ruled by *Shayks* (tribal chieftains) and *Emirs* (subject rulers) who in the main subscribe to the Shafi school of Sunni law, though the rulers of Kuwait follow the Maliki school, more usually found in northern Africa. Shafi'ism is slightly less traditionalist than Saudi Hanbali'ism, but still deeply conservative. A strict version of the *shari'ah* is theoretically enforced in all the Gulf States. But in Bahrain in particular its implementation is lax.

By the mid-1960s it became obvious that the growing oil wealth of the Emirs meant they could support themselves, and Kuwait, the most developed territory at the time, became independent in 1961, followed by Qatar and Bahrain. A group of smaller territories, led by Dubai, federated as the United Arab Emirates in 1971.

KUWAIT
Population: 2.7 million (UN 2005)

Historically Kuwait was part of Iraq, forming part of the
Ottoman-administered province of Basra from the seventeenth
century onwards. The city was established by Iraqi settlers and
for centuries functioned as Iraq's main port. The British bought
the city from the Ottomans in the nineteenth century and
Kuwait officially became a sub-division of British India, as a
base for domination of Iraq and Iran. A type of legal apartheid
was also introduced with a British-type judicial system for
Europeans and the *shari'ah* system for natives.

The discovery of oil in the 1930s and the development of the
oil industry in the following decades transformed the importance of the country and today makes up more than 90 per cent
of Kuwait's foreign currency earnings. The Constitution,
adopted in 1962 after independence, says, 'the religion of the
State is Islam, and the Islamic *shari'ah* shall be a main source
of legislation'.

In 1976 Shayk Sabah, the second shayk since independence,
abolished the limited consultative National Assembly and
reintroduced rule by decree after the Assembly had become a
platform for sympathisers with Kuwait's 300,000 exiled Palestinian residents. Palestinian organisations were curbed and five
years later new elections gave an absolute majority to the
Shayk's traditional conservative Bedouin allies, with a marked
decline in support for Sunni fundamentalists.

In the wake of the Iranian revolution in the 1980s the
government announced a programme of 'Islamisation' of the
country, fearing that Islamic revolution might spread from
neighbouring Iran to the country's significant Shi'ite minority.
Fearing the influence of Iran, Kuwait promised to support
Saddam Hussein in the Iran–Iraq war.

In 1991 the country was briefly occupied and annexed by
Iraq during the First Gulf War, claiming that Kuwait had failed
to deliver its oil revenues to pay for its share of the war effort
against Iran. A US-led military coalition based in Saudi Arabia
expelled the Iraqis, put the al-Sabah family back in charge of
the country and sales of cheap oil to the developed world

resumed. After an experiment with a limited form of democracy, the national assembly was again suspended and a move to grant political rights to women was quashed.

Most of the large Palestinian exile community fled Kuwait after the al-Sabah restoration, since they were blamed for collaborating with the Iraqis. The pre-war Palestinian population that had amounted to about a fifth of the total was reduced to only about 30,000. About 6,000 Palestinians were held in long-term detention and according to the US State Department between 45 and 50 were executed and tortured.

In 2002 relations between Iraq and Kuwait were normalised, but in the following year the country became the launch pad for the massive American- and British-led attack on Iraq leading to the destruction of Saddam Hussein's Ba'athist regime.

The war at first seemed popular with the Kuwaiti population, as expressed in electoral support for pro-government and moderate religious parties in a male-only 2003 parliamentary election. A decision by the Emir to appoint one of his relatives as Prime Minister – instead of ruling in his own right – was hailed as a step toward liberal constitutional reform. Reform continues with the extension of the vote to women for the first time.

But by 2005 conservative reaction and insurgency in Iraq, especially in nearby Basra, saw increasingly conflict with a number of bloody shoot-outs between police and Islamic militants.

UNITED ARAB EMIRATES

ABU DHABI, DUBAI, AJMAN, FUJAIRAH, RAS AL KHAIMAH, SHARJAH, UMM AL QAIWAIN
Population: 3.1 million (UN 2005)

This federation of former fishing villages, notable only for pearl-fishing and piracy before the discovery of oil in the 1950s, is one of the more liberal states in and around Arabia and the Gulf. This is mainly due to the fact that the indigenous population forms a small and self-contained minority content to regulate their own affairs and unable or unwilling to impose their will on the vast army of guest-workers and ex-pats who run the oil industry or work in the burgeoning tourist industry.

The British ruled the area from the middle of the nineteenth century, after being forced into military action to control piracy aimed at British ships trading with India. An 1853 treaty signed with local chieftains assigned permanent control of the 'pirate coast' to the British navy and the region was garrisoned and administered from British India.

The Emirates became theoretically independent after Britain abandoned all its colonial interests 'East of Suez' in the 1960s. In 1971 the former colonies were federated as the UAE.

The Emirs work together, mainly for the purposes of self-defence. Within their respective territories they are complete despots. In theory there are free elections for the presidency, but the 80 per cent of the population who are foreign are not entitled to vote. The same man, Shayk Zayed Bin-Sultan Al Nahyan, has been re-elected every five years since 1971.

The Shafi version of the *shari'ah* is enforced amongst the native population and the less strict Hanafi version amongst the vast community of Pakistani guest-workers in domestic service or labouring in the oil and leisure industries which completely dominate the Emirates.

OMAN
Population: 3 million

The sparsely populated state of Oman is the oldest continually existing state in the Muslim world, tracing its origins to the Khariji sect formed in the civil war following the death of the Prophet. The Kharijis turned their backs on the world, retreated to the remote Omani coast, lived in the desert and governed themselves with the Ibadite *shari'ah* legal code, which still forms the basis of the Omani monarchy today.

Fiercely independent, the warlike Omani chieftains resisted conquest by the Turkish and Portuguese overlords in early modern times. In the sixteenth century the Omanis even founded a slave-trading empire of their own, conquering much of the Gulf and the African island of Zanzibar (in modern

Tanzania) and becoming the main sea power in the Indian Ocean. Clashes between Oman and the French in Napoleonic times led the still-independent Omani Sultans into alliance with the British and in 1891 the state became part of the British Empire as a protectorate. In 1951 the British granted formal independence to Sultan Sa'id ibn Taimur. In 1970 Taimur was replaced by his strongly pro-Western son Qaboos in a palace coup supported by the British. Qaboos encouraged the British to deploy the SAS and other elite forces to help win a long-running guerrilla war against militant Palestinian and Marxist groups.

By 1975 the Sultan was claiming victory and expelled a large number of Palestinian guerrillas from his domains. But victory was bought at the cost of spending over a third of the national budget (almost entirely provided by oil) on the armed forces. Attempts were made at reform in the early 1980s with the introduction of a token Consultative Assembly (with no law-making powers) to advise the Sultan. At first the Sultan picked members of the assembly himself, but in 2002 elections were held, with all citizens over 21 entitled to vote.

The secretive British military presence in Oman continues to this day. British forces prepared for their supporting role in the attack on Afghanistan in 2001 with a series of large-scale military exercises in the Omani desert.

In 2005 the regime charged 100 Omanis with terrorist offences; 31 were convicted of attempting to overthrow the state and sentenced to death, only to be pardoned by the Sultan a few months later.

Despite relative liberalisation the Sultan can rule as a complete autocrat if he chooses to do so. He is the final authority on Ibadite Qur'anic law and can try individual cases in the fashion of a latter-day King Solomon

BAHRAIN
Population: 0.75 million (UN 2005)

After independence from Britain in 1971 the Emir experimented with limited democracy, but the National Assembly was closed down in 1975 when it proposed legal rights for trades unions and better wages for Pakistani guest-workers and support for the Palestinian cause. The Emir reverted to traditional autocratic rule. The second Emir Shayk Hamad Bin-Isa Al-Khalifah (who gave himself the title King in 2002) was brought up in the UK (Cambridge University and the Aldershot officer training academy). He has been the effective ruler of the state as crowned prince and head of the armed forces since 1964. He succeeded to the throne on the death of his father in 1999. All important positions in the government are held by members of his family. This now includes the director of internal security and secret intelligence, a post which until 1998 was held by a British citizen.

The *shari'ah* is enforced in Bahrain but the island has a reputation for being relatively liberal. Saudi Arabians visit in order to get away from the strict prohibition of alcohol and gambling in their own country. Bahrain is known in the Gulf as 'the pub at the end of the Causeway'.

From time to time 'coup' plots are reported, normally attributed to Iranian agents and Islamist groups such as Hezbollah, since Bahrain was once ruled by Iran. But otherwise the undemocratic microstate is stable and enjoys vast injections of money in the form of oil revenues and the backing of massive American military force in the region.

QATAR
Population 0.6 million (UN 2005)

This former Turkish and British military port and garrison town became independent in 1971, after – in the normal way for the end of British rule in the Gulf – a suitable pro-British clan was found and placed upon the throne.

In the two generations since discovery of oil in the 1950s the population of Qatar has rocketed from being amongst the poorest in the world to probably the richest. The delicate political balances which held this tribal community of 250,000 together have been torn apart and new centres of power have emerged with increasing wealth and self-confidence.

Emir Shayk Khalifah bin Hamad Al Thani's reaction was to insist on the absolute obedience of tribal leaders to his autocracy and strict adherence to Shafi Sunni Islam, whilst leaving the technical aspects of running the country to foreign advisers. The British were left in effective charge of military affairs after independence until, towards the end of the twentieth century, their place was taken by the Americans. During the Second Gulf War in 2003 American forces based their command centre in Qatar.

The vast majority of the native population have retired to rural estates, tended by Omani and Pakistani gardeners and servants, and the tribal pattern has stayed intact. Natives have little involvement with technical or industrial activity and more than 80 per cent of the workforce are foreigners.

In 1995 Shayk Al Thani's son grabbed power while his father was out of the country. Father and son then resorted to suing each other for possession of state funds, revealing in the most graphic way possible the state's true status as a private family business. In 1997 Al Thani diversified from oil to television, launching the Al-Jazeera satellite TV channel aimed at the rapidly growing market for satellite TV in the Gulf and the Arab world beyond.

In 2005 Qatar adopted its first ever written constitution, opening up the possibility of democratic reform in the future. At the same time Qatar and a consortium of large US corporations announced a $14 billion project to build the world's largest liquefied natural gas plant.

16. NORTHERN ARABIA AND EGYPT

EGYPT, SYRIA, LEBANON, PALESTINE/ISRAEL, JORDAN AND IRAQ

Total population: 133 million

In the eighth century Islam exploded out of its primitive origins in the Arabian peninsula and pushed north into the 'fertile crescent' linking Syria and Egypt along the eastern coast of the Mediterranean to Iraq, the 'fertile island' between the Euphrates and Tigris.

In these lands Islam flowered into a great multi-racial civilisation open to the influences of the Christian West and pagan Asiatic East. With the establishment of Damascus, Cairo and – above all – Baghdad, Islam left behind the narrow and traditionalist outlook of the peninsular Arabs and these northern Arabian lands became the true historical heartland of Islam in its Golden Age.

For five hundred years the area formed the territory of the Abbasid Empire ruled from Baghdad. Islam developed a sophisticated theology and philosophy and became highly heterodox. Great advances were made in the arts and sciences centuries before the European Renaissance.

This great civilisation of northern Arabia and Iraq came to an abrupt end in 1258 with the Mongol invasion and destruction of Baghdad. In the following six hundred years the region languished and became backward under the domination of the Ottoman Turkish Sultans.

The region remained culturally united under the Ottomans but was divided into two main administrative areas – Egypt and Greater Syria. Egypt achieved autonomy in the 1860s following a religious revival that fused nationalism and Islam. From then on Islam was seen as a potent force for pan-Arab nationalism – the idea of uniting all the northern Arabian lands into a single powerful and modern state.

The collapse of the Ottoman Empire in 1919 brought great expectations that the pan-Arab dream was about to become a reality. Instead the region turned into a steaming cauldron of political intrigue with France, Britain, Italy, Turkey and a variety of radical and conservative Arab factions competing for influence and power.

Egypt gained independence in 1923 but the former Ottoman province of Greater Syria was divided into League of Nations mandates administered by Britain and France. The mandate territory of Syria was reduced to a rump around Damascus, ruled by the French; the area round the former Syrian trading port of Beirut became the independent French mandate territory of Lebanon; and the new mandate states of Palestine and Jordan to the south, and Iraq to the east, came under British control.

All these new states were highly unstable. Various Arab attempts were made to reunite Greater Syria as a prelude to political union with Egypt, but all fell foul of dynastic disputes and tribal feuds manipulated by astute Anglo-French diplomacy.

After the Second World War the position was transformed by the creation of the state of Israel. This was seen not only as a direct attack by the Western powers on the Arab world but also an affront to Islam. In 1948 the Syrian, Egyptian, Jordanian and Iraqi monarchies jointly declared war on Israel and in so doing greatly strengthened pan-Arab feeling and fused it further with Islam.

The defeat of the Arab monarchies in the 1948 Arab–Israeli war shook the entire Arab world. The demand for pan-Arab unity became intense and there was a new factor – a growing pan-Arab 'Islamic Socialism' movement firmly rooted amongst both intellectuals and young officers of defeated Arab armies. In the two decades that followed the pan-Arab socialist movements overthrew the monarchies in all the northern Arab countries except Jordan. Military coups brought Nasser to power in Egypt and the Ba'ath (Arab Socialist Renaissance) Party to power in Syria and Iraq. Egypt and Syria federated as the United Arab Republic in 1958, but, after further coups, Iraq stayed outside the union.

In Jordan the Royal Family survived a Palestinian-led pan-Arabist insurrection and remained implacably hostile to the idea of union. Lebanon also refused to join. In 1961 the United Arab Republic collapsed when the Syrian Ba'ath Party pulled out, complaining of Egyptian domination.

Defeat for the Arab nations in the 1973 Yom Kippur war with Israel led to mutual recriminations, further coups and, eventually, the complete disintegration of the pan-Arab ideal. The Ba'ath Party remained in power in Syria and Iraq in the name of 'Islamic Socialism', but in practice the Syrian and Iraqi wings evolved separately and became extremely hostile to each other.

During the First Gulf War in 1990 Syria sent troops to fight with the Americans. Egypt made peace with Israel, Jordan recognised the Jewish state and the main 'hard-line' Ba'athist state – Iraq – was defeated in the Second Gulf War. Only Syria keeps alive the old idea of unification of all the Arab lands, but as a small and diplomatically isolated state is hardly in a position to lead a new drive for Arab unity.

The role played by Islam in the tragic conflicts of the Middle East was in formal terms slight, until the recent rise of the Islamist Hamas movement. The Muslim regimes of the area were officially highly secular and Islam was entirely secondary to Arab nationalism, but beneath the surface the Islamic traditions of *jihad* and martyrdom played a crucial role in Arab intransigence towards both Israel and rival Arab states which are seen as insufficiently hostile to the Jewish state.

Jerusalem, currently under Israeli occupation, is Islam's third Holy City after Mecca and Medina. The Dome of the Rock mosque in the centre of the city is a Muslim shrine second only in importance to the Holy *Ka'bah* in Mecca. Still further beneath the surface is traditional Muslim antipathy towards the Jews.

EGYPT
Population: 75 million (UN 2005)

Egypt is by far the largest and fastest-growing Arab nation, with twice the population of the next largest Arab country, Morocco. Egypt is home to approximately one quarter of the total population of all the Arab nations put together.

Of all the Arab Islamic nations Egypt has the longest tradition of effective modern nationhood and is the home of both Arab nationalism and modernising 'secularist' Islam. Cairo's Al-Azhar mosque and university is one of the oldest seats of learning in the Western world and today is the main source of doctrinal authority for Sunni Muslims.

The Islamic modernist movement began in Egypt in the 1860s with the first systematic revision of the *shari'ah* legal code, by Muhammad Abduh (died 1905), the chief legal officer (*mufti*) of the British colonial administration.

Abduh cut out many of the mystical, irrational and authority-worshipping customs that had been absorbed into the *shari'ah* during centuries of Ottoman despotism and Sufi sophistry. Instead he produced a simplified version of Islamic theology, developed a secular penal code to replace the draconian *hadd* punishments of the Qur'an, and relegated religious law to control of family and private matters.

Contemporary Islam in Egypt is still officially based on Abduh's approach, but since the 1920s there has been growing pressure from fundamentalists for full implementation of the *shari'ah*. The fundamentalist Muslim Brotherhood was formed in 1928 and is still the main focus of fundamentalist agitation.

The Brotherhood enjoys close relations with the Saudi Arabian government and, since the Saudis repeatedly bail out the bankrupt Egyptian economy, this gives them considerable protection and freedom to operate within the country, even at times when they have been officially outlawed.

At the other end of the political spectrum secular Egyptian 'Islamic Socialism' reached its peak in the 1950s and 1960s during the Presidency of Gamal Nasser, and formed the inspiration for similar regimes later formed in Iraq, Yemen and elsewhere. Following Nasser's death in 1970 his successor, Anwar Sadat, leaned on external Saudi and internal fundamentalist support to reverse the leftist domestic policies of the Nasser years and steer Egypt from the Soviet into the Western camp. The process culminated in the US-sponsored Camp David peace accords with Israel and the recognition of Israel's right to exist in a treaty signed in 1980. With this act, previous attempts to form a United Arab Republic by uniting Egypt, Syria, Iraq, Palestine and (at one time) Yemen came to an end, perhaps for good.

Following Camp David, Egypt was thrown out of the Arab League and Sadat was assassinated in 1981 by members of his own guard acting under the influence of a militant splinter group from the Muslim Brotherhood. His death was met with general rejoicing by 'hard-line' Arab leaders like Colonel al-Qaddafi of Libya, who declared a public holiday to mark the event.

Sadat's successor, President Muhammad Hosni Mubarak, built a closer relationship with the US and tried to rebuild bridges to the Arab world through increasing unofficial diplomatic contacts with Saudi Arabia.

Internally Mubarak continued Sadat's policy of reversing Nasserite 'Arab Socialism' by introducing free markets and encouraging foreign investment and tourism. The extra-parliamentary fundamentalists nevertheless have considerable support amongst the urban poor of Cairo and have gained in influence through attempts by both Sadat and Mubarak to use them as a counterbalance to what remains of the radical Nasserite left.

Fundamentalist groups led an open insurrection in the southern city of Asyut in 1982 and have been involved in isolated terrorist incidents and occasional riots against Cairo's soaring food prices (a consequence of Mubarak's World Bank-directed free market policies). In 1997 58 Western tourists were killed in Luxor by terrorists belonging to a fundamentalist Islamic terrorist group.

Similar outrages have taken place at the Westernised coastal resort of Sharm al-Sheikh.

In the meantime Egyptian politics, and the country's ageing ruling elite, has remained in a deep freeze reminiscent of the last years of the Communist regimes of Eastern Europe. In September 2005 President Mubarak was elected, essentially unopposed, for his fifth consecutive term of office. In the same election the once illegal Muslim Brotherhood increased its representation, winning a fifth of the scats in the national asscmbly.

Many commentators observed that living in Egypt was in some ways like living on the edge of a political volcano. The state's failure to deal with social problems, the ossified nature of the political system and the sheer strain of the country's rapidly growing population seemed to threaten a political eruption. Any sort of political revolution in Egypt, perhaps led by an anti-Western and anti-Israeli Hamas-type movement, would – in a country of such size – be an event of epoch-changing significance.

SYRIA
Population: 19 million (UN 2005)

Until the 1970s Syria was subject to chronic political instability, with coup and counter-coup establishing and deposing governments in an endless series of faction fights between the different wings of the Ba'ath Party, its allies and opponents.

The current ruler, Ba'athist President Bashar al-Assad, is the son of Lt General Hafez al-Assad, the man who shaped modern Syria after coming to power in a 1970 military coup. Assad has imposed a measure of stability by ruthlessly eliminating opponents and staffing the top levels of the army, civil service and largely nationalised industries with members of his own clan, who all subscribe to the minority Aluwyin ('Upholders of 'Ali' or Alawite) Shi'ite sub-sect.

The current Syrian constitution dates from 1973 and declares the country 'a democratic Arab nation' with government based on the principles of 'Socialism, Freedom, Economic Justice, Arab Unity and Islam'. There were riots when the first draft failed to mention Islam and it was duly amended, along with the provision that the President must be a Muslim (there are sizeable Christian and other minorities in Syria) and legislation based on *shari'ah* law. But Islam is mainly a political – or tribal – creed in Syria, manipulated as a support for the all-important concept of Syrian nationalism and its mission to unite the Arab lands.

Like his father, Bashar Assad uses the tightly knit structure of the Alawite sect to maintain control of the Ba'athist power structure which in turn permeates every sphere of public life. The sect dominates the economy and government whilst constituting only 10 per cent of the mainly Sunni-Hanafi population. Alawite power is concentrated in the Special Defence Units (SDUs) which are effectively above the law and used to terrorise the population and police the army and Ba'athist structure.

The SDU executed at least three hundred members of the Muslim Brotherhood following an assassination attempt on Assad in 1980 and shortly afterwards, according to press reports, two hundred more were buried alive in the compounds of the SDU's Tadmor prison in Palmyra, central Syria. In 1982 the Syrian Army, led by the SDU, occupied the town of Hama and slaughtered the entire population of about 15,000, including women and children, as a reprisal against an attempted insurrection allegedly started by the Brotherhood.

The regime is extremely hostile to all its Arab neighbours. Israel, Jordan and Lebanon to the south are regarded as occupying the historic lands of Greater Syria which must be reconquered. Jordan is particularly despised on religious-doctrinal grounds because the 'usurper' Jordanian kings have 'collaborated' with Israel, Britain and the US against the Palestinians, who are seen as Greater Syrian nationals.

Syria invaded Lebanon in 1976, beginning a process which brought this once prosperous multi-ethnic and multi-religious state to its current condition of anarchy (see Lebanon).

Syria enthusiastically supported the American-led coalition which evicted Saddam Hussein's Iraqi troops from Kuwait during the First Gulf War; but was more circumspect during the Second Gulf War, after having been named by American

President Bush as a member of the 'axis of evil' – regimes like Iraq and Iran which had used force or sponsored terrorism in the Middle East and beyond.

Bashar Assad made overtures to the West and to conservative Arab powers like Saudi Arabia by legalising the Muslim Brotherhood, releasing political prisoners, softening the regime's anti-Israeli rhetoric and liberalising the economy. Political liberalisation soon found its limits when in 2001 leading reformist members of the Syrian National Assembly were arrested.

In 2004 the US accused Syria of supporting insurgents in neighbouring Iraq, reviving the old 'axis of evil' allegation. Economic sanctions were imposed after the US claimed Syria was failing to prevent Iraqi insurgents crossing its borders. Relations worsened further when the Syrian army assassinated the democratically elected President of Lebanon, Rafik Hariri.

The death of Hariri led to massive anti-Syrian riots in Lebanon, resulting in the humiliating withdrawal of Syrian troops the following year. Syria continued, however, to exert influence in Lebanon through its support of Hezbollah (see Lebanon) and the commission of further assassinations of anti-Syrian journalists and politicians.

LEBANON
Population: 3.8 million (UN 2005)

The small state of Lebanon is the only ethnically Arab nation which is not overwhelmingly Muslim. Instead it is a fascinating, complex and frequently explosive mixture of mainstream and exotic Muslim and Christian sects including Shi'ites, Sunnis, Druzes, Egyptian Ismailis, Syrian Alawis, Christian Maronites, Greek Orthodox, Greek Catholics, Roman Catholics, Jacobites, Armenian Orthodox, Assyrians and Protestants. The once substantial Jewish minority has, however, been reduced to a few dozen.

As a crossroads and great trading centre, what is now Lebanon thrived under the Ottomans, and ex-Lebanese communities can be found spread throughout the former territory of the Turkish Empire. The partition of the Arab Ottoman lands by the British and French at the end of the Second World War saw Lebanon come under French rule as part of the French mandate territory of Greater Syria. In the 1920s Christian elements of the mainly Muslim Syrian army split away to form the Christian republic of Lebanon with a secular constitution based on that of France, but still under the ultimate control of Paris and incorporating a highly complex system of power-sharing between the religious communities.

Maronite Christians and Sunni and Shi'ite Muslims in the population changed significantly over the span of half a century, and updating the census data providing the bases for the system of power sharing is an issue that has proved difficult for the modern state of Lebanon to address. In 1941, during the occupation of France by Nazi Germany, the 'Free French' and the British declared Lebanon to be independent, with a new constitution which enshrined the power of the Lebanese Christians even though the great birth rate of the Muslims meant they had already become a minority in the country.

The Christian minority began to fear domination by the more numerous Muslims (or even reunification with Syria or an even larger United Arab Republic), while the Muslims resented Christian privileges. These tensions – remarkably similar to those experienced by the UK in Northern Ireland – were made more intense by the arrival of a huge Palestinian refugee population after the establishment of the state of Israel and led to a descent into civil war in 1975 which lasts, with various twists and turns, to this day.

Terrorist attacks on northern Israel, especially by the Iranian-allied Hezbollah continued after the end of the civil war in Lebanon itself, leading in 1996 to the bombing of southern Lebanon by the Israeli air force – a pattern of events which was repeated on a huge scale in 2006.

The conflict in 2006 led to widespread devastation which and seemed to have the potential to plunge the entire region into war. It began with the kidnap of two Israeli soldiers by Hezbollah, an Iranian-linked Shi'ite political and social movement with an armed wing and a record of terrorist atrocities. Israel reacted with air strikes on areas of southern Lebanon thought to be Hezbollah strongholds. Israeli action was widely condemned as 'collective punishment' of Hezbollah's constituency Lebanese Shi'ite population. Hezbollah escalated the conflict by launching rockets at northern Israel from bunkers and bases just over the Lebanese border.

Israel escalated the conflict further by invading Lebanon. The destruction was so extensive that it seemed that Israel, having failed to gain political control of the area after the defeat of their allies in the civil war, now wanted to depopulate southern Lebanon, turning it into uninhabitable buffer zone. At the same time Israeli politicians internationalised the conflict, claiming that they were engaged on the ground and in the front line in George W Bush's 'war on terror'. Their aim was to destroy Hezbollah – a key component of the 'axis of evil' which directly linked the Iranian and Syrian regimes and, in addition, forwarded the aims of Hamas terrorism in Palestine and Israel itself.

JORDAN
Population: 5.7 million (UN 2005)

The Hashemite Kingdom of Jordan was created by British diplomacy as a model secular, conservative and pro-Western Arab state. The country's ruling royal family, the Hashemites, claim direct descent from Muhammad and have enshrined Islam in the country's constitution as a means of legitimising their rule.

The first Hashemite ruler, King Abdullah, had plans to extend his rule throughout northern Arabia and thus became the direct and bitter opponent of radical republican pan-Arabists.

His power was largely based on the British who trained his army and made it the most effective in the Arab world, but he was badly let down in 1948 when his British allies allowed the state of Israel to be established in Palestine – previously claimed as part of the Hashemite Kingdom. Jordanian participation in the 1948 Arab–Israeli War was only lukewarm, and after the Arab defeat Abdullah was accused of collaborating with the 'imperialists' to bring Israel into being.

As a result the pan-Arabists passed the death sentence on the entire Jordanian Hashemite clan and, with the support of radical Palestinians who flocked into Jordan as exiles, pledged the destruction of the Jordanian state. In 1951 Abdullah was gunned down by Nasserite pan-Arabist terrorists on the steps of the main mosque in Amman, the Jordanian capital. He was succeeded by his son Hussein, an Anglicised graduate of the British military college at Sandhurst. King Hussein's first problem was the half million or more Palestinian refugees from Israel who doubled Jordan's population.

The refugee camps were soon seething with rebellion. One of the principal agitators was Yasser Arafat, who in the late 1950s founded the main Palestinian guerrilla movement al-Fatah (the fighters) with the aim of destroying both Israel and Jordan and creating a 'democratic secular' Palestinian state in their place. In 1964 al-Fatah launched a broadly based political wing, the Palestinian Liberation Organisation (PLO) which has since claimed to function as the Palestinian 'parliament' with Yasser Arafat being the 'President in exile' of the proposed Palestinian state. In 1967 the Arabs were again defeated in a war against Israel, and the Israelis occupied former Jordanian territory on the West Bank of the Jordan river, including all of Jerusalem, sending more Palestinian refugees into what remained of the country.

Hussein moved against the Palestinians in 1970 and defeated them in a brief but bloody civil war. Hundreds of thousands of Palestinians fled to Iraq, Syria and the Gulf States. Another large group of Palestinians ended up in Lebanon, setting off the tragic chain of events leading to that country's endemic civil war.

Minority factions of the PLO based in Syria remain implacably hostile to Jordan and there were dozens of assassination attempts on Hussein. In response the King developed a network of spies, informers and bodyguards legendary throughout the Middle East.

Through the 1990s Jordan was gripped by economic crisis caused to a large extent by economic sanctions imposed by the UN on its oil-rich neighbour Iraq. Jordan has few natural resources of its own, and the economy was badly hit by the loss of income from cross-border trade with Iraq.

In 1999 King Hussein died to be replaced by his son Abdullah, an even more Westernised figure than his father, who rules as Abdullah II. One of the new king's first acts was to order the execution of six Palestinians accused in a military court of plotting attacks against Israeli and US targets.

A brief flowering of democracy and free speech came to an end when the national assembly began an investigation into the corruption which emanates from the monarchy, reaching into every corner of official life in the country.

In 2002 Abdullah signed a massive economic development deal with Israel, designed as an alternative to the country's former economic dependency on Iraq. In the same year there were mass arrests of political activists and the closing down of the Qatar-based Al-Jazeera satellite TV station after it criticised the King.

After the outbreak of the Second Gulf War, Abdullah continued his strongly pro-Western stance. Suspected Islamic extremists or potential supporters of the insurgency in Iraq were routinely rounded up and there were multiple executions. Eventually Abu Musab al-Zarqawi, the Jordanian-born leader of the al-Qaeda fighters who had gone to Iraq to exploit the chaos after the American invasion, was killed by US forces.

The inevitable backlash included suicide bombings at international hotels and al-Qaeda rocket attacks on US military installations. A terrorist attempt to mount a major chemical warfare attack on US intelligence headquarters in Amman was only narrowly averted. By 2006 the profoundly undemocratic and authoritarian Jordanian regime, despite enjoying a positive image in the West (partly because of the charitable and fashionable activities of Princess Noor, a former film star) was more isolated from its increasingly hostile and disgruntled population than ever.

PALESTINE/ISRAEL

Population: Palestine: 3.8 million (UN 2005) Israel: 6.7 million (UN 2005)

In 1948 the new specifically Jewish state of Israel was created within the territory of British-administered Muslim Palestine mainly by European immigrants. Both Jews and Muslims claimed the city of Jerusalem in particular as integral to their historic homeland – for the Jews it is the capital of the ancient

Jewish Kingdom of David; for the Muslims the site of Muhammad's Night Journey, commemorated by the famous golden-roofed Dome of the Rock mosque – one of the most famous architectural monuments in the world. In a further complication Jerusalem is also a Holy City for Christians.

The creation of Israel forced hundreds of thousands of Palestinian Arabs (mostly Muslim, but some Christians) into exile throughout the Arab world, with particularly large concentrations at one time or another in neighbouring Jordan, Lebanon and in Egypt, North Africa and the Gulf States.

Decades of war between Arab states and Israel culminated in a 1979 peace agreement between Israel and Egypt which became the first Arab or Muslim country to recognise the right of Israel to exist in some form. Since then many of the more conservative Arab states have either explicitly or covertly come to terms with the existence of Israel and have tried to exert pressure for a general regional peace settlement.

The position was transformed by the First Gulf War in 1991. Iraq's Ba'athist leadership had long advocated a strong or 'rejectionist' anti-Israeli line and claimed to be champions of the Palestinian cause as part of the regime's claim to leadership of the Arab nation as a whole. After the occupation of Kuwait the Iraqis tried to broaden the conflict into a war between the 'Arab masses' including the dispersed Palestinian population on the one hand, and the US, Israel and their 'clients' among the leadership of Saudi Arabia, Jordan and the Gulf States on the other. This idea was popular with many Palestinians in the refugee camps – thousands of whom had been expelled or otherwise been badly treated by the oil *shayks*. When during the war Saddam Hussein managed to actually land missiles on targets in Israel as well as inflicting losses on American troops he became something of a hero – the latest in a line of potential saviours and unifiers of the Arab nation as a whole (by means of war on Israel) – stretching back to Nasser and the optimistic days of the United Arab Republic.

But, in diplomatic terms, the evident enthusiasm for the Iraqi cause among the Palestinian masses, and the vaguely supportive stance taken by Yasser Arafat and the Palestinian Liberation Organisation was a disaster. The PLO had alienated its wealthy supporters in the Gulf and in Saudi Arabia and, at the same time, had lost any of the dubious advantages Iraqi support had provided. Arafat's former allies in Baghdad were reduced to financial and strategic impotence after the imposition of sanctions and loss of control over oil revenues. At the same time the previously dictatorial and charismatic grip Yasser Arafat had exerted on the leadership of the Palestinian people as head of the secular and 'Arab socialist' (i.e. vaguely pro-Ba'athist) PLO (recognised by the UN as a sort of 'parliament of the PLO') was being undermined by Islamist Palestinian groups such as Hamas and Islamic Jihad. It was these explicitly Islamic groups who were leading the actual anti-Israeli fighting in the occupied territories and whom the PLO's more conservative wealthy backers (such as the Saudis and Gulf Emirs) were now more inclined to support and finance.

After Iraq's defeat, Arafat and the PLO found themselves more diplomatically isolated than ever, and Israel (as a recent victim of unprovoked Iraqi aggression) in a strong strategic position. The generally pro-Israeli US government took the opportunity to force through a new peace agreement, deciding that the collapse of Palestinian capacity for intransigence meant that Arafat could at least be persuaded to abandon his aim of replacing Israel with a Palestinian state, and adopt a more realistic plan of permanently dividing the territory of historic Palestine (including Jerusalem) between Israel and a new (much smaller) Palestinian state.

Nevertheless, the leadership of Israel – emboldened by the US victory in Kuwait and the evident disarray of the Palestinian leadership – was reluctant to take advantage of the situation. Instead of striking a deal with the Palestinians on extremely favourable terms (which might not come again in a generation) the newly elected hard-line government of Yitzhak Shamir was reluctant to talk and instead seemed to favour an ill-formed idea of somehow driving the Palestinians out of Israeli territory into neighbouring countries such as Jordan, or even out of the Middle East altogether.

US pressure on Shamir led to an international summit in Madrid which even Israel's bitter Ba'athist enemy Syria agreed to attend, tentatively offering recognition of Israel's right to exist in return for Israeli evacuation from the occupied Syrian Golan Heights. Jordan – still officially at war with Israel, home to millions of Palestinian refugees and often nominated by Israel as a possible new Palestine homeland – also became involved in the process.

Shamir refused to talk with PLO 'terrorists', so a fig leaf was provided by designating what was in practice Arafat's PLO negotiating team as a 'Jordanian–Palestinian' delegation. When Shamir said he was still not prepared to talk the US threatened to withdraw $10 billion in economic aid. The Summit took place with Arafat hinting, in front of a worldwide TV audience, that he might be prepared to recognise the state of Israel if its government offered concessions. He talked optimistically of the two states of Israel and Palestine co-operating peacefully within the region. The speech was in fact an admission of defeat and marked the formal end of ideas for a United Arab Republic in northern Arabia, brought into being by the need for war or military co-operation against Israel on behalf of the dispossessed Palestinians.

One effect of Arafat's Madrid declaration was to undermine support for his more moderate, secularist PLO in the refugee camps and amongst Islamic and Arab militants generally. In place of the PLO the Islamist groups Hamas and Islamic Jihad – which had links beyond Palestine to militants in Afghanistan and Chechnya possibly co-ordinated by Osama Bin Laden's al-Qaeda network – began to find support and recruit in the refugee camps. (In an attempt to win back some of this support it was alleged that Arafat, while officially talking peace with the Israelis and Americans, set up a Hamas-style Islamist organisation under PLO control called the al-Aqsa Martyrs' Brigade – the group claimed responsibility for suicide bombing throughout the 1990s.)

After Madrid, talks between Israel and the Palestinians continued in secret in Norway, developing into what became known as the 'Oslo process'. In 1993 the continuing talks were made public after the election of the new left-wing and 'peace'-orientated Israeli government of Yitzhak Rabin. The process led to the Joint Declaration of Principles, brokered by

US President Bill Clinton and signed on the White House lawn and sealed with a symbolic handshake between Rabin and Yasser Arafat, watched on TV by 400 million people around the world. Arafat had recognised the right of Israel to exist and Israel had agreed in principle to return occupied Jordanian, Syrian and Egyptian Arab territory taken after the 1967 Arab–Israeli War and that on these territories Israel would sanction the creation of a Palestinian state of some sort. Jordan and Syria, at the same time, formally ended their official states of war with Israel.

The following year plans were made for the establishment of what was to be called the Palestinian Authority in the former Egyptian territory of the Gaza Strip. It was recognised that the Palestinian–Jordanian territory of the West Bank, occupied by Israel, would present more problems since it now contained a large number of Israeli settlers – and these settlers were completely (and sometimes violently) opposed to the idea of a 'land for peace' deal with the Palestinians.

On 1 July 1994 Arafat nevertheless drove in triumph through the streets of Gaza to take up residence in the newly established PLO headquarters. Two years later he was elected president of the newly established Palestinian National Authority. The city of Jericho on the West Bank was also handed over to the new National Authority as the first step to extending Palestinian rule over all of the West Bank. But amid the celebration, conflict continued. The religious right in Israeli politics denounced the establishment of a 'terrorist state' within what had lately been Israeli-administered territory. They predicted that Arafat – an unreformed terrorist – would simply use his new territory as a base for further terrorist attacks throughout Israel. These fears seemed to be confirmed when Palestinian militants who remained unconvinced of the need to accept the existence of Israel began terrorist activities along the border and against Israeli settlers in the West Bank.

Meanwhile, extremists on the Israeli side also agitated against the peace agreement. Messianic Jewish settler communities in the West Bank became more militant, more heavily armed and sometimes got involved in shoot-outs with Palestinians and Jordanian Arabs in the surrounding countryside.

Eventually Jewish religious extremists assassinated Rabin, architect of the peace process, saying that he had sold Israel to the Americans and the Arabs, sanctioning the death and destruction of the entire Jewish nation.

Rabin's assassination and settler intransigence was followed by a series of devastating Hamas suicide bombings in Israel, and a three-week bombardment of Lebanon by Israel aimed at destroying Hamas's Iranian-backed and Lebanese-based Islamist allies, Hezbollah.

A new right-wing government in Israel, led by Benjamin Netanyahu, lifted the freeze on new settlements in the West Bank, thus reversing one of the key planks of the Oslo agreements. Netanyahu also enflamed Arab opinion by opening an archaeological tunnel under the compound of the al-Aqsa mosque in Jerusalem – one of Islam's holiest sites. Under US pressure, and to keep the failing peace process from falling apart, Netanyahu nevertheless handed over a further chunk of West Bank territory – 80 per cent of the land in and around Hebron – to formal Palestinian control and in 1998 signed a formal agreement to surrender more territory in future, according to a schedule which would eventually see almost all of the Jordanian West Bank (whether it had Jewish settlers present or not) under Palestinian rule.

Netanyahu was voted out of office in 1999, to be replaced by the more leftist Ehud Barak who pledged to 'end the hundred-year conflict' between Israel and the Arabs within one year. The election came at a critical moment. The original timetable set out in the Oslo Process promised the Palestinians full statehood and sovereignty before the year 2000. Arafat agreed to suspend a unilateral declaration of independence for the West Bank – which would almost certainly have led to all-out war between the Israeli army and Palestinian *intifada* fighters – in favour of talks with Barak.

Barak, however, dragged his feet in talks, adopting a policy of 'divide and rule', trying to play off the Syrians, Jordanians and Palestinians against each other. US President Clinton intervened, trying to force a rapid agreement from Barak at a Camp David Summit. But two weeks of talks failed to come up with a deal over the status of Jerusalem and the extent to which returning Palestinian West Bank refugees would be allowed to take over land now being farmed by Israelis.

As these arguments continued the right-wing Israeli opposition leader Ariel Sharon seemed to deliberately provoke Palestinian violence by touring the al-Aqsa mosque in Jerusalem, fuelling the Palestinian myth that the Israelis were on the point of demolishing it, or rededicating it as a synagogue. Violent Palestinian demonstrations broke out and, after the normal and depressing sequence of army repression and demonstrator counter-attacks, the whole country was engulfed in the violence and suicide bombings of what became known as the al-Aqsa *intifada*.

Palestinian violence led to political reaction in Israel. Barak lost an election to the much more hard-line Sharon, who won a landslide victory on a ticket of ending the peace process and starting all-out war on Palestinian 'terrorism'. The US-backed policy of Israel 'buying peace by giving away land' had come to an end. Israeli and Palestinian violence got worse and worse as Sharon sanctioned policies such as assassinating Palestinian militants, carrying out US-style air strikes on the newly-established Palestinian self-rule areas – including Arafat's headquarters – and reoccupation of evacuated areas of the West Bank. The US seemed powerless to intervene and, after the replacement of Bill Clinton by President George W Bush, seemed less interested in the affairs of the region (at least until the terrorist attacks on New York in September 2001).

Violence escalated through 2002 and 2003 as Israel began to reoccupy almost all of the West Bank and struck at the Gaza Strip at will. In April 2002, 52 Palestinian civilians were killed when Israeli forces attacked a refugee camp in the northern West Bank city of Jenin and Israel was later accused by Amnesty International of committing war crimes. The following month a five-week Israeli army siege of the Church of the Nativity in Bethlehem only ended when thirteen Palestinian militants went into exile. At the same time the number of suicide bombings increased and began to claim the lives of large numbers of Israeli citizens.

The US-led attack on Iraq – the Second Gulf War – switched international attention away from Israel but once again had the effect of isolating and weakening the Palestinians – potentially allies or sympathisers with the Iraqis – and strengthening the hand of the US allies, Israel. In fact the Israelis had done what they could to suggest Palestinian terrorist collusion with the September 2001 terrorist attacks in New York – releasing to the world's media, for example, footage of Palestinians apparently celebrating after seeing the destruction of the World Trade Center. The footage was in fact faked.

Partly to ensure British support for the attack on Iraq, US President Bush promised to address some of the problems and injustices of the Middle East which were the root cause of the endemic instability in the region, of which the persistence of regimes such as that of Saddam Hussein in Iraq could be seen as symptomatic. The result was the 'road map for peace' – the latest overarching plan for agreement between the Israelis and Palestinians based around a 'two-state solution'. President Bush then added the caveat that before the 'road map' could be any use there would have to be 'regime change' at the top of the PLO and in the Palestinian Authority. Yasser Arafat, Bush said, was 'compromised by contact with terrorists' and would have to be replaced before there could be progress.

On the ground, in the seething Palestinian refugee camps, things were moving in the opposite direction. The authority of the secularist PLO was giving way more and more to extreme Islamist groups who viewed the whole 'Oslo' peace process as a straightforward deception and who never accepted, or felt themselves party to, agreement that the state of Israel should be allowed to exist. The most important of these groups were Hamas and Islamic Jihad.

HAMAS

Hamas was formed in the late 1980s during the first Palestinian *intifada* by younger militants in the camps frustrated by the inability of Yasser Arafat to lead them to victory. As the official PLO leadership tried more sophisticated attempts to compromise with the US and Israel, Hamas's aim remained simple – to drive Israeli forces out of the occupied territories by means of violence directed against the Israeli army and civilian population. Hamas political leader Abdel Aziz Rantissi declared in 2002: 'It is forbidden in our religion to give up a part of our land, so we can't recognise Israel at all.'

Israeli military withdrawal would lead to the establishment of an Islamic Palestinian state which, in time, would end all Israeli and American influence in historic Palestine. More than this, just as the Palestinian cause had once been seen as the catalyst for a wider Arab national revolution and political unification, elements within Hamas believe that an Islamic triumph in Palestine would lead to Islamic revolution in neighbouring Syria, Jordan, Iraq and Egypt, creating a new Muslim superpower in the region.

Hamas appears to be loosely organised and dependent on cells run by an unknown number of activists and financed partly by smuggling and other illegal activities along the border of the Palestine Authority in Gaza and partly by voluntary contributions in the refugee camps. Over 40,000 people attended a rally in December 2002 to mark the organisation's fifteenth anniversary addressed by the spiritual leader Shayk Ahmad Yassin. The Shayk predicted the complete destruction of Israel and the establishment of an Islamic republic throughout Arabia by the year 2025. 'The march of martyrs will move forward,' he said. 'Resistance will move forward. *Jihad* will continue, and martyrdom operations will continue until the full liberation of Palestine.'

In the early 1990s Hamas operated mainly from Jordan where it was tolerated by the late King Hussein (and may have been welcomed as a thorn in the side and an alternative to the King's old enemy Yasser Arafat). But the new Jordanian King Abdullah II closed the group's headquarters and forced many leaders into exile in Qatar. The move, if anything, saw an increase in Hamas's activities.

After initial Palestinian euphoria over the creation of the Palestinian National Authority in Gaza, Hamas began to capitalise on grass-roots disillusionment with the slow progress towards the creation of a truly sovereign Palestinian state and – importantly – with the disappointingly corrupt, undemocratic and compromised nature of the Arafat-dominated Authority itself.

Hamas gained support by providing schools, clinics and basic social services (based on Qur'anic obligations such as the collection and distribution of the *zakat* poor tax) where the PNA failed to do so. Clever political leadership led the organisation into sickening terrorist attacks on Israeli citizens and – especially – Israeli civilian settlers in the West Bank, knowing that these attacks would provoke retaliation from Israel, further undermining Israel and the US's partners in the 'peace process' – namely the PLO and the secular governments of Jordan and Syria in the eyes of ordinary Palestinians.

In December 1995 the Israelis arrested Hamas's 'chief bomb-maker' Yahya Ayyash. The organisation retaliated by carrying out several suicide bus bombings, killing sixty Israeli civilians of all ages and effectively bringing the peace process to an end, as intended. Further attempts by the Israeli forces to arrest or assassinate Hamas leaders – such as the botched attempt to murder Hamas's Jordanian organiser Khalid Meshal in 1997 – merely revealed Hamas to be a hydra with many heads, a loose federation of local cells united by ideas rather than a more conventional organisation with membership, rules, policy and hierarchical organisation like the PLO.

The widespread support for Hamas has forced the PLO into a more hard-line position and there have been attempts to bring Hamas back within the fold as the 'Islamist' wing of the PLO and the PNA. In 2003 Hamas and Yasser Arafat's paramilitary al-Fatah faction of the PLO reportedly reached an agreement in Cairo – Hamas agreed to stop attacks on Israeli citizens if the PLO, by means of negotiation, could secure the removal of Israeli troops to positions occupied before the *intifada*.

In the meantime Israel has made its own attempts to wipe out Hamas – or at least some of its better-known leaders. Hamas guerrilla commander Salah Shehada was killed in 2002 by a guided missile fired into his apartment block in Gaza by an Israeli jet fighter. Shehada's successor, Mohammad Deif has so far escaped several attempts on his life.

In 2006 Hamas won the first free elections for the Palestinian Authority's legislature, narrowly defeating the Arafat Fatah faction of the PLO. By that time Arafat had passed away, mourned as the father of the nation, but with his reputation much tarnished by corruption and by the failure of his foreign policy strategy.

The popularity of Hamas seemed to come as a shock to many in the West, where the movement was viewed exclusively as a terrorist organisation. The reality, according to the US Council on Foreign Relations was that more than 90 per cent of Hamas's activities and budget went on social welfare. The group provided basic social services that were otherwise unavailable to ghettoised community of the PNA statelet and this, in contrast to the corruption or indifference of Fatah, was the key to its success.

The new Hamas government overturned Arafat's policy of recognising Israel but offered and maintained a ceasefire until the Israelis (they claimed by accident) shelled unarmed civilians on a Gaza beach. Hamas responded with its trademark tactic of suicide bombing, since it lacked conventional military forces. The Western world responded by cutting off the economic aid on which the Arafat regime had come to depend. The result was overnight destitution for most of the population. By 2006, when Israel launched its attack (or as it claimed 'counterattack') on Hezbollah in southern Lebanon, the Palestinian statelet was facing a major humanitarian crisis.

ISLAMIC JIHAD

This utterly ruthless terrorist network, also known as Palestinian Islamic Jihad or PIJ was founded by three Palestinian students – Fathi Shikaki, Abdul Aziz Odeh and Bashir Moussa – who had been inspired by the Islamic Revolution in Iran. At the time the three young men were studying in Egypt and, after initial agitation against the secular leadership of the PLO and (its then close ally) the Egyptian state, they were thrown out of the country and made their way to join the huge Palestinian exile community in Jordan. They may also have spent time in Lebanon and possibly Iran itself.

Unlike fellow Islamist movements such as Hamas in Palestine and Hezbollah in Lebanon, PIJ has made no attempt to build a mass organisation, or to supplant the secular authorities in such matters as housing, health and welfare. Instead it has remained a tiny 'vanguardist' movement, enrolling only those who are prepared to die fighting. In recent years this has increasingly meant suicide bombing and attacks designed to be spontaneously copied by other would-be martyrs.

The first attacks claimed by PIJ took place in the early 1980s, within months of Yasser Arafat's renunciation of violence on the part of his own al-Fatah faction of the PLO as a failed tactic. For most of the decade the attacks seemed to be random, reflecting PIJ's essentially informal and opportunist way of operating.

By 1988 PIJ 'incidents' were becoming frequent enough to provoke a counter-attack by Israeli forces who arrested many supporters of the movement and expelled Shikaki and Odeh, who had moved from Israeli-occupied Gaza to Lebanon. In October 1995 Israel's security forces assassinated Fathi Shikaki in Malta – in the very same week that Israel's pro-peace Labour government was negotiating a 'two-state' solution to the conflict with Arafat and the PLO.

But these security measures did little to curb PIJ. Dozens of terrorist attacks have since been attributed to or claimed by the group, especially since the outbreak of the second *intifada* in 2000. Attacks, which are designed to attract publicity and inflict psychological as well as physical wounds on Israeli public opinion, have included armed infiltrations and machine gun attacks on unarmed members of Jewish settlements – especially those with a reputation for advocating peace with the Arabs. There have also been car bombings, ambushes and suicide bombings on Israeli buses, deliberately targeting children and teenagers. Other psychological operations have included the abduction of children from West Bank settlements who are then stoned to death in public on Palestinian National Authority territory.

PIJ strategy is to foster the idea that Palestinians and Israelis can never live side by side and it is doing what it can to plant seeds of hatred which, it hopes, will flower into an inter-ethnic vendetta which will last until one side has completely wiped out the other. The group may be small but it has had a great deal of success in provoking anti-Palestinian and anti-Peace Process feeling in Israel.

Leadership of the organisation passed in 1995 to Ramadan Abdullah al-Shallah, whose academic links in the West (he has a doctorate from the University of Durham and had just left a post at the University of South Florida) caused some controversy.

IRAQ
Population: 26 million (UN 2005)

For five hundred years from the middle of the eighth to the thirteenth centuries, Iraq was the centre of the greatest civilisation and empire Islam ever produced. The capital, Baghdad, was the wonder of the world with magnificent mosques, palaces, gardens, markets, schools of law and art, universities, hospitals and libraries. In backward Europe the legend arose that the streets of Baghdad were paved with gold, and that its scientists had devised magic flying carpets and elixirs of eternal life.

As in the other countries of northern Arabia, the Islam practised in Iraq is of moderate Sunni Hanafi variety. Fundamentalism is rare amongst the Hanafi and they are the Muslims most likely to accept and support secular regimes. Sunni'ism, since Ottoman times, has been the religion of the educated ruling elite and, recently, of the Ba'ath regime of former President Saddam Hussein. More than half the population, however, is Shi'ite – the faith of Iraq's hostile eastern neighbour, Iran.

Saddam Hussein came to power in 1968 following a faction fight within the ruling Ba'ath Party. Hussein purged the party of its Marxist wing, banned the Communist Party (which had previously ruled in coalition with the Ba'athists) and turned the country into a totalitarian one-party state based on his absolute power.

The Shi'ite's holiest shrine of the martyr Imam Husayn is at Karbala in the eastern part of the country and annual Iranian Shi'ite pilgrimages have become a focus of fundamentalist opposition to the secular regime in recent years. Fear of growing Shi'ite fundamentalism was one of the main causes of Iraq's attempt to overthrow the Iranian regime with the 1980 invasion.

Saddam Hussein hoped to destroy the Iranian regime before the Shi'ite revolution could spread to his eastern provinces and in the process annexed small amounts of territory along the Iran–Iraq border which had been claimed since the 1930s. He clearly expected Iran to collapse quickly and when it did not was forced to abruptly change international alignment.

The war radically changed Iraq's international relations. Previously the country had been closely allied with what was then the USSR and Syria. But the Soviets remained neutral whilst Syria backed Iran. Hussein turned for help to Saudi Arabia and the West who, disturbed by the threat posed by the Iranian regime, unambiguously supported him.

During the war Iran attempted to incite the Iraqi Shi'ites to revolt and continued after peace was declared. Hezbollah, the foreign wing of the ruling Iranian Islamic Republican Party, became active in eastern Iraq and a new party, al-Da'wah al-Islamiyyah (Islamic Call) has been active since the mid-1980s. Neither attracted mass support and both were severely repressed by the Ba'athist regime. As the Iraqi Shi'ites are Arabs rather than Iranians (an entirely different ethno-linguistic group), Saddam Hussein was able to counter Iranian propaganda with appeals to Arab nationalism.

In August 1990 Iraq invaded and occupied Kuwait – long claimed as part of historic Iraqi territory – on the assumption that the rest of the world would accept the invasion as a fait accompli. But the adventure was a dramatic miscalculation. The US gathered an international coalition to liberate Kuwait and protect its allies Israel, Saudi Arabia and the Gulf States and Iraq's armed forces were completely destroyed within six weeks.

The continuing failure of the Saddam Hussein regime to co-operate with the West and, it was claimed, the regime's attempts to create nuclear weapons led to the imposition of economic sanctions which, according to critics, led to the deaths of millions of Iraqi citizens.

In March 2003 a second American-led coalition attacked

Iraq, over-running the weak Iraqi army, occupying Baghdad within a few weeks and deposing Saddam Hussein.

After the surrender of Baghdad, American forces moved to put down Shi'ite rebels in Falluja and at Najaf, an important pilgrimage site for Shi'ites from Iran as well as Iraq. Insurgents based themselves around the holy sites of the city, and the US had to be careful not to cause damage and thus further antagonise Muslim sentiment.

In 2005 roughly half the population voted in relatively free elections and, amid a rare mood of optimism, a new democratically elected national government took office with the hope that it would be capable of taking on the immense task of reconstructing a country ruined by two major wars, economic collapse, national humiliation, revived ethic rivalries and vendettas and a decade of harsh externally imposed economic sanctions. Most of these hopes were dashed in an escalating campaign of terrorism and unconventional warfare against the new regime, and the reawakening of sectarian violence between Sunnis and Shi'ite and, in addition, warfare with the Kurds in the north of the country.

THE KURDS

The Kurds are a non-Arabic Muslim people forming the majority of the population in the north-eastern provinces of Iraq. There are also groups of Kurds in neighbouring Turkey and Iran who, together with the main group in Iraq, proclaimed an independent state of Kurdistan in 1945. The state was crushed within weeks by the joint action of Turkey, Iran and Iraq and the Kurds have been denied statehood ever since.

Iraq's 1974 Kurdish autonomy plan did, however, grant them the right to speak their own language, but stopped short of self-government. Two Kurdish groups, the Patriotic Union and the Unified Socialist Party, have kept up a limited guerrilla war ever since.

In 1988 the Iraqi armed forces used chemical weapons against the Kurdish town of Halabjah, as part of a campaign of ethnic cleansing. An attempted Kurdish uprising at the end of the First Gulf War in 1990, when the bulk of the Iraqi army had been destroyed during its retreat from Kuwait, was ruthlessly repressed but thereafter a Kurdish zone enjoyed some protection, underpinned by American and British airpower.

In 2003 Kurdish fighters joined with American regular troops, waging war with the Iraqi army during the Second Gulf War, thereby establishing a degree of de facto autonomy over Iraqi Kurdistan.

17. NORTH AFRICA (THE MAGHREB)

MOROCCO, ALGERIA, LIBYA AND TUNISIA
Total population: 81 million

The coastal fringe of North Africa was conquered by the Islamic Army at the end of the seventh century at the same time as the centre of the Muslim world moved from Mecca and Medina to the north Arabian lands and Iraq. The indigenous population of Berbers or 'Moors' – an ancient Mediterranean people similar but ethnically distinct from the Arabs – retreated to the inland Maghreb desert and resisted Arab rule.

In the eighth century the Meccan traditionalists defeated in the civil wars over the Mohammedan succession were also forced into exile in the Maghreb (the Arabic word for the west, or the sunset), mingled with the Moors and converted them to a traditionalist version of 'pristine' Islam hostile to the Arab aristocracy of the coast.

The Moors and their new Meccan allies, known as the Ibadites ('upholders of religious law'), founded cities like Fez and Marrakech, deep in the Maghreb beyond the control of the heterodox Caliphs of Baghdad and their Arab governors on the North African coast.

By the tenth century the Ibadites and Moors had swept the Arabs out of North Africa and replaced them with a series of states ruled (unlike the 'usurper' Caliphs in Baghdad) by descendants of the Prophet via his daughter Fatima. The Moors also conquered Spain from its Arab Muslim rulers (Spain was conquered by the Arabs in 711 and became an Emirate under the overall rule of Baghdad) and held parts of it for two hundred years before the Christian reconquest.

The Moorish rulers of the Maghreb adopted the strictly conservative Maliki school of Sunni law which today is the official doctrine of most of Muslim Africa. For six hundred years Moorish descendants of Muhammad ruled most of the territory of modern Morocco, Algeria, Libya and western Egypt before slowly falling under Ottoman and then French colonial rule.

The influence of these Imperial powers – like that of the Arabs one thousand years before – did not penetrate much further than the coastal strip where, especially in Algeria, there was considerable French settlement. The Maghreb desert preserved a simple and highly traditional form of Islam tightly closed to outside influences. Today the Muslim regimes in the region – from the bizarre, messianic form of Islam adopted in radical Libya to the grandiose Imperial schemes of conservative Morocco – share the same tendency to act as though the rest of the world did not – or ought not to – exist.

MOROCCO
Population: 32 million (UN 2005)

Morocco's official title is Kingdom of the Maghreb and the state still claims sovereignty in theory over all the lands ruled by the fifteenth-century ancestors of the current ruler King Mohammed VI, who claims, like the Kings of Jordan, direct descent from the Prophet. The claimed territory includes all of Morocco's southern neighbour Mauritania, most of Mali, the southern half of Algeria, most of Libya, part of Sudan and Egypt as far east as the Nile.

Until 1956 Morocco formed part of the French North African Empire which encompassed most of the Maghreb except Libya. After the Second World War King Hassan's father Mohammed al-Sharif (Mohammed V) tried to persuade the French to make him king of all their North African possessions.

The French at first refused but in 1956, following the Anglo-French defeat at the hands of Colonel Nasser of Egypt and the start of the Algerian war of independence, they changed their minds. Mohammed was given the territory of the former French protectorate of Morocco and proclaimed King of the Maghreb as a conservative, pro-French alternative to the radical anti-Western Arab independence movements active in virtually every French colony.

King Mohammed purged the more radical nationalist element amongst his own supporters and the French built up his Royal Armed Forces in preparation for the day when, following the expected French victory in Algeria, he would annex it to the Kingdom.

Mohammed died in 1961 and was succeeded by his son Hassan, the current king's father. When the Algerians finally won their own independence in 1962 the plan to annex the territory was effectively shelved and a constitution adopted for the state of Morocco alone. The new constitution established a limited parliament which could be dissolved at will by the king and enshrined Islam as the state religion. A hybrid legal system was developed using both the Maliki version of the *shari'ah* and French criminal law.

In 1965 Hassan dissolved parliament, claiming that the Kingdom was threatened by Algerian-backed Communist subversion, and ruled by personal decree. During these years the King repeatedly recognised and then challenged the boundaries of the neighbouring countries of the Maghreb and appeared confused about his territorial demands in the region.

The confusion prompted two botched coups by the army and Hassan's conservative supporters who clung to their Imperial dreams. In 1972 Hassan re-established the Parliament, packed it with supporters of his own Royalist Party and has since ignored it.

In 1975 he restored much of his popularity with the army by annexing the newly independent territory of Western Sahara – a stretch of barren, inhospitable desert which nevertheless formed part of the Maghreb Kingdoms of the Middle Ages.

Hassan personally led the so-called 'Green March' – a mass exodus of Moroccan settlers into Western Sahara, forcing the indigenous population to flee across the border into neighbouring Algeria. Settled in camps in eastern Algeria the refugees have formed an effective guerrilla army called the Polisario Liberation Front which was armed by Algeria and Libya and diplomatically supported by the majority of African and Arab countries.

The problems caused by the faltering war in Western Sahara contributed to a wave of internal unrest in the early 1980s led by the secular left-wing political opposition and the Communist-influenced trades union movement. After serious urban rioting against food price increases in 1981 the trades unions and leftist parties were utterly crushed by the army. Over six hundred leading leftists are believed to have been killed and more than two thousand were sent to jail, where many remained for years.

Hassan took further dictatorial powers for the monarchy, including the right to overturn legislation and dissolve parliament at any time. He retains immense personal power as Commander in Chief of the armed forces and director of the national TV and radio service. As the country's supreme religious authority the king dictates what is taught in schools and what is preached in the mosques.

On inheriting the throne on his father's death in 1999 Mohammed VI resolved to end the draining war with the Polisario and, more generally, insulate the kingdom from the wave of Islamic fundamentalism and anti-Western feeling sweeping neighbouring Algeria in the wake of the First Gulf War in 1990.

In 2003 there were mass demonstrations against US plans to attack Iraq in the Second Gulf War. At the same time Moroccan authorities arrested three Saudi members of al-Qaeda who, it was claimed, were planning to blow up British and American warships in the straits of Gibraltar. Within months Morocco suffered one of its worst ever terrorist attacks when suicide bombers blew up the centre of the country's business capital, Casablanca.

ALGERIA
Population: 33 million (UN 2005)

Algeria became a French colony in 1830 and there was extensive settlement by French nationals in the large coastal cities. This large-scale foreign presence was something entirely new in the thousand-year history of the Maghreb's isolation and was to profoundly influence the post-independence development of Islam in the country. '

A significant number of ethnically Moorish (or Berber) Algerians became Westernised, adopted French habits, received French education and came into contact with the European political idea of socialism. In the early years of the twentieth century ethnically Algerian socialists – often lawyers or other professionals – began agitating for national independence.

But these Westernised Algerians were politically isolated. In 1945 there was a 'conventional' socialist-inspired uprising based around demands for nationalisation of French-owned agricultural estates. This was easily put down by the authorities with heavy loss of Algerian lives.

In the late 1940s a younger generation of Algerian nationalists became convinced that the traditional insularity and puritanism of Islam in the Maghreb interior was the only force powerful enough to overthrow French rule. Whilst the older generation of radicals had encouraged secularism and appealed to the Muslim population as 'workers', the new radicals, the National Liberation Front (NLF), adopted Islamic customs and traditional dress. They began to agitate against the flagrant breaches of the *shari'ah* – such as drinking, gambling, the display of female bodies – taking place in the French quarters of Algerian cities.

By the mid-1950s law and order had collapsed in the cities. Drinking clubs and casinos were bombed and French colonial restrictions on religious dress and practice were openly flouted. The inevitable French backlash produced a steady supply of martyrs whose deaths in defence of Islam caused the tribesmen of the interior to join the revolt.

By 1958 isolated terrorist outrages had escalated into a full-scale civil war with half a million French troops deployed

against an almost completely united Muslim Algerian population. Appalling massacres were committed on both sides and by
the end of the war in 1962 France had lost more soldiers in
Algeria than they had in the Second World War, the mainland
had been brought to the brink of civil war, and General de
Gaulle had become President of France with dictatorial powers.

The new Algerian NLF government, headed by the wartime
guerrilla leader Ben Bella, enshrined Islam as the national
religion but at the same time retained a largely secular legal
system. Most of the economy was nationalised along socialist
lines and simultaneously 'Islamised'.

Banks were forbidden to charge interest in line with the
Qur'anic injunction against 'usury' and the joint capital
venture method of finance – where a proportion of the profit
went to the capital lender or bank – was substituted.

Wages and prices were fixed by central government according to the classic socialist model, but the Qur'anic reference to
'moral contracts' was also invoked. The second *surah* states:
'When you [trade] with each other in contracting a debt for a
fixed time, then write it down; and let a scribe write it down
in fairness' (2:282). Measures like these, which upheld the
shari'ah and fitted well with centralised socialist economic
planning, became known as 'Islamic Socialism' and Algeria
quickly became the archetypal Islamic Socialist state.

In 1965 Ben Bella was replaced as NLF leader by his former
assistant Colonel Houari Boumédienne in a bloodless coup. On
the pretext of the continuing 'Imperialist' threat, Boumédienne
abolished the Constituent Assembly and replaced it with a
military junta constituted as the Revolutionary Command
Council.

The NLF under Boumédienne and his army-dominated
successor Colonel Chadli Bendjedid built a prosperous state by
Third World standards based on the export of oil and
minerals. Internationally Algeria became an important backer
of the non-aligned 'Tricontinental Movement', also sponsored
by Cuba and Burma. Within the Muslim world this meant
supporting Nasserism, nascent guerrilla movements like the
Palestine Liberation Organisation and the Fedayeen guerrillas
active against the Shah of Iran.

In 1986 Algeria adopted a new Political Charter to guide the future development of 'Islamic Socialism' which elevated the importance of the *shura* (religiously guided councils) in the running of the state and the nationalised industries. At the same time greater freedom for private enterprise was granted within an overall framework of state control.

Unrest caused by growing corruption and nepotism within the NLF along with falling oil revenues found expression in Islamic opposition to the reforms of the *shari'ah* in the early 1980s. These reforms had provoked Islamists by abolishing polygamy and granting full and formal equality to women. In 1988 and 1989 rioting sparked by food price increases, but with Islamist overtones, forced the NLF government to revoke a previous ban on Islamic political parties. A new fundamentalist party called the Islamic Salvation Front (FIS) made huge gains in local and national elections, but was kept out of office with a series of questionable constitutional manoeuvres devised by the army and government.

In 1992, after years of political crisis and growing internal violence, secularist President Chadli resigned. A new junta took charge of the country, declared a state of emergency and began to rule by decree, supported by the military. Within weeks the leader of the new junta was assassinated by a member of his own bodyguard who, in turn, was believed to be an agent on the FIS's military wing, the Islamic Salvation Army.

For the rest of the 1990s Algeria was in effect run by the military, though the ruling High State Council did submit itself to elections, which it always won by a landslide amid accusations of ballot rigging and intimidation of voters in FIS-supporting districts. Nevertheless a measure of stability was achieved. It was later conceded by the security forces that they had been responsible for many abuses of human rights including the disappearance of 6,000 people during the decade.

In 1999 the military and the FIS signed an accord pardoning members who had engaged in terrorism in return for the winding up of the guerrilla war. More elections followed, but these were boycotted by many parties as a 'sham'.

In 2004 and 2005, however, elections of increasing credibility were held, an amnesty was issued to former militants and

FIS was said to have ceased to function as any sort of power in the country. Algeria in the middle years of the first decade of the new millennium was thus a rare case of an Arab Muslim country which could look forward to growing stability and, perhaps, even a resumption of some of the optimism which surrounded the emergence of the country from colonialism fifty years earlier.

LIBYA
Population: 5.8 million (UN 2005)

From the nineteenth century onwards the Berber-Moors of the Libyan desert became the most extreme adherents to the highly traditionalist and insular form of Maliki Sunni Islam found throughout the Maghreb.

The cause of this renewed bout of extremism, which still profoundly marks Islam in Libya today, was the Sanusi movement launched by Zayid Mohammed 'Ali as-Sanusi (died 1859). Sanusi was an Algerian Berber who studied theology in Fez and Mecca and became a dedicated follower of the Wahhabi movement in the Arabian peninsula, the first group of modern Muslim fundamentalists. He returned to the Maghreb, settled in Libya and began propagating the Wahhabi message.

Sanusi attempted to rally the Berber tribes of the Maghreb to overthrow Ottoman Egypt in the way Wahhab and his followers had attacked the Ottoman authorities in the peninsula. The Libyan Berbers were enthusiastic. Contemporary Egypt was the centre of despised Muslim heterodoxy and the old enemy from dozens of Berber-Arab wars in the Middle Ages.

Sanusi died before he could unleash the rebellion and leadership of the movement passed to his son Sayyid al-Mahdi (the apocalyptic 'chosen one'). Al-Mahdi fought the Egyptians in Sudan and assisted in the establishment of the short-lived Mahdi'ist Republic in Khartoum. In Libya al-Mahdi set up a network of hundreds of secret Sanusi lodges (*zawiyah*) giving the movement a permanent structure – rare for a Sunni Muslim sect of this type.

Mohammed Idris, Sanusi's grandson, allied with the Italians in a short war against Ottoman Egypt, establishing himself as Emir of an independent Libya under Italian protection. Idris allowed himself to fall more and more under Italian control during the middle years of the twentieth century but, after the Italian defeat in the Second World War, emerged as King of an Independent Libya in 1951 with British and French support.

He had strengthened the grip of the Sanusi sect on the country and by 1951 at least one third of the population had joined local Sanusi zawiyah. As King, he tried to use the Sanusi network to establish a conservative fundamentalist regime friendly to the Western powers along the lines of Saudi Arabia. But lower down the Sanusi structure younger members grew frustrated with his conservatism and especially his failure to support the radical Nasserite regime in Egypt over Suez.

Nasser was greatly admired by the radical Sanusi as the man who had overthrown the despised British-backed Farouk monarchy and championed the cause of war against Israel. In 1969 a group of young Sanusi army officers formed themselves as the Free Unionist Officers Movement (MLCU), overthrew the monarchy, and pledged to root out foreign influence and impose Sanusi-influenced Muslim rule in the country.

Twelve leaders of the MLCU formed themselves into a Revolutionary Command Council (RCC) military junta under the chairmanship of Colonel Mu'ammar al-Qaddafi, who quickly emerged as the dominant figure in the new regime. In 1977, having reduced the RCC from twelve to six people and established complete personal control of the regime, al-Qaddafi published his 'Green Book' outlining the Colonel's 'Third Universal Theory' – the official ideology of the country.

The Book is a bizarre collection of traditionalist Berber, Sanusi and extremist socialist thinking. It calls for the revolutionary overthrow of all the governments of the world and their replacement with the direct rule of Allah by obedience to Qur'anic law (the *shari'ah*) and al-Qaddafi's own divinely inspired Green Ideology.

In 1973 the distinction between civil courts, administering Roman-based law and 'traditional' or 'native' *shari'ah* courts was abolished. In 1977 a new revolutionary constitution declared: 'The Holy Qur'an is the Constitution of the Socialist People's Libyan Arab Jamahiriya.'

Where the *shari'ah* is inadequate to deal with modern problems, as al-Qaddafi concedes is often the case, he believes that laws can only be made by a gathering of the entire people of the country (in Libya's case some 5.5 million adults) through a series of People's Assemblies and local committees.

In line with these ideas he 'dissolved' the Libyan state in 1977 and replaced it with a 'state of the masses' (*Jamahiriya*) composed of local committees dispensing the functions of the state and judiciary. The committees are also responsible for implementation of the *shari'ah*, though there is a national court of appeal and a supreme court in Tripoli.

The personnel of the appeal and supreme courts are selected by the People's General Congress which carries out the functions of central government. The General Congress meets from time to time to decide matters such as the national budget and is composed of up to one thousand delegates from local committees, trades unions, women's organisations and the like. These gatherings are reportedly chaotic and, in practice, controlled by the Congress Secretariat composed of nineteen regional representatives.

In 1979 al-Qaddafi resigned as General Secretary of the Congress Secretariat and retired to a tent in the Libyan desert. Moving about to avoid possible assassination he directs a parallel national structure of Revolutionary Committees whose cell-like structure extends into every corner of Libyan society. The Revolutionary Committees form a tightly knit and fanatical elite, based in turn on the secretive structure of the Sanusi *zawiyah*, which polices the whole committee system.

In 1980 a Sunni theological commission in Mecca accused al-Qaddafi of apostophy – reversion from Islam – and the Colonel is now widely described by other Islamic rulers as a non-Muslim (*kafir*). Despite this, he is widely regarded by his followers as *al-Mahdi* and uses his position as head of the armed forces to rule the country. Conscription is enforced and Libya is one of the most militarised nations in the world, with reportedly more aircraft, guns and tanks than it has people able to operate them.

The 1986 American air strike against Libyan targets was a response to Libyan sponsorship of international terrorist groups. According to Western intelligence, al-Qaddafi has at one time or another financed, trained or supplied arms to various factions of the PLO, the Red Brigades, the Baader-Meinhof group, the American Black Panthers and the Provisional IRA. He is also accused of sponsoring coup attempts or other forms of subversion in Egypt, Niger, Chad, Sudan, Mali, Tunisia, Saudi Arabia, Lebanon, Jordan, Guinea and The Gambia. He came to the brink of all-out war with France in 1984 over his role in Chad and, in addition, from time to time has been accused of masterminding the secret export of Niger uranium to Iraq as part of a plan to build an 'Islamic Bomb'.

After the US bombing al-Qaddafi appeared to moderate his stance and reduce his involvement in foreign adventures, though he did expel 30,000 Palestinian refugees from the country in protest at PLO leader Yasser Arafat's de facto recognition of the state of Israel during the Oslo peace talks in 1995.

In 1999 Libya finally handed over two of its citizens to the British who put them on trial in the Netherlands for their role in blowing up an American jumbo jet over Lockerbie in Scotland in 1998. One was found guilty and the other released. In 2002, in the wake of the attacks on the World Trade Center and the bombing of Afghanistan, US and Libyan officials held talks at restoring relations. Interestingly Libya was not named as a member of President Bush's 'axis of evil' and in 2003, amid much controversy, the US did not object to Libya being elected to the chairmanship of the United Nations Human Rights Commission, despite the regime's long record of human rights abuses.

The warming of relations with the West was crowned by a visit to the country by Tony Blair in 2004 and in 2005 granting of oil and gas extraction contracts to a US energy corporation for the first time in twenty years. The US resumed full diplomatic relations with Libya the following year.

TUNISIA
Population: 10 million (UN 2003)

Tunisia is too far north and too narrowly coastal to have been permanently included in any of the inland Berber-Moorish Maghreb Empires of the past. It has thus remained predominantly Arab both in population and culture and therefore slightly more open to outside influences.

The Tunisian Arabs nevertheless share the highly conservative Maliki version of Sunni Islam found in the neighbouring Berber-Moorish states. The country is also home to many small pockets of extreme fundamentalist Ibadites. The offshore island of D'Jerba – about the size of the Isle of Wight – is home to 50,000 fanatical Ibadites who live more or less as their ancestors did when they fled there from Mecca 1,300 years ago.

Tunisian independence was granted by France in 1955 without a fight, mainly because the country was an economic liability and had no large indigenous French population. Most of the rural population was scarcely touched by French rule and completely unexcited by its passing.

In the early 1970s post-independence leader Bourguiba abandoned socialism in favour of free market economic policies promoted by the World Bank, to which Tunisia is heavily in debt as a result of the high-spending socialist policies of the past. Through the 1970s food subsidies were steadily withdrawn and the economy was progressively denationalised. Service industries – particularly tourism – were encouraged.

In 1981 the pace of economic liberalisation increased and there were strikes and protests against unemployment and high food prices. The trades unions, traditional allies of the government, were placed under severe legal restraint and became largely ineffective. Left-wing opponents within the government party were expelled and independent left-wing groups curbed.

The repression is mild by the standards of nearby Morocco where similar economic and political action has been taken and has failed to stop the periodic unrest. In recent years anti-government demonstrations have become incoherent and violent and, as in Morocco, increasingly 'Islamic'.

Rising prices and falling wages are linked in the minds of many Tunisians with the arrival of foreign tourists and their shockingly un-Islamic behaviour. Measures have been taken to strictly segregate the alcohol-swilling, sun-bathing tourists but the impact on this highly traditionalist society has been profound.

The Islamic Tendency Movement, widely believed to be a 'front' organisation for the illegal pro-Saudi Arabian Muslim Brotherhood, emerged for the first time as an active force during the 1984 food riots. The Movement links popularist demands for lower food prices with demands for full implementation of *shari'ah* law, at present restricted to the personal affairs of practising Muslims. The Tendency also wants a ban on permissive activities by tourists – particularly female nakedness.

18. TURKEY AND THE BALKANS

TURKEY, ALBANIA, BOSNIA
Total population: 81 million

From the twelfth century onwards waves of pagan central Asian invaders began to sweep into the ancient Islamic heartlands attracted by the fabulous riches of Baghdad and its empire.

One such group of invaders, the Turks, settled in Iraq and had converted to Islam in significant numbers by about 1150. At first they were employed by Iraq's Arab rulers as mercenaries and palace guards but, as Arab rule became decadent, gained in power. By the start of the thirteenth century effective political power had passed from the Arab Emperors to the Turkish warlords.

In the middle of the thirteenth century AD, Ghengis Khan's pagan Mongol horde swept into Iraq and Syria and put Baghdad and Damascus to the sword in an orgy of destruction. The Turks fled west to Asia Minor – the territory of modern Turkey – capturing it from the declining Christian Empire of Byzantium. Damascus and Baghdad became backwaters, Mecca and the Arabian peninsula became even further removed from the historical stage, and only Cairo survived to preserve, in a greatly weakened form, the heritage of the Golden Age.

Under the leadership of the Ottoman dynasty of Sultans the Turks developed a highly efficient military machine which became legendary for its ferocity and frequent barbarity. In a century of unrelieved warfare they captured all the lands of the Byzantine Empire, extinguishing Christianity forever in Asia Minor and establishing their capital Istanbul in the former Byzantine capital of Constantinople.

Under the Ottomans Islam became the ideology of an Empire otherwise based on military ruthlessness and the despotic rule of the Sultans. Worship at the mosque became not only a mark of free submission to Allah, but of forced submission to the Sultan.

The Ottoman conquest of Balkan Europe was achieved at the cost of much bloodshed and great cruelty was shown to the indigenous Christian populations. As a result, Ottoman rule in the Balkans linked Islam with barbarism in the European mind. The reconquest of the Balkans by the Europeans left behind large Muslim minorities who were frequently despised by their Christian compatriots.

TURKEY
Population: 73 million (UN 2005)

Modern Turkey is on the face of it the least 'Islamic' of all major Muslim nations. The Turkish national state, established in 1923, was devised specifically to break the political grip of six hundred years of backward 'Islamic' Ottoman rule. Shari'ah courts were abolished, women were given the vote and it became illegal for members of the armed forces or the civil service to profess Islam in public by, for example, growing long beards or wearing religious dress.

Islamic education was banned in schools, the Latin alphabet replaced Arabic (the sacred script of Islam), and the considerable endowments of various Islamic organisations – especially the Sufi monastic Orders which had grown rich under Ottoman patronage – were confiscated by the state. Turkish Islam was thus reduced to being a purely private religion of conscience. The Sufi orders promptly rose in revolt but were crushed and have remained banned ever since.

Religious observance has declined enormously, especially in the cities and amongst the young, and many mosques – other than those preserved for the tourist trade in Istanbul – are deserted and face dereliction (a mosque, however, may never be used for any purpose other than worship and may not be demolished – a rule upheld even in secular Turkey).

Endemic economic crisis in the 1990s led however to the election of the moderately Islamist 'Welfare' party in 1996 – forming the first avowedly Islamic government of Turkey since 1923. Within a year the Welfare government was forced out of office by the army, to be replaced by a centre-right government. Within twelve months the Welfare Party was banned. Islamic activists reconstituted the Welfare Party first as the Virtue Party and then the Happiness Party, but these were also banned – making Turkey the first state in history to officially outlaw welfare, virtue and happiness as political objectives.

The country is now being promoted as a European tourist destination to rival Greece and this is as good an indicator of Islam's position within the country as any. Semi-naked sun bathing would be out of the question in a country like Saudi Arabia and has to be confined to highly segregated areas even in relatively liberal Muslim tourist destinations like Tunisia. No such provision for the sensibilities of the faithful is being made in Turkey.

Far away from the beaches the Turkish state is still prosecuting a civil war against the fighters of the PKK who demand independence for Turkey's eastern Kurdish-speaking region. This terrorist group is Marxist and nationalist rather than Islamic. But the violence involved in suppressing the separatists appears to rule out the government's objective of joining the European Union for the time being at least.

ALBANIA
Population: 3.2 million (UN 2005)

The Muslim majority countries of Albania and Bosnia and the large minorities in Serbia and nearby Bulgaria are all that remains of six hundred years of Ottoman rule in the region which began with the defeat of the Serbian Orthodox Christian

Empire following the Battle of the Field of Blackbirds, in the disputed Serbian-Albanian province of Kosovo, in 1389.

Albania became an officially atheist Socialist state at the end of the Second World War. All religions, including Islam, were officially discouraged. In 1967 the Albanian authorities, inspired by the Chinese Communist Cultural Revolution, closed all the country's churches and mosques. At the same time the extreme isolationism of Albania's Maoist-Marxist government meant that Albania became Europe's poorest and most closed society.

Elections in 1992 ended 47 years of Communist rule but brought with it new problems of ethnic strife, corruption, economic collapse and organised crime. The collapse of neighbouring Yugoslavia, meanwhile, threatened to destabilise the country after thousands of ethnic Albanians fled repression in the neighbouring Serbian (but majority-Albanian populated) province of Kosovo.

In 1998 intense persecution of Kosovan Albanians by the Serbs led to a flood of refugees and the start in 1999 of the NATO bombing campaign against Serbia (then still part of the rump federation of Yugoslavia). The refugees brought with them an estimated one million machine guns and other firearms looted from army stores, adding to the general lawlessness of the country. In 2003, nevertheless, Albania began 'stabilisation and association' talks with the EU, seen as the first step in the very long road to eventual membership of the European Union.

BOSNIA
Population 4.2 million (UN 2005)

The new state of Bosnia-Herzegovina was carved out of the ruins of Yugoslavia effectively as a homeland for Yugoslav Muslims. Before its disintegration Yugoslavia was the only European country apart from Albania to have Muslim majorities on parts of its territory, and direct Muslim input and representation in its political systems.

There was always significant anti-Muslim feeling among the various other nationalities and religious groups that made up

Yugoslavia, particularly the dominant Serbs and Croats. In 1918 Slavic Muslims made up over 90 per cent of the landowning class, enjoying privileges and the military protection of their Ottoman Turkish overlords. The expropriated Slavic peasant class were little better off than slaves, and felt they had suffered for their loyalty to the original national creed of Orthodox Christianity. Further resentment was caused by the noted collaboration of Muslim Bosnians with the Nazi Germans during the dismemberment of Yugoslavia during the Second World War.

These long-held tensions exploded in the early 1990s with the fall of Communism through Eastern Europe, including Yugoslavia and Albania. Around 250,000 people died during the civil war between Bosnian Muslims, Croats and Serbs amid atrocities and massacres on a scale not seen in Europe since the days of the Nazi extermination camps.

The war was brought to an end in 1995 by the intervention of the US and NATO and the boundaries of the new Bosnian state were established as part of the Dayton accords within which two sub-states – one for Muslims and Croats, the other for Bosnian Serbs – were established, along with an international peacekeeping force to keep each community from attacking the other.

By the turn of the century US intelligence began to suspect that Arab Muslim extremists were recruiting disaffected Bosnian youths – who look like any other ethnic European – for terrorist activities. In 2002, after the attack on the World Trade Center in New York and the subsequent toppling of the Taliban in Afghanistan, US forces arrested six Bosnians with suspected Arab links and took them for questioning to Guantanamo Bay in Cuba.

19. IRAN

Population: 71 million (UN 2005)

Iran, known as Persia until the 1930s, is unique amongst the Islamic nations for its overwhelming Shi'ite, rather than Sunni, population. It is also the only modern Muslim nation apart from Afghanistan with a centuries-old tradition of national independence – gained at the cost of long and bloody struggles against both Sunni Muslim Empires and European Colonialists. Shi'ism and ancient Persian nationhood combine to make Islam in modern Iran quite different from that found in the other Muslim 'worlds'.

Shi'ism was established as the dominant form of Islam in Persia in 1500 by the Safavid dynasty of Shahs after a century of bitter guerrilla war against the Sunni Ottoman Turks at the height of their military power. But as Ottoman Islam began to decline Safavid Persia became the centre of an Islamic civilisation deeply influenced by the ancient and sophisticated culture of pre-Islamic Persia.

The Safavid capital of Isfahan became one of the greatest cities of later Islam and, in its architectural and artistic achievements (not least the living arts of poetry, cuisine, clothing and – above all – carpet making) came to rival the heyday of Baghdad.

From the eighteenth to the twentieth centuries Persia declined under the rule of Afghan dynasties with Mongol ethnic roots. For two hundred years Islam and the state were separated along the lines of the division between church and state roles in many Western countries. The Shi'ites developed a ramified religious hierarchy – the only one of its type found in Islam – which allowed the Shahs to run the state but maintained a tight grip on the religious life of the people.

In 1906 the Afghan Qajar dynasty of Shahs framed a Western-type constitution granting autonomy to the Shi'ite clergy and allowing them to run schools, charities and religious foundations. The separation was maintained by the short-lived Pahlavi dynasty of Shahs, founded by Reza Khan Pahlavi, an army officer who overthrew the pro-British Qajars in 1925 with a military coup.

After the Second World War Shah Muhammad Reza (the 'last Shah') developed the separation of state and clergy still further in the belief that if the Shi'ite authorities were granted greater control over education and the moral, religious and private lives of the population, they would leave him free to develop the country into a Western-style secular state.

But by the 1970s the Shi'ite clergy had decided that Muhammad Reza Shah had gone too far in his campaign of Westernisation. Since the 1950s rapid economic development had been threatening the grip of Shi'ism, based on the traditional peasant structure of the countryside and the bazaar economy of the cities. Eventually the governing religious body of the Shi'ites – the *ulama* – began to preach that the Shah was working to destroy Shi'ite Islam through a wave of secularisation and Western permissiveness.

THE MULLAHS' REVOLUTION

The *ulama* was particularly incensed by the lavish celebrations marking the 50th anniversary of the Pahlavi dynasty in 1975, which clashed with Islamic religious festivals and peaked with parades glorifying the pre-Islamic pagan gods of ancient Persia accompanied by drinking binges and Western pop music.

At first the religious opposition joined the secular left in the so-called movement of the Red Mullahs, led by Ayatollahs

Kashani and Shariati, focusing on the cultural and economic effects of Western-style capitalism and the enormous American military presence within the country. This movement was crushed by SAVAK, the Shah's notorious secret police, but the conservative religious wing of the opposition, led by Ayatollah Khomeini, was largely ignored.

Exiled to Iraq and then to Paris, Khomeini began to preach the overthrow of the Shah and the imposition of rule by the *ulama* ('the rule of the jurists') under his leadership as Imam. Finally, in April 1979 an incoherent coalition of what remained of the left-wing and liberal movements, bazaar merchants threatened by the Shah's capitalist reforms and Shi'ite clergy (*mullahs*) rooted in every part of the country, deposed the Shah and proclaimed an Islamic Republic.

New institutions were formed in 1980 but the real power in revolutionary Iran passed to the *ulama* and Imam Khomeini – who was officially held to be the divinely guided representative on earth of the 'concealed' Twelfth Imam of the Shi'ites (see Part 3 – Islamic Sects).

A new constitution was adopted in 1979. Article 4 provides that all civil, penal, financial, economic, administrative, cultural, military, political, and any other laws must be based on Islamic criteria. Article 12 provides that the official state religion is Islam and the twelver Ja'fari school; other schools of law are tolerated as, in theory, are Judaism, Christianity and other monotheistic religions.

The *ulama*, working through the larger 83-member Council of Experts, appoints all judges and can overturn their decisions. It also functions as the supreme command of the Iranian armed forces and revolutionary guard, ratifies the election of the Iranian President and can dismiss the Majlis (National Consultative Assembly or Parliament) or overturn its decisions. The *ulama* also directs foreign policy and may declare war or make peace.

The *ulama* is the top layer in a hierarchical clerical system similar in many ways to that of the Roman Catholic Church. Its power is based on about 100,000 *mullahs* (priest-teachers) who transmit its decisions and instructions to every town and village in the country. The *mullahs* are, in the main, 'lay' clerics who have jobs as peasant farmers or bazaar merchants and thus penetrate Iranian society far more effectively than a full-time professional clergy.

About 40,000 *mullahs* have the rank of *mojtahidi* – clerics sufficiently learned to give legal ruling in the local *shari'ah* courts. Above them are several thousand *hojatoleslami* (regional judges or 'deputy Ayatollahs') and about 100 Ayatollahs (national judges).

The five most senior Ayatollahs, the *Ozma* (Grand Ayatollahs), form the highest religious and judicial authority in the country. The Ozma sit with seven other Qur'anic scholars – who may or may not be Ayatollahs – as the *ulama*. The *ulama* in turn elects the *Imam* – the Shi'ite 'Pope' – from within its number.

The decade of the 1980s, the first after the Islamic revolution, was dominated by a devastating war with neighbouring Iraq whose leader Saddam Hussein attacked his eastern neighbour – according to some at the behest of the Kuwaitis, Saudis and the West – evidently expecting a quick victory and substantial territorial gains. Instead the conflict dragged on for eight years, resulting in millions of deaths. The conflict was marked by such horrors as Iranian 'human wave attacks' and the first widespread use of chemical weapons on the battlefield since the First World War.

The war ended in 1988 and Ayatollah Khomeini died in the following year, to be replaced by President Ali Akbar Hashemi-Rafsanjani. Under Rafsanjani diplomatic relations were resumed with Iraq. Iran stayed neutral during the First Gulf War, denounced the presence of the US military in the Middle East and may have helped Saddam Hussein by allowing him to hide all or some of his air force in Iran.

Declining relations between Iran and the US in the 1990s led to the imposition of economic sanctions, after US claims that Iran was the 'largest sponsor of terrorism' in the world. Internally, however, the late 1990s saw a new younger generation come to the fore and liberal reforms which meant that Iran became one of the few functioning democracies in the region. In 1997 the liberal and reformist Mohammad Khatami was elected president by a landslide after promising to reduce the constitutional power of the Shi'ite clergy. In 2001 he was elected for a second term, with his Liberal supporters taking 170 of the 290 seats in the Majlis. The remnant of the once all-powerful Islamic Revolutionary Party was reduced to only 44 seats.

These liberalising trends came to an end, at least at the level of state policy, after a general election in 2005 brought Mahmoud Ahmadinejad to power as president. The former mayor of Tehran was usually described as 'ultra conservative', meaning that he wanted a return to the principles of the Khomeni revolution in both domestic and foreign policy spheres.

President Bush had already accused Iran of supporting external terrorist groups, including Hezbollah in Lebanon. Of equal concern was Iran's evident intent to produce nuclear weapons.

Throughout 2005 and 2006 the US took an increasingly belligerent stance against Iran and it even seemed that a pre-emptive strike against Iranian nuclear facilities might be on the cards. Relations declined further when the sporadic military exchanges between Hezbollah and the Israelis escalated in the summer of 2006 into all-out war.

The nuclear weapons issue, taken together with a statement by the new president demanding the complete destruction of the already nuclear-armed state of Israel, brought the new and chilling dimension of possible nuclear war into middle-eastern politics.

20. THE SUB-CONTINENT AND SOUTH ASIA

PAKISTAN, KASHMIR, AFGHANISTAN, BANGLADESH
Total population: 340 million

Islam was established in north-west India and Afghanistan in the eighth century AD but languished under a series of local Emirs and Sultans during the Golden Age of the Abbasids. The lands of Islam were forever divided between west and east by the Mongol destruction of Baghdad in 1258. Thereafter the 'eastern' Islam of the sub-continent developed independently of the dominant Ottoman west.

With the Ottoman Empire entering its last phase of decline in the sixteenth century, Islam in India experienced a spectacular revival in the form of the heterodox, Hindu-influenced Mogul Empire. For two hundred years Muslims and Hindus co-operated to create a great civilisation, now chiefly remembered for great architectural monuments such as the Taj Mahal.

During the peak of the Mogul Empire traders and missionaries set out from western India to Bengal (part of which now forms the territory of Bangladesh) and the Malay-Indonesian archipelago. Local Hindu and pagan princes converted to a tolerant and localised manifestation of Islam, creating dozens of religiously heterodox and prosperous Sultanates – later welded together by European colonialists to form the modern states of Indonesia and Malaysia.

In India itself the later Mogul emperors reversed the policy of religious toleration and embraced a narrow and sectarian version of Ottoman-type Hanafi Islam. Countless Hindu–Muslim wars sapped the power of the Empire and led to its conquest by the British. Under British rule Indian Muslims became a despised minority in a hostile Hindu-dominated nation.

Partition of the sub-continent into the states of Pakistan and India in 1947 was an unsatisfactory attempt to reconcile the rival political ambitions of Muslims and Hindus. But from the beginning there were great doubts that the partition would be stable and, in practice, the new state of Pakistan quickly began to disintegrate.

In West Pakistan Islam inherited the narrow sectarian creed of the late Mogul period and the Afghan tribesmen. The elusive search for Islamic purity was expressed as an increasingly dogmatic and intolerant 'fundamentalism', deeply hostile towards Hindu-influenced Muslim refugees from the central and southern parts of the sub-continent.

In East Pakistan (later Bangladesh) the Muslim community was based on relatively recent Bengali converts from Hinduism who had little in common with the West Pakistanis and retained ethnic, cultural and linguistic ties with the Hindus of the neighbouring Indian state of West Bengal. Islam here remains relatively heterodox, moderate and secularist in outlook.

In remote Afghanistan, meanwhile, ferocious highland tribesmen and warlords remained untouched by both Mogul civilisation and British influence. Like the Bedouins of the Arabian peninsula, they preserved a highly traditionalist form of Islam, rebelling against foreign rulers and attempts to change their ancient way of life.

PAKISTAN
Population: 161 million (UN 2005)

The state of Pakistan is a purely political invention designed as a homeland for the Muslims of the Indian sub-continent following the dissolution of the British Indian Empire.

In recent times the state's politics have been shaped by struggles between two sources of power – the secularist and pro-Western military and militant Islamists. These two groups are united only by antipathy towards India. The state has also been destabilised by the terrible conflicts in Afghanistan, its northern neighbour (to which it is connected by historic, linguistic and ethnic ties) and the presence of millions of Afghan refugees.

In the 1930s and 1940s, the last decades of British rule in India, many Muslims supported Mahatma Ghandi's All-Indian Congress movement in its campaign for a secular, multi-religious Indian state free from British rule and encompassing the entire territory of the sub-continent.

But as independence grew nearer they began to fear that, as a religious minority within India as a whole, they would become second-class citizens. In 1930 Muhammad 'Ali Jinnah withdrew from the Congress and began agitation for the establishment of a Muslim 'homeland', based on the old Mogul territories in north-west India and federated with distant Muslim majority territories scattered throughout the sub-continent.

In 1947 the British and the Hindus compromised with Jinnah and granted him the Muslim majority territories of Punjab and Sind, which became West Pakistan. East Bengal – separated from West Pakistan by 1,600 kilometres of Hindu majority territory – became East Pakistan. Amid much bloodshed millions of Hindu and Muslim refugees migrated between the two new states of Pakistan and India, the borders of which were often no more than arbitrary lines drawn on the map.

The largest group of Muslim refugees – the *Mujahdirs* (literally 'foreigners') – came from Hyderabad in the centre of India, fleeing mainly to West Pakistan. The Mujahdirs, although a minority in Hyderabad, had formed its ruling class. They were heterodox Isma'ilite Shi'ites and had absorbed many Hindu customs and religious practices including an Islamised version of the main Hindu festival of *Diwali* (known throughout the sub-continent as the festival of the Night of Forgiveness – *Shab-i-Barat*).

The Mujahdirs were not only religiously heterodox but highly educated and cultured by Pakistani standards. They soon came to dominate commerce and public life in West Pakistan and were deeply resented by the more orthodox native Sunni Hanafi Punjabis and Sindis. The Sunni desire to sweep the Mujahdirs out of the government and civil service fuelled a campaign for 'Islamisation' of Pakistan, leading to the declaration of an Islamic republic in 1956.

Mujahdirs, Muslim secularists and modernists were hounded and a stifling Hanafi orthodoxy was imposed. Celebration of non-orthodox Muslim festivals such as *Shab-i-Barat* was banned, narrow 'Islamic' education was imposed in the schools and the capital was moved from cosmopolitan Karachi to the new citadel of orthodoxy – Islamabad. A paranoiac desire to root out Hindu influence and Indian 'traitors' swept Pakistan, setting in motion the chain of events leading to the 1971 Indo-Pakistani war over Kashmir and the secession of East Pakistan as Bangladesh.

The creation of Bangladesh disturbed the internal balance of Pakistani politics. Islamisation was blamed for the secession of East Pakistan and a short-lived, but intense, secularist backlash took place. Zulfikar 'Ali Bhutto's secularist Pakistan People's Party won a large majority in 1972 elections on a platform of halting the Islamisation campaign.

Bhutto's new 1973 constitution gave more power to the secularising PPP-dominated parliament and limited the power of the army. During his Presidency Pakistan's endemic economic crisis worsened causing strikes, food riots and a fresh wave of anti-Mujahdir feeling. The growing unrest was exploited by the 'fundamentalist' Jam'at-i-Islami Party which had strong support in the army. In 1977 a military junta under General Zia ul-Haq seized control, imposed martial law, executed Bhutto and revived the Islamisation campaign.

Panels of Islamic judges were attached to all higher courts, and a federal *shari'ah* court given the power to overturn the decisions of lower courts. The country adopted the *hadd* penal code of Qur'anic punishments – the first modern country, other than Saudi Arabia, to do so.

Islamisation remained largely superficial. A grandiose new mosque was built in Islamabad with Saudi finance and daily attendance at the mosque for the five prayer cycles of *salat* was imposed in the army and civil service, but the communal Friday prayers remained the main form of observance for Pakistani Muslims. As ever, the changes at the top of the country had only a limited impact on the vast mass of the illiterate Pakistani peasantry.

Military rule brought a measure of stability to the country and, with the help of massive Saudi Arabian and American aid (the US provided $3.2 billion over five years), Pakistan adopted a strongly anti-Soviet foreign policy and became the main base for the guerrilla war against the neighbouring Soviet allied state of Afghanistan.

The alliance of Saudi Arabia – an Islamic monarchy with a tiny population but huge wealth – and Pakistan – an Islamic Republic with a huge population but little wealth – became one of the most dynamic in the Islamic world and still provides the backbone of contemporary conservative Sunni fundamentalism. It is underpinned by the presence of millions of Pakistani 'guest-workers' in oil fields of Saudi Arabia and other Gulf States whose remittances provide one of Pakistan's main sources of foreign currency.

In 1986 martial law was lifted and General Zia was killed two years later in a mystery plane crash. Soviet-sponsored terrorism was suspected, but never proved. Also in 1986 Bhutto's daughter Benazir returned from exile to narrowly win a general election for the secularist Pakistan People's Party, but her room for political manoeuvre was slight since a supreme *shari'ah* court retained power to overturn any 'non-Islamic' legislation enacted by her government. The army also wielded a de facto veto over any policy initiatives and within two years Mrs Bhutto had been run out of office and faced corruption charges. In 1991 newly elected President Nawaz Sharif strengthened the Islamic character of the state by incorporating *shari'ah* law into the constitution and making it the basis of the country's legal code.

Since the defeat of the Soviet-backed regime in Afghanistan the endemic civil war in Pakistan's northern neighbour has tended to destabilise Pakistan, giving a far greater role to the military in the country's affairs. By 1990 at least five million destitute Afghan refugees had flooded into Pakistan's northern provinces. Fearing the growing influence of militant clerics under Nawaz Sharif's pro-Islamist regime, the army intervened again in 1996 to remove him from office and bring back Benazir Bhutto. Mrs Bhutto ruled over growing economic chaos until forced into exile after finally being found guilty on corruption charges. (A few months later Nawaz Sharif was also found guilty in a military dominated court on charges of corruption and sponsoring terrorism – he went into exile in Saudi Arabia.)

In 2001 the head of the Pakistani army General Pervez Musharraf appointed himself President and head of state, just in time to give the US full and unconditional support in the bombing of the Taliban regime in Afghanistan. In October of the same year conflict broke out between India and Pakistan over the disputed state of Kashmir. In 2002, in light of the military crisis, Musharraf confirmed his constitutional status as military dictator, taking powers which would enable him to dismiss parliament at any time and appoint ministers as he saw fit.

The main opposition to the military regime comes from militant Islamists in the 'tribal lands' in the north of the country where support for remnants of the Taliban regime in Afghanistan is strong among both Afghan refugees and their ethnic northern Pakistani kinsmen. Al-Qaeda is known to be active in the region and it has been suggested that Osama Bin Laden is hiding in the area.

The regime has mounted military operations against Islamic militants in the territories and in 2006 tolerated a US cruise missile attack on border villages suspected of sheltering al-Qaeda and Taliban leaders.

The 2005 al-Qaeda-inspired suicide bombings in London, carried out by British Muslims of Pakistani extraction, focused attention on Pakistan's network of thousands of Madrassa religious schools which, in fact, were the main source of elementary education in much of the country. The British suicide bombers had spent time at a Pakistani Madrassa and following this revelation Pakistan arrested and detained two hundred officials from Madrassas as part of the investigation into the outrage.

KASHMIR

Population: 15 million (77% Muslim, 20% Hindus, 3% Buddhists, 7% others including Sikhs and Christians, according to the Asian Human Rights Commission, 2003)

The beautiful but sparsely populated mountain state of Jammu and Kashmir on the Indo-Pakistani border has a Muslim majority in the state as a whole, which is concentrated in the entirely Muslim western provinces on the border with Pakistan.

Kashmir was claimed by Pakistan in the partition settlement of 1947, but invaded and annexed by India in 1948. The two countries have clashed over it many times, but an uneasy peace has been established since 1972 when it was placed under military occupation and partitioned between them.

The Hindu majority of east Kashmir is now the target of a concerted missionary campaign led by the wealthy Shi'ite Isma'ilite sect whose members are found in small concentrations throughout India. The Isma'ilites provide clinics and schools which are highly popular with low-caste 'untouchables' who are otherwise denied access to education.

In recent years entire untouchable villages have converted to Islam throughout India but especially in Kashmir. As Muslims they are immediately released from their status as virtual slaves and, in east Kashmir, enjoy effective Pakistani protection as a religious minority.

Islam is growing faster in India than in any other major Muslim minority country and Muslims may well already constitute the majority in Indian East Kashmir as well as in the western part of the region. In 1990 Muslim separatists began a campaign of violence in Kashmir which, the Indian government claimed, was officially sanctioned by the government of Pakistan. Since that time the two countries have been locked into a cold war, occasionally breaking out into actual shooting, made still worse by the development of nuclear weapons by both countries.

A Hindu nationalist backlash in India, expressed as support for the nationalist BJP Party, has further complicated relations between the two countries. In 1992 Hindu extremists demolished a mosque in Ayodhya, claiming it as the site of an ancient Hindu temple. The action triggered widespread sectarian violence throughout India. The worst incident in a decade of inter-communal violence came in 2002 after Muslims set fire to a train carrying Hindus travelling back from pilgrimage to the new Hindu temple built on the ruins of the mosque at Ayodhya.

The turn of the century saw a crisis in Indian–Pakistani relations which seemed likely to develop into all-out war. In 2002 India threatened to invade Pakistan if terrorist attacks in and from Kashmir did not stop. Pakistan said that it would respond with 'full force' if attacked. To underline the threat, Pakistan test-fired missiles capable of delivering nuclear warheads.

In 2003 relations between India and Pakistan warmed slightly after the election of a Muslim, Dr Abdul Kalam, as Indian President. While nuclear war seemed to have been averted, a solution to the Kashmir problem seemed as far away as ever.

AFGHANISTAN
Population: 26 million (UN 2005)

The inhospitable mountains of the Hindu Kush in Afghanistan, which became a province of the Arab Islamic Empire in the first century after Muhammad, have served as Islam's impregnable Asian fortress ever since. The highly traditionalist Afghan warlords have preserved an ancient and conservative form of Islam strikingly resembling that of the equally ungovernable Bedouin Arabs.

Afghanistan, unlike central Asia to the north and the Muslim lands of India to the south east, never came under the rule of either Imperial Russia or Britain (though in the early part of the twentieth century it did briefly become a protectorate of the British Raj as a guarantee against Russian domination).

As in Iran, the only other Muslim country to remain independent since the Middle Ages, Afghani Islam has become fused with militant nationalism and *jihad*. And at the same time Afghan independence has become a potent symbol of how 'fundamentalism' can survive European domination.

For centuries dynasties of Turkic, Iranian, Mongol and indigenous Pashtan Afghani rulers have attempted to limit the power of the chieftains and impose centralised rule on the country, but have failed without exception. In the twentieth century a limited amount of economic development based on tourism and mining opened the country to foreign influences and the small educated middle class began to blame the power of the chiefs for the backwardness and dire poverty of the country.

In the early 1960s a student-based radical movement began agitating for land reform and other modernising policies. The movement culminated in the overthrow of the king who had hitherto maintained his power by manipulating a fragile alliance of tribal chiefs and regional warlords.

The new secular republic which was established was popular with the urban population of Kabul and with the poorer peasants, who were promised land of their own and freedom from virtual slave status in the service of the chiefs, but the pace of change was slow and fiercely opposed by traditionalist Muslim groups led by the Muslim Brotherhood.

In 1977 a further coup brought a Marxist government to power, proposing the immediate collectivisation of agriculture and other measures such as education for women, bitterly opposed by the chiefs. Uniting under the title *Mujahideen* (literally 'fighters' or 'Crusaders') the chiefs declared *jihad* on the government.

The Marxist government came under Soviet influence and, after early Mujahideen successes, a pro-Soviet faction widely seen as Soviet 'puppets' came to power and requested Soviet military assistance. Western and Soviet involvement led to a bitter war which ruined the country's economy and caused five million refugees to flee to neighbouring Pakistan.

Predictions that the Mujahideen would quickly overthrow the Afghan government following the withdrawal of Soviet troops in 1988 were premature. The various rebel groups were divided along tribal grounds, or represented the local or regional following of some warlord or other, often more interested in extending control over the production and exportation of heroin – the only business which boomed in Afghanistan in the era of civil war.

The emergence of the Pol Pot-like ethnically Pashtan Taliban movement brought a measure of stability to the country after they seized power in 1996. Rival warlords, led by a Tajik faction, formed the 'northern alliance' which fought the Taliban (whose power base was in Kabul, southern Afghanistan and Pakistan) for control of territory and the heroin trade.

The Taliban imposed an extreme version of *shari'ah* law in the lawless country. Their complete intolerance of the non-Muslim world was symbolised by the demolition of the giant and ancient Buddhas carved out of the cliffs at Bamiyan. The prevailing chaos and the huge numbers of refugees also made the country the ideal base for Osama Bin Laden's al-Qaeda network. The former Saudi businessman gathered his exiled Saudi followers, together with other militants expelled from Yemen, the Sudan, Egypt, the Gulf States, Kashmir and other trouble spots. This new generation of fighters was hostile above all to conservative Muslim rulers such as the Saudi royal family and – for other reasons – the governments of Iran and Iraq. In 1998 the US fired cruise missiles at refugee camps in southern Afghanistan suspected of being training camps for al-Qaeda, after Bin Laden was accused of bombing US embassies in Africa.

In 2001 the US imposed sanctions on Afghanistan after the Taliban's refusal to hand over their ally Osama Bin Laden when he was accused of organising the terror attacks on the World Trade Center on 11 September 2001. The US air force attacked Afghanistan when the Taliban refused to co-operate. The entire country was overrun in a matter of weeks and an interim government was placed in power. Clashes between the new government and its US and British military backers continued thereafter at a lower level of intensity. Al-Qaeda lost some of its bases, but Bin Laden was not found. It seemed likely that he had been killed. But it was equally as likely that he or his successor would continue to hide amid the mass of refugees in southern Afghanistan and northern Pakistan, doubtless planning further attacks and political campaigns

against the West and 'collaborationist' Muslim states throughout the world.

In 2005 Hamid Karzai was elected president but it was
immediately clear that his authority could not be upheld in
much of the country which quickly reverted to a patchwork of
rival tribal areas ruled by local leaders and warlords. Attempts
to eradicate the heroin trade which had financed the country's
rival bands of 'narco-terrorists' came to nothing and record
opium poppy harvests were recorded.

By 2006 Afghanistan required vast subventions of aid money
as well as a significant and growing military presence, including a large contingent of British forces.

BANGLADESH
Population: 153 million (UN 2005)

Bangladesh comprises the territory of the eastern part of the
old Mogul outpost of Bengal, a densely populated peasant
province based on the fertile Ganges delta. Islam in Bengal is
a comparatively recent addition to the religious landscape
which, for one thousand years, was dominated by Hinduism
and Buddhism.

The ancestors of today's Bangladeshi Muslims were mostly
low-caste Hindus who escaped from their status by converting
to Islam during the Mogul heyday three hundred years ago. As
a far-flung outpost of Islam they escaped much of the
sectarianism of the late Mogul years and today have strong
linguistic and cultural ties to the Hindus of Indian West Bengal.

Bangladeshi Islam, in stark contrast to the version dominant
in Pakistan, is mainly secular in outlook and highly tolerant of
other religions including the large Hindu minority (12 per cent)
within the country.

The incorporation of the Muslims of Bengal into the state of
Pakistan in 1947 must now be judged as one of the greatest
political and economic disasters of the twentieth century. The
new province of East Pakistan was denied access to its
traditional markets in Calcutta, 80 kilometres across the new
border, and was instead put under the control of Karachi,
2,400 kilometres away in West Pakistan.

As well as economic unviability the partition brought chronic political instability as West Pakistan attempted to force 'Islamisation' on the reluctant Bengalis. In 1971 East Pakistan declared itself neutral in the Indo-Pakistani war over distant Kashmir and, after a nine-month civil war, became the independent state of Bangladesh.

In December 1972 a secular constitution was brought in which, in contrast to West Pakistan's status as an Islamic Republic, proclaimed Bangladesh a secular, socialist and non-aligned People's Republic, with no legal status for the *shari'ah*.

Hopes of a new beginning were quickly dashed. The economic plight of the country worsened as Bangladesh moved towards the Soviet Union and India in Asian affairs and thus, unlike Pakistan, cut itself off from US and Saudi Arabian aid. And from the late 1970s onwards the low-lying delta – home to the vast majority of the poverty-stricken population – began to be hit by a series of increasingly disastrous floods.

Political instability continued as factions accused each other variously of pro-Indian, pro-Pakistani, pro-Chinese or pro-Western treachery. Between 1973 and 1977 three civilian Presidents were assassinated in a series of coups. Reaction against the left-wing secular political parties brought the Bangladesh Nationalist Party to power under the leadership of Hossain Muhammad Ershad on a platform of mild Islamisation which was designed to rebuild bridges to Pakistan and Saudi Arabia. Bangladesh's 1972 constitution had enshrined secularism. In 1977 the constitution was amended to include a clause saying the basis of the state was 'absolute trust and faith in Almighty Allah'.

In 1983 Ershad seized total power in a military coup, imposed martial law, banned political opposition and reorganised the judiciary and local government. Islam was enshrined as the state religion and a much more far-reaching Islamisation campaign was begun. In 1986 martial law was lifted and new elections were held in 1988, which Ershad's Nationalist Party won on a very low turn-out amid accusations of ballot-rigging. In 1990 Ershad was forced out of office after mass demonstrations. In the following year he was jailed on charges of corruption. A type of ramshackle democracy was re-established in the 1990s with power alternating between the secularist Awami League and Ershad's Islamising Nationalists.

Since the 1980s, political events in Bangladesh have been overshadowed by continuing floods, crop failures and famine, provoking fears that Bangladesh may never become economically or even ecologically viable. There are signs that the course of the Ganges has been irreparably altered by erosion and irrigation schemes in the Indian Himalayas and, combined with the phenomenon of rising sea-levels, this may mean that within the near future the fertile Ganges delta may disappear under water. If the worst forecasts are correct then almost the entire population of Bangladesh – perhaps 150 million people – may eventually be forced to evacuate.

As the country's ecological problems began to mount a new and worrying trend towards political violence emerged in the form of random murders of moderate, secular Awami league politicians by shadowy groups of Islamic militants.

21. INDONESIA AND THE EAST INDIES

INDONESIA, MALAYSIA, BRUNEI, PHILIPPINES/MINDANAO
Total population: 270 million

The East Indian archipelago is made up of 13,000 islands stretching nearly 5,000 kilometres from Sumatra and the Indian Ocean in the west to New Guinea and the Pacific in the east. The hundreds of millions of inhabitants speak over three hundred different languages and belong to many different tribal groups.

Islam was first established as a major force in the early sixteenth century when Hindu-influenced Muslim merchants and missionaries from Mogul India clashed with the Chinese for control of the declining indigenous Hindu and pagan tribal civilisations.

Fearful of growing Chinese power, the Hindu princes turned to the Hindu-influenced Mogul Empire for help. In the century that followed dozens of Hindu princes converted to heterodox Mogul forms of Islam, sometimes under the influence of Sufi missionaries who established themselves as physicians and advisers in Hindu courts.

By the middle of the seventeenth century most of the islands were under the rule of indigenous Muslim Sultans and the southward spread of the Chinese religions of Buddhism and

Confucianism was halted and confined to the mainland of south-east Asia.

The Sultans adopted the Shafi school of Sunni Islam, a variant of the *shari'ah* which has always been associated with Muslim traders and explorers, because it is particularly forgiving of non-performance of the pilgrimage (*hajj*) to Mecca.

Hajj is a subject of some importance for distant Muslim communities such as these. Performance of the pilgrimage is one of the Five Pillars but is obligatory only for those who can 'find their way' (3:97). Despite this, many early East Indian Muslims made the trip on foot – a journey of at least 8,000 kilometres each way through jungles and across mountain ranges and deserts.

Over the past two hundred or so years, hundreds of poorer East Indian Muslims have settled in Mecca and Medina rather than attempt the return journey. Together with other long-distance *hajji*, such as the Chinese and West Africans, the East Indians now form a distinct ethnic minority in the Holy Cities. Many have sold themselves into slavery (which is still officially sanctioned in Saudi Arabia) and sent a large remittance home to meet the Qur'anic obligation to care for families placed on *hajji*.

Apart from Shafi Islam's special approach to the problem of long-distance *hajj* it is otherwise slightly more traditionalist than the Hanafi'ism practised in Pakistan and Bangladesh. The early Muslim Sultans nevertheless pursued a policy of religious toleration towards the indigenous Hindu population. Conversion of the mass of the population from Hinduism to Islam was a slow process and the full Islamisation of the archipelago has not been completed even today.

The division of the Sultanates between the British and Dutch Empires, the two largest powers in the region, resulted in the eventual creation of the states of Malaysia (a federation of formerly British-controlled Sultanates) and Indonesia (the former Dutch Sultanates) after the Second World War.

The Sultanate of Brunei, although controlled by the British, was left out of Malaya and is now a tiny – but extremely rich – independent Muslim state.

INDONESIA
Population: 225 million (UN 2005)

Islam in Indonesia is moderate and influenced by Hinduism, Buddhism and heterodox Sufi'ism. Since the formation of the country in 1945 most Indonesian Muslims have been happy to live under a secular, nationalist government and to tolerate large Hindu and other religious minorities. Although about 80 per cent of Indonesians are Muslims, Islam is only one of five state-recognised religions alongside Christianity, Confucianism, Buddhism and Hinduism.

After promoting Islam as an anti-Communist force in the 1960s and 1970s, the thirty-year authoritarian and military-backed rule of pro-Western Nationalist President Suharto saw the role of religion in the country eclipsed by attempts at Western-style economic development. For a while Indonesia did experience rapid economic growth, based on export of oil, gas and tropical hardwoods; and by assembling Japanese consumer electronics goods. But status as an Asian 'Tiger Economy' was undermined by the Asian financial crisis in the late 1990s and continuing weaknesses in the Japanese economy.

Under Suharto, who came to power in a 1965 military coup, Indonesian politics was dominated by official attempts to forge 'New Indonesian Man' from the bewildering ethnic patchwork of islands. A highly secularised version of Islam was included in the official make-up of 'New Indonesian Man' but nationalism was more important – the official line was that an Indonesian's first allegiance must not be to religion but to 'Indonesia-ism'.

The main effects of the official policy were felt in remote eastern islands such as Timor and Irian Jaya (the Indonesian half of New Guinea) where Stone Age tribes have been virtually wiped out to make room for 'New Man' settlements of 'New Order' Muslims from densely populated areas such as Java. Large areas of tropical rain forest in these areas are now under threat from Javanese developers using Japanese and American multinational capital. In 1976 Indonesia invaded, occupied and attempted to settle and 'ethnically cleanse' East Timor, after Portugal granted the colony independency. After decades of conflict East Timor was restored to independence in 2002.

From the time of Suharto onwards opposition in Indonesia – both religious and secular – was severely repressed by the army-linked New Order Party (The Golkar) and is confined to state-controlled official opposition parties. One of these, the Development Unity Party, is in favour of introduction of *shari'ah* law and other conservative pro-Islamic reforms. But the main function of the DUP is to institutionalise and confine Islam as a political force and the party's demands have generally been ignored by the secularist government.

However, further secularisation campaigns in 1984 and 1985 provoked rioting by Muslim youths in urban areas, campaigning against a ban on 'Islamic ideology' in public life and the allegedly privileged status of Christian and Chinese Confucians in the civil service and army.

Unrest continued for more than a decade until riots in the wake of the Asian economic crisis caused Suharto to fall from office in 1997. Elections resulted in a quick succession of democratically elected – but highly corrupt – administrations and there were signs that, as in so much of the former 'Third World', the masses of people left out by economic development were starting to turn their back on secularism and looking towards Islam.

In October 2002, in the wake of the US and British attacks on Afghanistan, Indonesian supporters of Osama Bin Laden blew up a nightclub in Bali killing 180 Western tourists. At the same time an increasingly violent struggle between the central government and Islamist separatists in the oil-rich Indonesian province of Aceh in northern Sumatra was beginning to develop.

In 2005 Aceh separatists came to a disarmament agreement with the central government in the wake of the huge destruction inflicted on the area by the 2004 Tsunami.

MALAYSIA
Population: 25.3 million (UN 2005)

Islam in Malaysia is very similar to that found in Indonesia but is marginally more sectarian, feeling more threatened by the larger and more confident Buddhist and Chinese religious minorities who constitute about a quarter of the population.

During the Second World War the Chinese Malaysians fought a guerrilla war against the Japanese, whilst the Muslim majority either acquiesced or actively collaborated. After the war the guerrillas, under the influence of the new Communist People's Republic of China, continued their war against the British.

By the early 1960s the British had put down the pro-Communist rebellion with great barbarity and in 1963, underwritten by a large continuing British military presence in the country, Malaysia was granted independence as a secular Muslim majority federation.

In 1966 the Malaysian government recognised Islam as the official religion of state but did not apply the *shari'ah* for fear of upsetting the fragile balance of ethnic and religious groups in the community.

BRUNEI
Population: 0.4 million (UN 2005)

The independent Sultanate of Brunei, a tiny enclave on the Malaysian north coast of Borneo island, is all that remains of the powerful Muslim Sultanate of Borneo which, at the height of its power in the fifteenth century, dominated the East Indian islands as far as the Philippines and the South China Sea. The ancestors of the large Muslim minority now found in the Philippines were merchants and settlers from Muslim Borneo.

In 1888, reduced to an 80-kilometre strip of coastline, the Sultanate became the British protectorate of Brunei within its present borders. The Sultanate would probably have been included in the Federation of Malaysia if it had not been for the discovery of vast quantities of oil. The Sultan was determined to keep this new source of wealth for himself and his subjects.

Sultan Hassanal Bolkiah ruled the 250,000 population – mostly Malay Muslims with a large Chinese minority – as an autocrat after independence from Britain in 1985. The *shari'ah* is strictly enforced. Political opposition was legalised in 2004.

The Sultan's rule is underpinned by massive oil wealth, passed on to the small population through free education, medical care, state loans and padded civil service salaries (the annual income per person was calculated by the World Bank in 1997 as $26,000 per capita, the highest in Asia outside the Gulf). The Sultan also rents a force of eight hundred British Ghurkha troops, which are used to underpin his autocratic rule over the Sultanate.

SOUTH WEST PHILIPPINES (MINDANOA MOROS)
Muslim population approx. 20 million (Philippines government)

The term *Moros* (Filipino Muslims) was coined by Spanish conquistadors in the sixteenth century and defines thirteen ethno-linguistic groups in the south-western Philippines. The Muslim areas remained independent during the period of Spanish rule in the Philippines, regulated by *shari'ah* law and subject to the Sultan of Sulu. This autonomy was abolished after the conquest of the Philippines by the US in 1899. The US encouraged Christian settlement in Muslim areas and abolished *shari'ah* courts (though minor modifications to US law – for example in the matter of polygamy or divorce – were allowed if both parties appearing in the US court were Muslim).

After independence a Muslim separatist movement gained support which led to intercommunal violence and the declaration of martial law in 1972, and to an intermittent guerrilla war fought by the Moro National Liberation Front for the next thirty years. The fall of Ferdinand Marcos's US-backed regime in 1986 led to the creation of an autonomous Muslim region in Mindanao and a respite in the fighting. In 2002 the US and the Philippine armed forces organised joint training and exercises in counter-insurgency after it was claimed by US intelligence that the most militant Moros guerrilla fighters, gathered in the Abu Sayyaf group, were linked to Osama Bin Laden.

A 2003 ceasefire between Abu Sayyaf and the government collapsed in 2005 and hundreds were killed in armed clashes throughout the south, but centred on the island of Jolo. In 2006 President Arroyo declared a week-long state of emergency and took extraordinary powers to impose order in the south, claiming that rebels were attempting a military coup.

22. SAHARAN AND SUB-SAHARAN AFRICA

SUDAN, CHAD, NIGER AND NORTHERN NIGERIA, MALI AND
BURKINO FASO, MAURITANIA, SENEGAL, THE GAMBIA,
GUINEA AND GUINEA-BISSAU
Total population: 240 million (UN 2005)

Islam in, and on the southern fringes of, the Sahara is the result
of contact between the Berber-Arab Muslim civilisation of the
Maghreb and the indigenous pagan religions of great pre-
Islamic Negro Empires such as Malinke (Mali), Benin and
Ghana. For eight hundred years Muslims and pagans alternate-
ly co-operated and fought and the result is two very different
trends within Islam as practised in the region.

In the south the Negro population has developed an
idiosyncratic form of 'African Islam' which becomes steadily
more heterodox as the semi-desert and grassland gives way to
the Negro heartlands. Magic, idol worship and ancient pre-
Islamic customs such as 'female circumcision' are all practised
in the name of Islam.

The most widespread form of magic is fortune-telling based
on the *mandalah* – a five-pointed star with an ink blot at the
centre, usually drawn on the palm of a virgin boy. A Qur'anic
verse is inscribed at each point of the star and the verse: 'Yea!
we have removed your veil and today your sight is penetrating'

(50:22) is chanted as an incantation. The boy is then believed to be capable of having visions by concentrating on the ink blot.

The *mandalah*-palm design is also worn as a piece of metallic jewellery known as the 'Hand of Fatima' – a reference to the daughter of the Prophet who is repeatedly described in Muhammedan *hadith* as knowing the 'right way'. These objects are thought to have originated as crude 'loadstone' compasses used for divining the direction of Mecca and are now used for casting spells and divining water.

Many African Muslims fear the continuing power of the surrounding tribal religions and protect themselves from spells with *gri-gri* – leather amulets worn around the neck. These amulets contain inscriptions from the Qur'anic 'verses of refuge' which describe how Muhammad was protected from Arabian black magic. A typical *gri-gri* verse is: 'And we have guarded [the Prophet] from every outcast devil' (15:17).

The continuing influence of pre-Islamic traditions is one reason for African Islam's extreme heterodoxy. The other is the all-pervasive influence of heterodox Sufi orders often sharing the indigenous population's enthusiasm for magic and mysticism.

Islam was first carried across the Sahara in the mid-eleventh century by Berber-Arab traders who dominated the gold trade between Negro Africa and the rest of the world. These merchants established ghettos within the cities of the great pre-Islamic Negro Empire such as Ghana and Malinke (Mali) but made no attempt to convert the local population.

By the late thirteenth century these Muslim trading communities were wealthy enough to support Sufi *madrasahs* (college-hospitals) which were to be the key to converting the region to Islam. Under the rule of the great Malian King Sundiata in the thirteenth century AD the Sufis (known as *karamoro* in the Malian language) replaced the traditional witch doctors and magicians as advisers to the Malian court. Some of Sundiata's many sons converted to Islam and ruled in the name of the religion following his death. But there was no attempt to convert the Malian tribesmen, who clung to their pagan religions, treating Islam as an auxiliary religion of state.

The Malian Empire reached the peak of its power in the fourteenth century under Emperor Mansa Musas, who established Sufi institutions in Timbuktu run by Negroes independently of the Arab and Moorish Sufi orders. In the middle of the fifteenth century Muslim Mali was conquered by surrounding Songhay pagan tribes. Sufi'ism preserved a core of believers who eventually converted the Songhays, but Islam in the region diverged from the strict orthodoxy of the Berber-Arab Maghreb for two hundred years, taking on its distinctively Sufi-magical form.

Following the Islamic millennium in AD 1622 (AH 1000) a wave of religious fervour swept all branches of Islam and was expressed in the Maghreb as the 'Jihad Movement'. Waves of Berber-Arab invaders swept across the Sahara determined to convert the entire population by force. A hundred years of Berber-Arab war on the pagan Negro tribes to the south followed. Defeated tribes who would not submit to the Berber version of orthodox Islam were taken as slaves and sold to the European powers.

Sufi-influenced 'African Islam' was only one of many religions in the region before the Jihad Movement, but by the end of the seventeenth century it became dominant. Almost all the population of the present day states of Mali, Mauritania, Niger and Chad converted to Islam during the early stage of the Movement.

However, the spread of the religion was bitterly resisted further south in the present day countries of the African coast such as Nigeria, Togo and Ghana. For two centuries the Negroes of the far south held out against repeated Berber invasions from the north until the process of forced conversion (or slavery for those who would not) was arrested by the arrival of the European colonialists. Islam never managed to convert the majority of the population in any significant area south of the 10N line of latitude.

The French colonised sub-Saharan Africa, which by that time overwhelmingly subscribed to the Maliki Sunni'ism of the Maghreb whilst the British took most of the west coast, which remained pagan with Muslim minorities in the north. (Later, owing to British missionary activity, many of these countries also became largely Christianised.)

During the half century of French rule the sub-Saharan Muslim countries generally stagnated and the religion began to diverge into the southern Negro heterodoxy and northern Berber-Arab orthodoxy found before the Jihad Movement. The influence of Sufi'ism in the south, however, remained all-important and it is rare these days to find a Negro Muslim who is not affiliated to one or other of the Sufi orders.

Since independence all the sub-Saharan countries have experienced tension between the Berber-Arab north and Negro Muslim or pagan south. As a result the various regimes have, unlike the Maghrebian countries to the north, followed secularist policies designed to prevent power struggles between different Islamic factions.

SUDAN
Population: 35 million (UN 2005)

Sudan is a huge country – the biggest in Africa – stretching across the Sahara desert and bridging the course of the Nile from Egypt in the north to the grasslands and jungles of central Africa in the south. The country thus straddles the Muslim world of Berber and Arab Egypt and the Maghreb in the north and the Christian and pagan world of black Africa in the south.

Official Islam in Sudan is Sunni Maliki, shaped by contact with the Hanafi'ism of Cairo and Egypt which borders the country to the north. The country's latest Constitution came into effect in 1998, and proclaims Islam as 'the religion of the majority of the population'.

There have been backlashes against Hanafi influence throughout the history of Sudan. The most important Maliki rebellion took place in the last two decades of the nineteenth century AD in the form of the Mahdist revolt – the high point of the late Maliki Jihad Movements.

In 1881, with Egypt under the effective control of the British, the Sudanese Muslims declared their leader *al-Mahdi* – the long awaited 'chosen one' who will cleanse and reunite Islam – and proclaimed a Mahdist state independent from Egypt and their British overlords.

The Mahdists practised a fundamentalist version of Islam purged both of Hanafi modernism and pagan-influenced Negro 'African Islam'. Britain declared war on them and after bitter fighting, including the celebrated loss of a British force under General Gordon, recaptured Khartoum in 1898.

The Mahdists were crushed and Hanafi-based secular Anglo-Muhammedan law was re-established, administered from Cairo. But, as in Libya, the spirit of Mahdi'ism lives on in the form of bouts of religious extremism and sectarianism.

These days Sudanese Muslim sectarianism is mainly directed against the sizeable Christian and pagan minority left in the south by arbitrary borders drawn up by the British when the country became a part of their African Empire.

During the Mahdist revolt the French claimed the territory of what is now southern Sudan for their African empire, which would have given them control of an uninterrupted chain of possessions stretching across the entire continent from west to east and cutting off British Egypt from the British colonies of East Africa. The British fought the claim, defeated the French in minor skirmishes, and annexed the southern and Negro part of the country. The annexation created a nonsensical hybrid nation which was immediately plunged into a smouldering civil war as soon as modern Sudan became independent in 1956.

There was a brief respite in 1969 when the army under the skilful leadership of General Ja'far Mohammed Numiery seized power in Khartoum. Numiery tried to appease the southerners by granting them religious freedom and political self-rule, but when he attempted to retain 'Islamic' support by introducing and strictly enforcing *shari'ah* law in the north, sometimes with great brutality, he provoked a renewed flare-up of the civil war.

The rebels quickly gained ground and the Sudan People's Liberation Army, led by John Garang, became the dominant and most effective southern rebel force after a series of military successes. In the face of the worsening military situation Numiery was deposed in 1985 by a bloodless coup and power passed to the Transitional Military Council under the leadership of General Siwar al-Dahab, who offered talks with the

SPLA. The rebels refused to co-operate until *shari'ah* law was revoked in the south.

Al-Dahab abolished much of the *hadd* penal code, but was unable to lift *shari'ah* rule in its entirety for fear of provoking a fundamentalist revolt and counter-coup. The result was deadlock, with the framework of moderated *shari'ah* law in force throughout the whole country and continued rebel activity in the south.

In 1986 the Sudanese government sponsored multi-party elections after abolishing the one-party state machinery of Numiery's Sudanese Socialist Union. But there was no voting in most of the southern provinces because of the civil war. The election was won by a coalition of two moderate parties, the secular conservative Democratic Unionists and the moderately Islamising Muslim People's Party (The Umma Party). The National Islamic Front, a creation of the Sudanese Muslim Brotherhood, formed the opposition.

The democratically elected government under the Prime Ministership of Sadiq *al-Mahdi* faced formidable economic problems caused by the decline in world commodity prices, a reduction in Saudi Arabian aid, and the burden of hundreds of thousands of refugees from its own civil war, aggravated by refugees from the wars and famines in neighbouring Uganda, Ethiopia and Chad. On top of this the country was hit by a series of alternating floods and droughts, which left at least half the population homeless and a quarter at starvation level.

In 1989 a military coup brought a new regime to power which has sought to maintain the status quo over implementation of the *shari'ah* whilst abolishing democracy and attempting to restore order.

In 1991 relations between Sudan and the West began to decline sharply after Sudan diplomatically supported Saddam Hussein and Iraq during the First Gulf War. The country was then accused of renewed human rights violations against the Christians of the south, of backing Islamic extremists in Egypt and of attempting to assassinate Egypt's pro-Western leader President Mubarak. In 1998 the US air force bombed the Sudanese capital Khartoum after claiming that the Sudanese regime was manufacturing chemical weapons for possible use by al-Qaeda or other Islamic terrorists.

After 1999 the war on the non-Muslim south was intensified in an attempt to 'ethnically cleanse' areas where new discoveries of oil had been made. More light was thrown on the nature of the conflict in Sudan when it was reported by Human Rights officials that 14,500 slaves from the non-Muslim south had escaped from oil producing areas.

Violence increasingly centred on the western region of Darfur where irregular Arab 'Janajaweed' militias were reportedly carrying out systematic mass killings on non-Muslim ethnically African local people. The Sudanese government at first claimed that the Janajaweed fighters were beyond their control, but this was widely doubted. In 2004 US Secretary of State Colin Powell described events in Darfur as 'genocide'.

The following year, under pressure from the African Union and the international community, the Sudanese government signed a peace treaty with southern Christian separatists. A ceasefire was enforced and the government accepted targets for disarming the Janajaweed fighters. The ceasefire was to be policed by soldiers from the African Union.

The south was given a measure of independence and the former southern rebel leader John Garang joined the Sudanese government as Vice President. The policy of 'forced Islamisation' of the south was abandoned, and a multibillion-dollar aid programme to assist national recovery was also agreed.

The reaction of the Islamists was to attempt a military coup led by Hassan al-Turabi, an ally of Osama Bin Laden dating back to the time when the al-Qaeda leader had based himself in the Sudanese desert. Soon afterwards President Bush requested permission to deploy US and UN troops to enforce the Darfur ceasefire, since the African force was not up to the job. The Sudanese government rejected the suggestion, saying it would amount to foreign occupation.

CHAD
Population: 9.1 million (UN 2005)

Like Sudan, Chad, the adjoining slice of desert just to the west, is divided between a Muslim majority region in the north and a significant pagan and Christian minority in the south. The northern Muslim majority has been unable to assert its control over the south at any time.

At independence in 1960 the northern Muslim provinces remained under French military occupation and politics was dominated by the non-Muslim south where a process of de-Islamisation and reversion to paganism was already under way.

The reunification of north and south in 1965 immediately resulted in a debilitating civil war which continues today. The degree of violence, fuelled by *jihad*-type feelings in the north, and hateful memories of Muslim slave trading and persecution in the south, has few parallels anywhere in the world and sickening massacres have taken place on both sides.

At first the civil war ran along the simple north–south religious fault on the 16N line of latitude roughly marking the southern extent of Muslim settlement in Africa. The southern borders of the Muslim countries of Senegal, Mali and Niger run roughly along this line, but Chad extends another 950 kilometres south, deep into the non-Muslim belt. N'Djamena, 320 kilometres south of 16N, is the furthest south of any major Muslim settlement in central West Africa.

Since the 1960s the region south of N'Djamena has been in the hands of an anarchic collection of armed tribal groups controlling dozens of small fiefdoms at war with each other as well as N'Djamena itself. These groups, known collectively as the *Codos*, are held together only by their hatred of Islam.

Since 1969, when Colonel al-Qaddafi seized power in Libya, as Chad's northern neighbour he has provided military support for President Goukouni Oueddi. As a result Oueddi made substantial military progress in the south in the late 1970s. By 1981 the Libyans were effectively occupying Chad and conducting the war in the south independently of the small Chadian army. But in 1982 Col Hissene Habre, a Muslim, led a French-backed military coup and, with at least two thousand French paratroopers, secured control of N'Djamena from Oueddi and the Libyans, who retreated north of the 16N line. The Libyans and their Chadian allies fought a rearguard war, but by 1987 they had been forced out of all but a tiny strip of land along the northern border.

In 1990 another military coup saw Habre, the French client-ruler, replaced by the Libyan and Sudanese-backed Patriotic Salvation Movement. Three years later a constitutional conference confirmed the Salvation Movement's leader Idriss Derby as President. In 1997 Derby claimed to have won a landslide victory in Chad's first ever free multi-party elections.

The non-Muslim south had been quelled, but sporadic outbreaks of civil war continued. A new armed insurgency began in the north, but Libya refused to support rebels and a peace was brokered in 2002. Almost immediately another armed group, this time believed to be linked to fundamentalist Sudan, rose against government authority in the east.

In the early years of the new century Chad faced the challenge of absorbing thousands of non-Muslim refugee fleeing Janajaweed terror in the Darfur region of neighbouring Sudan.

President Deby remained firmly in the Western camp, allowing the US to establish military bases in the country extending the superpower's military influence in Muslim Africa and giving it the capacity to strike at periodically more anti-Western regimes in the region, including Sudan. In 2006 Chadian forces were reported as taking part in joint action with the US army against the Salafist Group for Preaching and Combat, an Algerian Islamic militant group associated with al-Qaeda and which operated widely across the Sahara.

NIGER
Population: 13 million (UN 2005)

The two African nations of Niger and Nigeria span the same latitudes from mid-Saharan 2°N in the north to equatorial 5° in the south. Like Sudan, this vast tract of land is inhabited by a Muslim Berber population in the desert north, mixed Muslim and non-Muslim black African populations in the middle and mainly pagan and Christian black African communities in the fertile and more densely populated south, right down to the metropolis of Lagos on the West African coast.

But unlike Sudan, the Muslim northern Niger formed part of the French African Empire while Christian southern Niger was conquered by the British. Therefore at independence the region was broken into two separate countries – French-speaking Niger in the north, and the much more populous English-speaking state of Nigeria in the south.

One fortunate result of the colonial borders was that the sort of civil war between north and south which has done so much terrible damage to Sudan has been avoided. Niger is homogeneously Muslim.

But being cut off from the more prosperous and fertile territory held by its more populous neighbour means that Niger is one of the poorest countries in the world, with most of the population scraping a living farming the poor semi-desert scrub lands of the vast territory.

Almost all the settled population is in the western part of the country on the thin strip of land irrigated by the Niger river around the capital city Niamey. The east and north of the country is desert which is slowly spreading. The population faced famine from 1984 to 1986 because of drought.

Islamic organisations appear to play only a very limited role in the official life of the country and religious observance in the country's only towns has declined markedly from the high point of the later *Jihad* Movements which swept Niger and the surrounding countries from the seventeenth to the nineteenth centuries. In contrast, Niger's large nomadic desert-dwelling Tuareg and Bedouin population are devoted followers of Ibadite and Sufi traditions.

In 1990 the Tuaregs revolted, sparking a series of coups and counter-coups as a succession of military governments in Niamey struggled to come to terms with demands for further Islamisation of the country and autonomy for the Tuareg desert regions of the north, bordering on Algeria, Chad and Libya. At stake is control of territory believed to be rich in both oil and uranium.

It was wrongly – or inconclusively – claimed during the Second Gulf War that Iraq had attempted to import uranium from Niger in order to make a nuclear bomb. Nevertheless, much of Niger's strategic significance lies in the fact that it is the Muslim and Arab world's only potential secure source of uranium for weapons purposes.

NIGERIA

Population: 130 million (of which approximately 50% are Muslim, 40% Christian and 10% Pagan) (UN and Nigerian Federal Government, 2005)

Nigeria is the most populous nation in Africa, the home to around sixty million mostly black African Muslims living in six arid northern provinces, grouped around the regional capital of Kano, now enjoying considerable autonomy.

The British annexed the territory around Lagos, the capital of the non-Muslim south in 1861 and then extended their power by making alliances with local Yoruba chieftains. They were drawn towards conquest of the Muslim north of the country by competition with the French whose African Empire at the time spread from Algeria and the north coast of the continent across the Sahara desert and was encroaching on British interests on the more valuable West African coast.

The British established control of the north by encouraging the Muslim Sultans of northern Nigeria to wage *jihad* against the pagan African rulers of the ancient Hausa Kingdom of Gobir. A new Muslim Empire was created at Sokoto in north-western Nigeria and *shari'ah* law was established across the whole of northern Nigeria. French influence was resisted and the Sokoto empire became dependent on British power, eventually being reduced to the status of a protectorate or puppet regime. Full incorporation into the British Empire as a colony followed.

Nigeria became independent as a secular federation in 1960. There was immediate tension between the three main quasi-national groups – the Muslims of the North and the African Yorubas and Ibos of the south – forced together into an essentially artificial state originally as an expedient of British Imperial policy. Civil war broke out between the Ibos and Yorubas in 1967. The following decades saw chronic political instability marked by military rule and corruption on a massive scale emanating from Nigeria's position as one of the world's largest oil producers.

In 2000 *shari'ah* law was adopted by six northern Muslim-majority provinces in defiance of Nigeria's original constitution.

Immediate clashes between Christian minorities who refused to be bound by Islamic law quickly developed into large-scale rioting and inter-communal violence. It quickly emerged that almost every major decision made by a *shari'ah* court would be controversial and carry the threat of violence, possibly escalating towards civil war. In 2002 the imposition by a *shari'ah* court of the penalty of death by stoning on a woman accused of adultery caused riots in the south. And when the federal court of appeal reversed the decision there were riots amongst Muslims in the north.

In the same year international attention was drawn to the death of two hundred people in rioting which followed the decision to hold the annual Miss World beauty contest in Kaduna, a city in the Muslim north. The event was rescheduled to take place in London.

More-deeply-rooted sectarian conflict continues to flare from time to time in Nigeria. In 2004 as many as three hundred Muslims were massacred by Christian paramilitaries in city of Yelwa. The underlaying cause was competition for scarce farmland in the central plateau where the Muslim immigrants are seen as interlopers. The massacre sparked revenge attacks by Muslim youths in towns and cities throughout Nigeria.

MALI AND BURKINO FASO
Population: Mali, 14 million (UN 2005); Burkino Faso, 14 million (of which approximately 50% are Muslim)

Mali is an ancient centre of African Muslim civilisation, though one of its few cities – Timbuktu – has passed into the languages of the world as a symbol of remoteness. Islam was established by traders from Arabia and North Africa in the ninth century who established settlements along the Niger river, a natural east–west border which divides the desert to the north from the more temperate grasslands to the south. In the fourteenth century Mali – more fertile then than now, due to climate change – was the centre of a vast and advanced African Muslim empire peaking under the rule of Mansa Musa who ruled from 1312 until 1337.

In the nineteenth century historic Mali fell under the rule of the French and was split three ways. The former coastal provinces of the Mansa Musa Empire, the most fertile area, became Senegal, ruled from the coastal colonial administrative centre of Dakar. The equatorial south became the territory of Upper Volta where the black African population was made up of traditional tribal pagan believers and what was, at the time, a Muslim minority. The desert regions of ancient Mali formed part of the French Saharan Empire.

Modern independent Mali was established as a democratic secular republic in 1960, still shorn of its ancient African Senegalese and Upper Voltarian territories. Upper Volta became independent in the same year (and was later renamed Burkino Faso).

In Mali itself the newly established one-party National Assembly was dominated by the left-wing African Democratic Party of Modibo Keita. His government followed 'anti-Imperialist' policies aimed at rooting out French influence and naively trying to create a viable Malian national economy free from dependence on France by refusing French economic aid.

The economic policy was a disaster and reduced Mali to one of the poorest countries on the continent. In 1968, in an attempt to smother growing opposition, Keita dissolved the National Assembly and declared a socialist one-party state.

He was immediately overthrown by a military coup led by Brigadier General Moussa Traore, who ruled as the head of a military junta until 1979 when a limited National Assembly was re-established. Traore was elected President, Prime Minister, Commander in Chief of the Armed Forces, Foreign Minister and Minister without Portfolio by an unlikely 95 per cent of votes in an equally unlikely 99 per cent turnout.

His party, the Democratic Union of the Malian People (UDPM), won all the seats in the National Assembly, again with a suspiciously huge majority, and declared itself henceforth the only legal party. Traore was deposed in a military coup in 1991 which was the trigger for an uprising by the nomadic tribal Tuareg inhabitants of the desert (linked to a similar tribal uprising against the government of neighbouring Niger).

As an agricultural country Mali's economy has been devastated by numerous droughts in recent years. The country has become entirely dependent on foreign food aid. In 2002 France announced it would cancel 40 per cent of Mali's debt if political stability could be achieved. A few weeks later the government resigned to be replaced by a 'Committee of National Unity' pledged to reach a settlement with the Tuaregs and new elections for the Presidency and the National Assembly.

MAURITANIA
Population: 3 million (UN 2005)

The Islamic Republic of Mauritania is a remote, vast, inaccessible desert nation divided into three distinct ethnic groups. The three million population is united only in adherence to a narrow version of traditionalist Maliki Islam now enshrined as the basic constitution of the country.

In Mauritania ancient Berber-Moorish Islam in the north begins to give way to the more heterodox and recent Islam of Negro sub-Sahara. The dominant ethnic group, making up only about 25 per cent of the population, is known as the White Moors and forms the ruling class of the country. The White Moors are linked by clan ties to the Moroccan aristocracy.

The remaining 75 per cent of the population is divided between the Negro Hausa, concentrated on the southern border with Mali and Senegal, and the so-called Black Moors – descendants of Arabised Negro slaves who are ethnically Negro but culturally Moorish. The slave trade was made illegal under French rule but resumed after independence in 1960.

The Mauritanian state was at first secular but highly traditionalist. The government was dominated by the White Moor ruling class, many of whom favoured the immediate incorporation of Mauritania into Morocco as part of a revived Maghreb Empire.

In 1978 a coup led by army officers belonging to the Negro Hausa tribe brought down the government, installed a Hausa regime and brought the country close to civil war.

Mauritania's foreign policy moved sharply against Morocco and evolved into diplomatic support for the Polisario guerrillas. The war and the coup had brought the Hausa population of the south and the Moorish population of the north close to civil war.

The new Hausa regime sought to broaden its base amongst the Moors and found an ally in the form of the Muslim Brotherhood. The regime accepted a Brotherhood proposal to turn the country into an Islamic Republic based on full implementation of the *shari'ah* law as the price of continuing Moorish support.

The Islamic Republic of Mauritania was proclaimed in 1980 and the first public hand amputations for theft took place in September of that year. At the same time, slavery was abolished and many Black Moors were freed.

Nevertheless there was by the end of the 1980s renewed racial tension between Berber-Arabs and Black Africans sparked by competition for scarce resources. In 1989 violence forced tens of thousands of black Mauritanians to flee over the border to Senegal, where they now live as refugees. The US later withdrew all development aid to the country – ostensibly because of the regime's treatment of black citizens, but also because it loudly supported Saddam Hussein's Iraqi regime during the First Gulf War in 1991.

The Mauritanian economy, based on copper mining, has suffered from the decline in world commodity prices since their peak in the 1970s. A further and terrifying problem is the rapid increase in 'desertification' of the few cultivatable areas of the country as a result of global warming, population and economic pressures. In the 1990s seven of the ten harvests failed, and the country has become dependent on food aid to avoid famine.

In 2004 Mauritania was accused of being a training group for al-Qaeda militants based in Alegria and operating widely throughout Muslim Africa.

In 2005 the civilian President Maaouiya Ould Sid Ahmed Taya was deposed by the army who accused him of acting as a dictator. The new military regime arranged for new elections to take place and, at the same time, released more than twenty people previously held without trial on terrorism charges.

SENEGAL
Population 10.6 million (UN 2005)

Senegal is the most developed of the Muslim countries of the former French African Empire, but still has a mainly agricultural economy based on exporting peanuts, a crop which has been badly hit by droughts in recent years. But the country has a remarkably stable and democratic political constitution based on moderate secularism, free elections, relatively free media and an independent judiciary.

The vast majority of the population is Maliki Sunni Muslim – the faith of the Maghreb to the north across the Sahara. But the constitution adopted when Senegal became independent in 1960 is robustly secular and a full separation of religion and state exists on the classic French and American republican model. As the colonial power France had administered separate *shari'ah*-type courts dealing with family matters for Muslims. After independence these were abolished in favour of attempts to create a modern unified secular legal system.

Senegal was ruled by Socialist Party leader President Sedar Senghor from independence in 1960 until his retirement twenty years later, making him the first African head of state to retire voluntarily and then be replaced by free elections without military supervision. At first the Socialist party followed a type of Third World Marxism, similar perhaps to that espoused by elements of the Algerian national liberation movement. Senghor's successor, Adbou Diouf, also represented the Senegalese Socialist Party, but led a programme of internal reform to get rid of the party's Marxist wing and liberalise the country's socialist economy. In 2000 Diouf handed over power to the opposition Democratic Party after losing a general election. The change of government marked the end of forty years of Socialist Party rule and was claimed to be the first example of a peaceful change of regime anywhere in Muslim Africa.

The main threats to Senegalese political stability are external or territorial. In 1989 violence forced tens of thousands of ethnically black citizens of neighbouring Mauritania to flee over the border to Senegal, where they now live as refugees, in order to escape persecution – and even enslavement – by

Mauritania's ethnically Berber-Arabic elite. Another source of potential instability comes from separatists in the southern province of Casamance, a region cut off from Senegal by the former British enclave of The Gambia.

However, refugee problems and the separatist agitation are of a secular nature. Islam has been pushed into the fringes of Senegalese political life and Muslim extremism is rare.

THE GAMBIA
Population: 1.6 million (UN 2005)

The former British colonial enclave of The Gambia is a tiny country with narrow strips of territory along the banks of the Gambia river flowing through central Senegal. The country is essentially a curiosity left over from Anglo-Franco political intrigues of over one hundred years ago.

The Gambia became independent in 1965 and was declared a republic in 1970. The population, being culturally and ethnically Senegalese, is mainly Sunni Maliki Muslim, though with more significant Christian minorities than Senegal itself. The legal system is based on an amalgam of English common law, Islamic law and traditional African customs. A colonial-style dual system of secular higher courts supervising *shari'ah*, which have powers only over the Muslim community, operates.

In its first decade of independence The Gambia was far less stable than Senegal. In 1981 the pro-Western government had to call on Senegalese troops and, it is widely accepted, the British SAS, to put down a Libyan-inspired attempt at forced integration of both nations under Marxist rule. In fact between 1982 and 1989 the two countries were formally confederated as Senegambia. But the arrangement fell apart after Senegalese complaints of Gambian domination.

The 1990s saw political instability, economic collapse and military coups and accusations of gross violations of human rights by the military government. 2002 saw attempts to reintroduce multiparty democracy, but religiously based parties, including those based on Islam, were not encouraged.

GUINEA AND GUINEA-BISSAU
Populations: 8.8 million and 1.6 million (UN 2005)

From 1958 to 1984 Guinea was ruled by President Ahmad Sekou Touré, a moderate socialist and secularist, and his Guinea Democratic Party (PDG). Although democratically elected, the PDG dominated the small National Assembly and, on the well-established African pattern, began to move towards a one-party state. After gaining total power Touré formed a cold war alliance with the Soviet Union after which his regime became increasingly anti-Western and repressive. A combination of economic devastation brought on by economic mismanagement and repression led to more than one million Guineans – almost a quarter of the entire population – fleeing into exile in neighbouring countries and in France.

Touré was overthrown by a military coup in 1984 and a junta under the control of Colonels Lansana Conte and Diarra Traore was set up. In 1985 Traore launched a further coup against his partner but failed, thereby firmly establishing Conte as President. His rule has been more liberal than Touré's and many exiles have returned. But the country faced a grave economic crisis despite the adoption of IMF-approved free market policies.

In 1990, after the fall of the Soviet Union, a new democratic constitution was adopted and the country's first relatively free multiparty elections were held in 1993. Conte was confirmed in office. But within three years parts of the army mutinied and rioted over the non-payment of wages. After that the country was increasingly sucked into the desperate civil war in neighbouring Liberia and Sierra Leone – with much of the national army becoming mercenaries for diamond-trading gangs fighting for control of territory.

By the turn of the century the fighting between the different militias had spread into Guinea, prompting the government to attack large tracts of its own border territory with helicopter gunships. Conflict has displaced much of the rural population and, coming on top of the population movements of the 1970s and 1980s, this means that Guinea has one of the worst refugee problems of any country in Africa.

Islam plays a limited role in the political life of Guinea. The religion is less well established than in the neighbouring Islamic countries of Mali and Mauritania – an official Islamic republic – and a third of the population cling to pre-Islamic ancestor worship and animistic tribal religions.

It is likely many nominal Guinean Muslims in actual fact practise traditional religions and the official figure of a 70 per cent Muslim proportion of the population is almost certainly an overestimate.

GUINEA-BISSAU

This small slice of historic pre-colonial Guinea won independence from Portugal in 1974 after a long and bloody guerrilla war fought by the Marxist African Party for the Liberation of Guinea and Cape Verde (PAIGC). A secular Marxist republic was established, allied to the Soviet Union and depending on a command economy. Rapid economic decline led to instability and a military coup in 1980. The army mutinied in 1998 after receiving no wages or food, and many may have joined private militias fighting over diamonds and territory in neighbouring 'failed states' such as Sierra Leone.

Guinea-Bissau functions as a state only at the most basic and symbolic level. The country's leader, President Kumba Yala, rules in an increasingly erratic and idiosyncratic manner: moving the capital city from the historic seaport of Bissau to the tiny village of Buba and demanding the expulsion of Muslim religious leaders on the grounds that they are engaged in black magic.

The exact number of Muslims in the country is difficult to gauge and it is probable that the majority of the population of less than two million follow traditional tribal cults, with Islam as the largest monotheistic religion practised in urban areas.

23. EAST AFRICA

SOMALIA, DJIBOUTI, ERITREA, TANZANIA AND THE INDIAN OCEAN ISLANDS
Total population: 17 million

Islam in East Africa is older than in the African interior. It was founded by small enclaves of Arab merchants shortly after the death of Muhammad but was never able to penetrate beyond a thin coastal strip because of the power of the ancient Christian Abyssinian Empire (now reduced to the modern state of Ethiopia).

Instead Islam spread down a series of merchant towns on the east coast of the continent such as Dar es Salaam (in modern Tanzania), and onwards to hundreds of tiny islands in the Indian Ocean. Islam in this region is almost entirely of the Sunni Shafi variety – the law school most closely associated with the merchant class of the Abbasid Empire during its Golden Age.

Muslims are in the majority in countries like Somalia and Eritrea, where the territory consists of strips along the coast of the horn of Africa. In the countries to the south, all of which have vast territories in the non-Muslim sub-Saharan African interior, the coastal Muslims form a minority. The classic case is Tanzania where the seaport capital Dar es Salaam and the fertile offshore island of Zanzibar are overwhelmingly Muslim and the adjacent African mainland almost entirely non-Muslim.

SOMALIA
Population: 10.7 million (UN 2005)

The Somali Republic was formed in 1960 by the union of the former colonies of British and Italian Somaliland under the supervision of the UN (which had administered Italian Somaliland since Italy's defeat in the Second World War). In 1969 a Marxist revolution, led by military officers, led to the creation of an African Socialist Republic with a secular constitution based on 'the principles of Scientific Socialism'. The dual system justice with *shari'ah* courts for natives was abolished, though the Shafi school of Sunni Islam, to which most Somali's subscribe, was made the residual source of law in family courts dealing with matters such as bigamy, divorce and child protection.

The new military junta abolished the country's parliament and ruled as a dictatorship. But it was secular and Marxist in outlook. The administration of Islam was placed under state-directed Spiritual Boards.

The country's new leader, President Siad Barre, espoused a version of Islamic Socialism similar to that found in Algeria. He also moved the country firmly into the Soviet orbit by accepting large-scale military and economic aid. In 1975, prompted by a law granting formal equality to women, the feuding chieftains united against him and rebelled in the name of Islam.

The revolt had a tribal as well as a political dimension. It was easily crushed with Soviet military help and Barre, himself the head of the third largest tribe in the country, was able to establish himself as unchallenged tribal leader by executing the ten most important rival chiefs.

In 1977 Somalia invaded neighbouring Ethiopia, claiming the province of Ogaden belonged to Barre's tribe and therefore to his country. When the Soviet Union refused to help him he moved to the Western camp and accepted French military aid.

The Soviet Union backed the new Marxist leadership in Ethiopia, which repulsed the Somali invasion with the help of Cuban forces.

In the early 1980s opposition to Siad Barre's rule emerged among the Mijertyn and Isaq tribal-Sufi sects which began a civil war against the leader's own tribe-sect the Marehan. After ten years of escalating wars and vendettas among the clans, Barre was forced to leave Somalia in 1991 and the country began to disintegrate. In 1992 the US established a peace-keeping force in the capital city Mogadishu (impossible before the end of the cold war, because the horn of Africa had been a Soviet zone of influence) which, after initial defeats at the hands of local insurgents, eventually grew into a rapid reaction force capable of delivering elite US troops to any part of east Africa and the Gulf in a matter of hours.

Since 1997 the US has been trying to broker a peace treaty between the tribes and territorial warlords. But the picture has been one of brief periods of national agreement followed by bouts of civil war and disintegration. As an archetypal 'failed state' Somalia, like new breakaway entities such as Somaliland, is awash with refugees and the camps doubtless have the effect of breeding support for groups like al-Qaeda.

By 2006 the Somalian capital of Mogadishu had become possibly the most violent place on earth, reduced to anarchy by rival armed gangs engaged in constant firefights amid the ruins. Developments were to follow the pattern of Afghanistan in the run up to rule by the Taliban. In the spring of that year one militia managed to assert itself over the others and took control in the name of the Union of Islamic Courts, establishing effective control and ignoring the non-functioning official institutions of the vapourised Somali 'state' entirely.

The Union was a loose federation of local *shari'ah* courts which had used the draconian Islamic '*hadd*' punishments (such as hand amputation for theft) to restore order after the official state forces ceased to function.

At least one of the eleven regional courts was administered by a man said by the US to be a terrorist leader – this was Hassan Aweys, the leader of an Islamic movement said to be the Somali arm of al-Qaeda. But the international spokesman for the Union of Islamic Courts, Sharif Sheikh Ahmed was at pains to assure the US that the movement was moderate and concerned only with establishing internal order. Aweys said that he no longer had dealings with al-Qaeda and denied that he had been involved in establishing terrorist training camps in areas under his control.

ERITREA
Population: 4.4 million (UN 2005)

The former colonial territory of Muslim Eritrea, part of the historically Arab-influenced coastal strip of the horn of Africa, was awarded to independent Christian Ethiopia in 1952 as an autonomous region within a relatively loose federation. Ethiopia's full incorporation of Eritrea as a subject province in 1962 set off a thirty-year guerrilla war for independence. In 1991, after the collapse of the Soviet-supported Marxist regime in Ethiopia, Eritrean rebels finally routed Ethiopian forces, independence was declared and ratified in a 1993 referendum. The new state was secular, though the justice system incorporates *shari'ah* law and courts for the trial of civil cases between Muslims. There are significant Coptic and Ethiopian Christian minorities, and small communities of Roman Catholics and Protestants established by missionaries during the years of colonial rule.

A border war with Ethiopia broke out within a few years and continued until 2000 when a border readjustment was brokered by the UN, backed by the arrival of a UN peacekeeping force. Like most of the region, Eritrea is a desperately poor country, threatened by repeated drought and the additional local problem of locust swarms.

DJIBOUTI
Population: 0.8 million (UN 2005)

The Republic of Djibouti consists of the ancient Arab fortress town of Djibouti and a tiny strip of adjacent coastline. Since independence four thousand French troops have remained to guard it against possible invasion from neighbouring Somalia and Ethiopia. Both states have territorial claims to ownership of the historically and strategically important seaport.

The Republic's politics are dominated by two main clans –
the Muslim Somalian Issas and the Muslim Ethiopian Afars.
Neither clan favours union with its respective homeland. The
Somali Issas are a minority tribe in Somalia itself and have
been sucked into the fighting and the civil war there; the Afars
are likewise fearful of becoming a minority in Christian
Ethiopia.

The two tribes have thus been forced together to defend
Djibouti and now carve up political power between them.

THE INDIAN OCEAN ISLANDS

All these islands have sizeable Muslim communities founded
by merchants who converted the population. They tend to
have Arab Muslim aristocracies, descended from the original
traders and explorers, and indigenous Bantu-related lower
classes who converted to Islam much later.

Generally the smaller the island the more complete was the
conversion, and Muslims of all classes speak Swahili, the East
African Arab–African trading language.

COMOROS ISLANDS
Population: 812,000 (UN 2005)

This former French colony was declared an Islamic Republic in
1975 by President Ahmad Abdullah. But within a month he
was overthrown by a Maoist-type secularising movement.
Abdullah won back power with a counter-coup, using a band
of French mercenaries under the command of the extraordinary French adventurer Colonel Bob Denard.

Abdullah redeclared the Islamic Republic in 1978 and
declared himself Sultan. But there was little doubt that Denard,
whose mercenary band formed Abdullah's new Palace Guard,
were in effective control of the country.

In 1990 Abdullah himself was overthrown by Denard who,
for a short while, attempted to rule the country as a type of
private pirate state. Denard was in turn deposed by French
special forces who put the pro-Western figure of Said Mohamed Djohar in power. Denard briefly went into exile, but
returned at the head of a mercenary force in 1995 to depose

Djohar and reclaim 'his' country. The French again invaded and expelled Denard. In 1997 a modicum of stability returned to the Islands as Mohamed Abdul Karin Taki was elected president, introducing a new Islamic constitution for the Islands. Denard was no longer around, but Taki immediately faced a crisis when half the Island group declared themselves independent. Taki attempted to invade the rebel islands, but his forces were routed. Shortly afterwards he died of a heart attack, leaving a country in which a bewildering series of coups and counter-coups took place every few months.

ZANZIBAR/TANZANIA
Muslim population approximately 17 million (Government of Tanzania)

The island of Zanzibar and the associated mainland port of Dar es Salaam are ancient centres of Muslim and Arab civilisation. The island is currently federated with the Republic of Tanzania. Zanzibar is almost entirely Muslim and much wealthier than the Christian and pagan Bantu-African mainland. But the federated state of Tanzania is resolutely secular.

The union of these two very different countries has been surprisingly successful. The previous President of Tanzania, Ndugu Ali Hassan Mwinyi, was a Zanzibar Muslim. In 1995 he surrendered power to a mainland African Benjamin Mkapa, after the country's first multiparty elections.

THE MALDIVE ISLANDS
Population: 338,000 (UN 2005)

This chain of two hundred islands, scattered across 800 kilometres of Indian Ocean, were ruled by a Muslim Sultan for seven hundred years before the British placed the Maldives under joint British and Hindu–Buddhist rule from Sri Lanka.

The islands have now reverted to a Sultanate-type of rule with a series of Presidents and Prime Ministers drawn entirely from the traditional Arab ruling class. The *shari'ah* is enforced but the penal regime is liberal and women have many formal civil rights.

The majority of the islands remain extremely orthodox Muslim, and Islam dominates everyday life. The islands, which are extremely beautiful, have been developed as a tourist destination, but tourists are strictly segregated and allowed little contact with the islanders.

The official religion of the islands is Islam and the legal system is a mixture of *shari'ah* and English common law. Maldivians are mainly Shafi Sunnis with a Shi'ite Ja'fari minority. Adherence to Islam is a condition of possessing Maldive citizenship.

THE LACCADIVE ISLANDS
Population: 56,000 (Government of India)

The Laccadive Muslims are a stranded community, arbitrarily incorporated into the state of India in 1948 and constituted as Union Territory in 1956. The small population is packed on to the habitable surface at a density of 1,300 per sq. km. The population is entirely Muslim.

24. THE CAUCASUS AND VOLGA REGION

AZERBAIJAN, CHECHNYA, DAGESTAN, OSSETIA AND THE TARTAR AND CHECO-INGUSH REGIONS OF RUSSIA AND THE FORMER USSR
Total population: 12 million

The history of the Caucasus and Volga regions, which border each other, is a story of two thousand years of war and continuous migration by tribal peoples from the east. The area has been ruled at various times by an extraordinary collection of states including Armenian and Byzantine Christian empires, Mongol and Jewish Khazar Khanates, a pagan Bulgarian kingdom, Islamic Ottoman and Mongol Sultanates, Ukrainian Catholic Cossack Republics and others. In more recent times the entire area was subject to rule first by the Czarist Russian Empire, then Soviet Communists, the German Nazis, independent nationalists and contemporary warlords.

As a result the region is a dense patchwork of ethnically and linguistically distinct Christian and Islamic peoples. Until the fall of the Soviet Union in 1989 the region was divided into four Soviet republics and then further divided into thirteen autonomous areas within them. The total number of nationalities and sub-linguist groups is estimated at over fifty.

About half of the population in the region as a whole is Muslim. But Muslims only form the clear majority in

Azerbaijan. The Azerbaijani, or Azeri, Muslims are ethnically Turkish, but belong to the Shi'ite Ithna ('Twelver') sect of neighbouring Iran.

The rest of the Muslims in the region are Sunnis – a legacy of Ottoman rule and Turkish ethnicity – and are only slightly in the minority in the territories which made up the former Tartar, Dagestan, Checho-Ingush and Kalmyk Autonomous Areas of the Russian Federation. These countries and ethno-linguistic territories form a chain of historically Muslim lands stretching down the length of the Volga Valley from Kazan and the Russian heartland in the north to the Caspian and Black Seas and the borders of Turkey and Iran in the south.

Muslims lost their majority status in the Volga region after the Second World War, partly because of increasing settlement by ethnic Russians and Ukrainians and partly because of mass deportation of the indigenous populations to central Asia (particularly the Chechens and Ingushi).

After the destruction of the USSR, Islam has become more important in a region dominated by a vicious war between the Russian army and Chechen separatists.

The Russian Empire conquered the region in the early nineteenth century. The Imperial administration attempted to introduce backward Ottoman Sunni Islam by placing Imams imported from Balkan territories captured from the Ottoman Empire. However, this tactic backfired. Sunni rule was deeply resented by the Shi'ites and became a focus for discontent. Furthermore, some of the Sunni Imams were members of clandestine Sufi Orders who, regardless of doctrinal differences, led Azeri rebellions against the Russians.

The Naqshbandi Sufi Order provided the backbone for a guerrilla movement based in the Caucasus mountains, and therefore known as the Mountaineer Movement. The mountains remained outside Russian control until 1859, when the local leader of the Order, Mohammed Sham'ail, was captured and executed. Many of the Naqshbandi were deported to Siberia and central Asia where they unsuccessfully attempted a fundamentalist reformation and also founded the guerrilla movement in Transoxia known as the Basmachi (Bandits).

The Naqshbandi were replaced in the forefront of the anti-Russian movement by the Qadiriyah Sufis, who originated in Persia. Following the execution of Sham'ail, the Qadiriyah declared a military *jihad* against the Russians.

Meanwhile, in 1878 the Ingush Muslims of the Volga had declared their own anti-Russian *jihad* through full-scale revolt which the Russians ruthlessly crushed, executing hundreds of village leaders and transporting hundreds to Siberia and central Asia.

The events of 1878 turned many Ingush and Chechens into fanatical anti-Russian nationalists and they remained in a continuous state of revolt until the 1940s when the bulk of the population, about two million people, was transported to central Asia by Stalin.

With the collapse of the Russian Empire in 1917 the Qadiriyah rose in open revolt in Azerbaijan and the Volga where, as the Mussavat (Tartar Nationalist) Party, they dominated the Baku Soviet (revolutionary national committee). By 1920 the Red Army had occupied Azerbaijan and the neighbouring Christian republics of Armenia and Georgia in the name of defending them against Kemal Ataturk's new Turkish national army which occupied part of Armenia and was threatening Azerbaijan.

The Red Army backed successful coups by Bolshevik minorities in the Soviets of each of the three republics, securing their federation as the Transcaucasian Socialist Federal Soviet Republic (TSFSR) in 1922. The TSFSR then federated with the Ukrainian and Russian Soviet Republics in the same year to form the Union of the Soviet Socialist Republics (USSR).

Whilst Azerbaijan remained passive during the early years of the Soviet dictatorship, there were major Sufi-inspired revolts further north in the Kazan area throughout the 1920s and 1930s. During the Second World War the Naqshbandi sided with the German invaders, helping recruit Tartars, Ingushi and Azeris into paramilitary SS 'punishment squads' and regular Waffen-SS units. Anti-Semitism flared, especially amongst the Tartars and Ingush (whose conversion to Islam had been secured by the Qadiriyah on the basis of racial hatred of the

Russians and Jews), and lower Volga Muslims played an important role in the Nazi 'final solution' in the area.

After the decisive Battle of Stalingrad the Red Army regained control of the Volga and Azerbaijan regions and punished the collaborators severely. In 1941 two million Ingush – over half the total population – were transported to the Muslim territories of Soviet central Asia. Hundreds of thousands of Tartars were likewise transported or executed. The Tartar and Ingush Autonomous Republics still existed on paper but after the deportations the areas had ethnically Russian majority populations. For several decades Islam as a publically practised religion all but ceased to exist.

The Soviet government also established the (Sunni) Muslim Spiritual Boards of Dagestan and the Northern Caucasus, and the separate (Shi'ite) Muslim Spiritual Board of Transcaucasia (Azerbaijan). The aim of both boards was to purge Volga and Azeri Islam of pro-Nazi, anti-Jewish teaching and replace the anti-Russian Sufi Orders.

After the disintegration of the Soviet Union the area was thrown into chaos. Ethnic conflict broke out between Muslim Azeris and Christian Armenians in disputed areas of the Armenian territorial enclave of Nagorno-Karabakh. Violence peaked in the mid-1990s, but the dispute is still unresolved. Further to the north there was even more serious violence when in 1991 the former Soviet Russian Federation's autonomous territory of Chechnya declared complete independence as a secular Muslim state in 1991. A decade of war – including the complete destruction of the Chechyan capital city Grozny and the creation of vast numbers of refugees – followed, which at various points threatened to destablise the whole region and perhaps even prompt a military or anti-democratic coup in Russia itself.

AZERBAIJAN
Population: 8.5 million (UN 2005)

Azerbaijan is one of the most developed nations in the Muslim world and has some of the best prospects of constructing a prosperous, peaceful civil society and democratic state along Western lines.

The country has huge oil wealth and a developed oil industry which dates back to the nineteenth century. Inefficiency and corruption were rife during Azerbaijan's time as part of the Soviet Union, and in the immediate years of post-Soviet independence, but the benefits of oil wealth are more widely spread than in the Gulf and many other oil-rich states. In Soviet times there was extensive associated industrialisation and at least some development of infrastructure and the provision of health care and education for most of the population.

In theory Azeri Muslims are subject to the religious authority of the Shi'ite Ayatollahs of the *ulama* in Tehran. But the federal Soviet government established a local Shi'ite hierarchy, the Muslim Spiritual Board of Transcaucasia, under the leadership of a local Shi'ite cleric with the title of Shayk al-Islami.

Public worship has declined markedly since the war – a trend well established throughout the developed world – and many mosques have closed, further reducing demand for clerics.

The most serious threat to stability is ethnic rivalries between the patchwork of autonomous ethnic regions and republics established within their current borders during the Soviet period. The boundaries of ethnic areas enclose the heartland of each linguistic group, but may contain towns and areas belonging to ethnic neighbours. Within Azerbaijan, for example, there are 4,500 sq. km of solidly Christian Armenian territory constituted as the Autonomous Region of Nagorno-Karabakh.

In 1988 and 1989 there was serious rioting by the Christian Armenians of Nagorno-Karabakh demanding elevation to the status of a full Soviet republic, with the ethnic Armenian population demanding the creation of a land corridor linking Karabakh through the majority-Muslim territory dividing it from the rest of Armenia. Meanwhile the Azeri minority in the region, about 20 per cent of the total population, rioted for full incorporation into Azerbaijan and Soviet troops were deployed to stop the fighting.

Once the Soviet Union collapsed and Russian-Soviet troops left the region, the Armenians attacked the Azeris, slaughtering thousands and provoking a backlash from Azeri militias. Large slices of Azeri territory remained under Armenian occupation, creating a refugee population of about 800,000.

In Azerbaijan the sense of nationhood is inextricably linked to the country's Islamic history, so Azeri nationalism involved a rival of religious practice. The fall of the Soviet Union also meant that the border with fundamentalist Iran to the south was open.

Independent Azerbaijan has not, however, followed the path of Islamic Revolution chosen by its southern neighbour. The country remains secular and has become increasingly orientated towards the West and, to a lesser extent, Turkey. In 2000 Azerbaijan joined the Council of Europe and, despite objections to the country's human rights record and worries over corruption and electoral fraud, began the process of creating closer formal links with the European Union.

CHECHNYA
Population: approx. 1 million

After the fall of the Soviet Union local officials and army officers grabbed power, declaring an independent secular republic in 1991. But in the absence of Russian or Soviet military power the country quickly disintegrated into rival mini-states run by competing warlords along Afghan lines. The warlords fought each other until 1994 when Russia tried to regain control. Two years of guerrilla war followed, with heavy Russian losses.

In 1996 Moscow effectively admitted defeat and offered Chechnya extensive autonomy within Russia, amounting in effect to independence. But, despite retaining titular control, the Russians failed to rebuild the country, most of which remained under the control of warlords. Organised crime flourished, with local gang leaders growing rich on the proceeds of kidnap and ransom, and other types of organised crime including drug trafficking.

In 1999 conflict threatened to spread to the hitherto peaceful Muslim-majority region of Dagestan where Muslim fundamentalists had declared an independent Islamic Republic and then called on all fellow Muslims in the Caucasus to wage a Holy War on the Russians. Numerous terrorist attacks in Moscow and throughout Russia followed and the Russians retaliated with a brutal military campaign which saw the complete destruction of the Chechnyan capital Grozny.

After the 11 September 2001 attacks on the World Trade Center the US gave some support to the Russian military campaign on the grounds that Chechnya was a breeding ground for terrorism. Attempts at a peace agreement between the Russians and the Chechens came to an end after a dramatic Chechnyan terrorist siege and gas attack on a Moscow theatre in 2002.

In 2003 the Russians imposed a new constitution on Chechnya, reincorporating it as an autonomous region within the Russian Federation. The settlement was resisted and there were suicide bombings against Russian-controlled buildings in the north of the country.

The following year saw one of the most harrowing terrorist incidents of modern times – the Beslan massacre of schoolchildren carried out by Chechen terrorists as a reprisal for Russian military action against civilians in their homeland. Chechen warlord Shamil Basayev claimed responsibility for the torture and murder of 344 people, including 186 children who were held amongst 1,200 hostages in a school hall. The actual killing was done by his deputy Magomet Yevloyev.

In the same year Chechen terrorist were blamed for a bombing on the Moscow metro system and for exploding a bomb on a Russian civilian airliner. Violent clashes between separatists and Russian forces continued, despite some Russian success in hunting down and executing terrorist and separatist leaders.

By 2006 Chechnya was still a focus for Islamic internationalism and, for example, Russian diplomats in Iraq were targeted by Sunni insurgents as a reprisal for the execution of the separatist leader Aslan Maskhadov.

25. TRANSOXIA, CENTRAL ASIA AND CHINA

UZBEKISTAN, KAZAKHSTAN, TURKMENISTAN, TAJIKISTAN, KYRGYZSTAN AND XINJIANG
Total population: 75 million

The Turkic peoples of Transoxia are directly related to the Muslim populations of modern Turkey and the Balkans three thousand kilometres to the west – areas settled by Turkic tribes migrating westwards in the Middle Ages, eventually founding the Ottoman Empire.

Today the Muslims of central Asia are the most remote of the major Islamic communities. For centuries they were cut off from the Islamic heartlands of north Arabia by the simple facts of geography as well as pagan invasions from China in the east. In the twentieth century Communist states kept the faithful tightly controlled until the fall of the USSR in 1989.

They are amongst the most secularised Muslims in the world, the result of relatively high educational and living standards and eighty years of secularising, atheist Communist propaganda.

Islam was originally founded in Transoxia in AD 649 when 'Uthman, the third Caliph, crossed the river Oxus separating central Asia from Afghanistan, Iran and Arabia to the south, and began the rapid conversion of the Turkic peoples of

'Transoxia' to Islam. For five hundred years Transoxian Turkic Islamic civilisation flourished under benign Abbasid overlordship, eventually pushing even further east to establish Islam in the northern Chinese region of Xinjiang.

In 1219 Ghengis Khan's pagan Mongol Horde captured Transoxia and destroyed much of the original Abbasid civilisation. But by 1300 the Mongols had converted to Islam and in 1360 the Mongol Khan Tamberlaine established his capital in the Transoxian city of Samarkand.

Tamberlaine's 'Islamic' Horde, made up of Mongols and the indigenous Turks, quickly conquered the whole of central Asia and European Russia as far as the borders of modern Poland in the west, and China in the east. The Russian cities of Kiev and Moscow both came under Muslim rule.

In the following centuries Tamberlaine's empire slowly disintegrated. The eastern part (Xinjiang) came under Chinese rule and the western part (the Volga region and Transoxia) under Russian. Thereafter Transoxian and Chinese Islam developed separately. Russian colonisation of the Islamic lands started in the 1720s with the capture of Azerbaijan in the Caucasus and the steady acquisition of the former Tartar territories in the Volga and southern Ukrainian regions from the declining Ottoman Empire.

Colonisation of Transoxia did not begin until the mid nineteenth century, but when it did it was achieved quickly. Kazakhstan was incorporated into the Empire in 1854, followed by Turkmenia (1864), Uzbekistan (1868), Tajikstan (1884) and Kirgizia (1895).

Under Russian rule the Muslims of Transoxian cities such as Samarkand and Tashkent were ghettoised. Muslims were not regarded as citizens but as subject colonials with no rights and were excluded from the army and police, which remained Russian or Cossack. The Russians, whilst permitting freedom of worship in the mosques, persecuted leaders of the various Islamic modernising movements of the time.

They also backed the most arcane and backward Ottoman Sunni-type trends which preached a fatalistic acceptance of rule by any power, regardless of religion, so long as the basic rules of the *ibadah* were not flouted. The only organised resistance came from Sufi orders which had preserved Transoxian Islam under pagan Mongol rule seven hundred years previously and now launched an intermittent guerrilla war against the Russians.

The Kazakhstan Soviet Socialist Republic (SSR) was established in 1920 and the Turkmenistan SSR in 1924. Kirgizia and Tajikstan were, however, directly annexed to the territory of the Russian Federal SSR. The Sunni establishment accepted Bolshevik rule as easily as they had accepted Russian rule, with many Sunni clerics becoming Communist Party secretaries, but the Sufi Basmachi rebels (from the Uzbek word 'bandit'), provoked by the introduction of atheist secular education in schools and proposals to give Muslim women civil rights for the first time, resumed their guerrilla war. The Basmachi fought bravely and viciously. But they had little support amongst the majority of the Muslim population and were easily defeated by the Red Army, ceasing to be an effective military force by 1928.

Meanwhile, the central Asian republics enjoyed a national renaissance in the 1920s and the population benefited greatly from the break-up of the old feudal land-owning system and a continuous series of literacy drives. Hundreds of native languages were revived and recorded for the first time and Arabic and Russian Cyrillic script abolished in favour of the more flexible Roman alphabet. But in the 1930s this all ended when the republics were subjected to the same Stalinist terror as the rest of the Soviet Union.

In the 1920s the Communist Party had emphasised the ideological points of contact between Marxism and Islam – of which there are many. But under Stalin in the 1930s all religion was denounced as backward, and Islam, in addition, was said to be worse by being 'foreign'. Sufi institutions were closed as part of a campaign to root out fictitious Basmachi threats and British agents. Separate Muslim schools were abolished and religious endowments, used for missionary work, were confiscated.

Devout Muslims were denounced as fanatics, religious dress was discouraged and in the mood of terror many Muslims began to pray in private, causing the closure of many mosques.

Islam declined to the status of a religion of private conscience, as in Turkey, and Russification in the name of emergency industrialisation resumed. In 1940 Cyrillic script was reintroduced and native languages downgraded in the education system.

The mood of terror increased during the Second World War when many Tartar and Azeri Muslims in the territories far to the west of Transoxia collaborated on a large scale with the Germans, forming their own anti-Soviet units under German command. Partly in response to this, Stalin further tightened the Communist state's grip on Islam with the establishment of the Muslim Spiritual Board of Central Asia in 1943.

The Board was given considerable state funds, powers of patronage and lavish headquarters in Tashkent. As in Azerbaijan, Muslim clerics were required to register with the Board and only registered clerics could lead prayers in mosques or perform funeral rites. In addition the Board controlled the two *madrasahs* expropriated in the 1930s. The Board was also responsible for the upkeep of mosques. Those with obvious tourist potential, such as the great mosque of Samarkand, were renovated, but the rest were allowed to fall derelict. Towards the end of the Soviet era the number of functioning mosques in Transoxia was estimated at less than two hundred.

The main destabilising factor in central Asia is intercommunal strife between the different Turkic nations. The borders of the central Asian republics have been redrawn several times since 1917 and there is continuing discontent with Uzbeks claiming Turkmenian land, and vice versa. These problems are further aggravated by the growing presence of Mongol Muslim immigrants from former Tartar territories in the Volga valley, hundreds of kilometres to the west.

This immigrant group comprises about two million Tartars from the Volga valley and about one million Crimean Tartars and Volga Chechen and Ingush Mongols who were forcibly deported east because they had collaborated extensively with the Germans during the Second World War. In recent years there have been serious clashes between these groups and the indigenous population.

UZBEKISTAN
Population: 27 million (UN 2005)

In 1991 former Communist officials declared Uzbekistan to be an independent secular republic, federated with Russia as part of the short-lived Commonwealth of Independent States, the successor to the federal USSR. Former Communist Party leader Islam Karimov declared a one-party state with himself as dictator. Through the early 1990s Karimov steered the country towards reintegration with Russia and other former Soviet central Asian republics.

In 1999 Uzbekistan experienced a wave of terrorist attacks attributed to the Islamic Movement of Uzbekistan, a fundamentalist group linked to factions in Afghanistan and supported by the Iranian government.

The Islamic movement was severely repressed, leading to accusations of civil rights abuses and torture amid reports of mass arrests.

Unrest in the country culminated in mass demonstrations and an attack on a prison in the eastern city of Andijan aimed at the release of inmates accused of Islamic militancy. Troops opened fire on the crowds killing at least 180. Partly to appease pan-Islamist feeling, the Uzbek parliament voted later in the same year to evict the US air force from bases in the country, previously held to be vital for prosecution of operations in neighbouring Afghanistan. Thereafter there were further arrests of opposition and Islamist figures, including those who had organised the Andijan protests.

KAZAKHSTAN
Population: 15.4 million (UN 2005)

Kazakhstan became independent in 1992 as a neutral, non-aligned, secular state. One of the new state's first acts was to close the remote, but major, Russia-Soviet military base at Semipalatinsk, where nuclear weapons were developed and tested.

As in Uzbekistan, the former Communist elite has remained in power and has tended to maintain links with Russia, leaving the large ethnically Russian settler population relatively unmolested and cracking down on any signs of Islamic militancy while, at the same time, seeking closer links with the West.

Kazakhstan, much of which is thinly populated desert, has remained a dictatorship and has been slow to embrace Western-style liberal economic reform. Private ownership of land, for example, was not allowed until 2003. The regime gave diplomatic support for the US attack on Afghanistan, but was more reluctant to support the invasion of Iraq in 2003.

TURKMENISTAN
Population: 5 million (UN 2005)

The former Communist power structure was left largely intact after disintegration and slowly evolved into an extraordinary North Korean-style despotism based around the personal cult of the country's president-for-life Saparmyrat Niyazov.

Niyazov has forced all opposition out of the country, which is the poorest of all the central Asian republics – consisting mostly of desert with potential for oil and gas production thwarted by lack of pipelines or access to the sea.

TAJIKISTAN
Population: 6.3 million (UN 2005)

Independence from the USSR in 1991 rapidly led to civil war in Tajikistan, the most 'Islamic' and, also, the most troubled of the former Soviet republics of central Asia. The population has close ethnic and tribal links with Afghanistan – where a significant Tajik minority has been one of the groups fighting for control of the country.

The country has also been destabilised by the drug trade – Tajikistan is the first stop on the distribution route for Afghan heroin – and 'narco-terrorists' are alleged to have established bases along the Tajik side of the Tajik–Afghan border.

In 2002 the Tajiki government, a dictatorship in the hands of former officials of the Soviet Communist regime, gave considerable support to the US during the attacks on Afghanistan and received military aid from Russia and the Americans to close its border to al-Qaeda fighters fleeing from Afghanistan.

Thereafter the country's large and militant pro-Islamic movement was severely repressed amid allegations of human rights abuses and ever closer military co-operation with Russia and the US.

In 2004 the Russians re-established military bases in the country. In 2006 the main Tajik secular political opposition leader was arrested while he was on holiday in Moscow and returned to the country in Russian custody.

KYRGYZSTAN
Population: 5.3 million (UN 2005)

In 1992 Kirgizia, as it was then called, became an independent secular republic under the effective rule of former Communist officials. Islamic-type opposition is active, but severely repressed.

In 2001 Kyrgyzstan took a leading role in the creation of the Shanghai Co-operation Organisation, an internal security pact aimed against Islamic insurgency in China and throughout central Asia. In 2002 Kyrgyzstani and Chinese forces took part in joint anti-insurgency exercises in the mountainous borderland between central Asia and the Chinese-ruled Muslim majority region of Xinjiang.

XINJIANG AND NORTH WEST CHINA
Population: 19 million (Government of China)

There is a substantial Muslim minority spread throughout China, but Muslims predominate only in the north-western province of Xinjiang, bordered by Muslim Transoxia to the west and Buddhist Mongolia and Tibet to the north and south. Xinjiang is vast, sparsely populated and has a very low level of economic development, even by contemporary Chinese standards.

The first Muslims to arrive in Xinjiang were merchants from the Abbasid Persian Empire along the Silk Road through Transoxia. The growth of Muslim influence followed the same pattern as other areas remote from Islam's north Arabian heartlands. Merchants first formed themselves into autonomous settlements under local Chinese rulers and steadily converted local people. When the Muslim community was well established Sufi missionaries arrived from Baghdad and, with their mastery of science and medicine, become advisers to the courts of local pagan or Confucian Chinese chieftains.

The Chinese, reaching the height of their power under the T'ang Dynasty at the time the first Muslim communities were formed, appear to have had no objection to this alien presence, regarding the Muslims as people of inferior race and culture who would eventually be assimilated.

Islam's great advance in China came with the fall of the T'ang Dynasty and the conquest of northern China by the Mongol Horde. When the pagan Kublai Khan ('Khan of the East') took power in China he called upon his brother Hagalu Ill-Khan ('Khan of the West') to supply thousands of literate Muslims from the territories of the conquered Persian Empire to administer China on his behalf.

From the fifteenth century onwards the ethnically Han Chinese Muslim converts in Xinjiang, known as the Hui, outnumbered the ethnically Turkic and Persian trading community and Mongol administrative class. The first settlers have been assimilated and are no longer ethnically distinct, but in modern Xinjiang there are Muslims in ethnic minority tribes such as the Turkic Tajiks and Uighurs, who migrated east from Transoxia to escape Russian expansion in the nineteenth century.

With the fall of the Chinese Manchu Dynasty in 1911 Xinjiang gained autonomy under the rule of local warlords – often doubling as Sunni Imams. The local warlord, Yang Tseng-Hsin, was an enlightened ruler who reduced taxation, allowed full religious freedom, and ended persecution of the minority Uighurs and Tajiks by the majority Hui. After the Bolshevik revolution he developed relations with the new Muslim Soviet Republics of Transoxia as a further counterbalance to central Chinese influence.

The warlords who ruled after Yang's death, however, were less supportive of Islam, discouraging religious practice, resuming persecution of the Tajiks and Uighurs, and attempting to assimilate the Hui with the dominant Han Chinese ethnic group. There were numerous revolts amongst the Muslims, especially the Uighurs who, with Soviet backing, declared a fully independent Uighur Republic sympathetic to the Chinese Communists.

With the proclamation of the Communist People's Republic of China in 1949, Beijing imposed its authority over Xinjiang for the first time since 1911. Muslims were granted a degree of religious freedom and Xinjiang given limited self-government as the Xinjiang-Uighur Autonomous Region (later Republic). Imam Saifudin, an Uighur, became governor with Communist Party support. At the same time the Communist government established the Chinese Islamic Association, which was given funds to renovate mosques, print copies of the Qur'an and supervise the Muslim clergy.

Between 1966 and 1976 – the period of government-inspired atheist-Communist fanaticism which became known as the Cultural Revolution, gangs of Communist teenagers – the Red Guards – arrived in Xinjiang from other parts of China to interrupt prayer meetings, attack Imams with clubs and vandalise mosques.

Muslims who continued to worship did so in secret and the mosques which had not been actually destroyed by the Red Guard fell into disrepair. The Chinese Islamic Association ceased to print the Qur'an and delivered atheist tracts to the Imams, who were expected to distribute them to the faithful. Many thousands of Muslims, especially of Turkic ethnic minorities, fled to the relatively liberal religious regime of Transoxia to the west. Others fought back and there were serious riots and clashes between Muslims and Red Guards in cities such as Kashgar, Urumchi and Khotan.

Since the end of the Cultural Revolution the Chinese regime's Islamic Association has attempted to gain the co-operation of Muslims but the organisation was discredited during the Cultural Revolution and has still not recovered, while continuing Muslim resentment over the aftermath of this period occasionally breaks out into mass demonstrations in favour of greater national independence. Muslim demonstrations took place in Beijing in the early part of 1989 a few months before the wider 'Democracy Movement' exploded on to the streets.

In 1996 China, Russia and the newly independent secular Muslim majority states of central Asia signed a treaty of mutual aid aimed at the danger of Islamic insurgency spreading north east from Afghanistan.

In the following year the death of veteran dictator Deng Xiaoping was greeted by rioting in the major cities of Xinjiang aimed at securing greater autonomy. Separatists planted bombs aimed at members of the settler Chinese community, killing nine and injuring 74 people. The bombing campaign escalated and in 2000 sixty people were killed in a single bombing in the Xinjiang city of Urumqi. The Chinese central government claimed that those responsible were linked to Osama Bin Laden.

The violence, coinciding with similar terrorist campaigns in Kyrgyzstan and Tajikistan and continuing guerrilla fighting in Afghanistan and Chechnya, prompted China, Russia and the central Asian republics to strengthen counter-insurgency co-operation. In 2002 Chinese and Kyrgyzstani forces mounted joint anti-terrorist exercises in the Kyrgyzstan–Xinjiang border region.

In 2003 the Chinese central government announced that the local Uighur language, which is spoken by the Muslim population, would be replaced by Chinese in the country's university and throughout much of its education system. Human rights groups claimed that Beijing was attempting to destroy the separate culture and identity of Xinjiang.

26. BRITAIN AND WESTERN EUROPE

T here have been communities of Muslims in Europe since the Middle Ages but, until recently (and with the exception of Spain, the Balkans and parts of the territory of the old Russian Empire) these communities have been tiny and practically invisible.

Muslim expansion was inhibited by the difficulty of performing the duties of the Five Pillars at higher latitudes. It would be impossible, for example, to observe the sun-up to sun-down fast of *Ramadan* in the Arctic Circle, where it would have to last of six months.

To answer this practical problem for European Islam, a standing conference of the four law schools has agreed that places on earth further north or south than the 45 constitute an 'abnormal zone'. The argument is an extension of the principle of exempting the ill from fasting, and the poor from alms-giving and performance of *hajj*. In this abnormal zone Muslim are encouraged to use the prayer times of the nearest mosque or *umma* (Muslim community) in a 'normal zone'.

All of the UK is an 'abnormal' zone, as is the whole of Scandinavia and the Netherlands. Northern France, including (just about) Paris, also falls within the abnormal zone, as does most of Germany. Southern France, Italy, Spain and the Mediterranean fall within the normal zone, and prayers and fasting must be observed according to the rise and fall of the sun.

In practice in the UK most Muslims tend to use the times used in Pakistan, Bangladesh or East Africa, which is where in most cases their families originated. This co-ordination of prayer and fasting times is one of the many ways that UK and European Muslims maintain ties, and in some ways a cultural focus, on 'home' countries. Likewise, French Muslims will observe times determined in Algeria, West Africa or Morocco, and in Germany and Holland Muslims (who in the main have family origins in Turkey and the Balkans) will look to Istanbul.

The other reason for the arrested spread of Islam is, of course, political and strategic. Contact between the Christian and Islamic world were hampered by centuries of military conflict and imperialism. These conflicts have also shaped the nature and outlook of European Muslim communities most notably in Bosnia, Kosovo and the Balkans, but also in Britain and France.

MIGRATION FROM INDIA AND PAKISTAN

Economic migration of large numbers of Muslims and others from India and Pakistan began in the 1930s and 1940s, some as refugees from the violence between Hindus and Muslims in the British-ruled sub-continent. In the 1950s the partition of the sub-continent into India and Pakistan – one of the bloodiest episodes in the history of the twentieth century – brought waves of Muslim migrants from disputed north-western border areas such as Mipur in Kashmir, former Muslim-majority states such as Hydrabad in the centre of the country and Sylhet in the east where they had been subjected to a form of 'ethnic cleansing'.

These substantial communities were joined from the 1960s onwards with further waves of migrants fleeing disasters and injustices of one sort or another, as well as dire poverty. In the 1960s, for example, as many as 100,000 people from Mipur arrived after 250 villages were flooded as part of a dam building project.

These new Muslim migrants found themselves ghettoised in areas of unwanted housing in the decaying inner city areas of

London and Birmingham and in declining Victorian northern mill towns such as Rochdale, Blackburn and Burnley which had never really pulled out of the great depression of the 1930s. This process of 'ghettoisation' was present from the start of the migration, and persisted in patterns of social disadvantage, poverty and a markedly insular mind-set well into the new century.

Prior to the new immigration from India and Pakistan there had been small but notable Muslim communities formed mainly by 'native' sailors, cooks and deck-hands from British colonies. There had about 10,000 British Muslims at the start of the twentieth century, with identifiable communities of Yemenis in the north east and Yorkshire and Somalians in Liverpool and Cardiff. Alongside these were tiny and fluctuating communities of 'white' Muslim converts. Since the eighteenth century there had been a phenomenon of indigenous Protestant Christian Unitarian believers converting to Islam, or incorporating Muslim ideas into their own form of monotheism, during bouts of religious revivalism.

Significantly there seems to have been little contact between the new and larger communities from the sub-continent and these more established communities – showing that whatever else it might be, British Islam was not monolithic and that national background played at least as much role as religion in defining their identity.

The original migrants from Mipur and Sylhet were joined through the 1960s and 1970s by large numbers from nearby parts of Pakistan such as Punjab and the Wazir region stretching up towards the border with Afghanistan. Many of these workers took jobs in the declining UK textile industry, in public service, as drivers and relatively unskilled positions in manufacturing and processing factories. Until 1962 the right to settle in the UK was automatically granted to any citizen of the British Commonwealth. After the passage of the 1962 Immigration Act migrants had to show that they could support themselves and that they had a job to go to.

Migrants of the 1960s were thus overwhelmingly male, since the Act would exclude dependants who would require support or other benefits from the British state. The men who arrived were thus determined to live as cheaply as they could and earn as much as they could with a view to either supporting a family back in Pakistan and one day returning there, or saving enough to bring their family over to settle in Britain at a later date.

This new and overwhelmingly male community was centred in areas of cheap housing, boosting the process of 'ghetto-isation' which had befallen the refugees of the previous generation. The need to have a work permit meant that they were destined to work in factories and in industries where previous migrants were already concentrated, or in family businesses. They thus lacked much interest in the affairs of the country around them and often did not see the need to learn to speak English. They were thus beginning to form what the British Prime Minister Margaret Thatcher was to call an 'alien wedge' of self-contained Muslim settlement in several British towns and cities. From the mid-1960s onwards these newly British Muslims, who probably regarded themselves as being Pakistanis living in Britain, were subjected to forms of discrimination based on the resentment of economically in-secure 'white' communities, who saw them as pushing down wage rates for less skilled jobs and as competition for housing, health and other social services.

The 1971 Immigration Act ended automatic entry for single males with a work permit. Immigration from the sub-continent declined and was in practice restricted to those who had both existing family and work ties with earlier migrants. The decade of the 1970s saw a new rush of mainly male immigration from Pakistan in anticipation of a full and final ban on immigration of all sorts.

There was more immigration in the form of both Muslim and Hindu refugees from former British East African colonies such as Kenya and Uganda where dictatorial regimes were persecuting Asians who had settled there during British rule.

The anticipated ban on further finally came in the form of the 1981 Immigration Act which effectively ended what was described as 'fresh' migration from 'new' (i.e. black) Common-wealth countries such as India, Pakistan and Bangladesh.

The Muslim population nevertheless continued to grow, partly as a result of a differentially high birth rate. Members of Muslim families who arrived before the draconian restrictions, particularly the second- and third-generation British Muslims of the 1960s or 1980s coming of age in the 1990s and at the turn of the century, began to develop a vibrant Anglo-Pakistani popular culture which began to be adopted as part of the mainstream by many younger 'white' and Afro-Caribbean Britons. At the same time sub-continent languages such as Urdu came under pressure and, according to some, even faced the possibility of extinction in the UK.

The 2001 UK census found that there were just over 1.5 million Muslims in the UK representing just under 3 per cent of the population in England and Wales and less than 1 per cent of the population in Scotland and in Northern Ireland. This community was overwhelmingly concentrated in a few urban areas such as Bradford, central Birmingham, Luton, the east end of London and central Lancashire where Muslim communities could represent up to a third of the population. In the London borough of Tower Hamlets some 36 per cent of the population was Muslim (2001 census) – the highest proportion anywhere in the UK. It was in these mostly deprived inner city urban areas such as this that the six hundred or so mosques and sixty dedicated 'faith schools' could be found. But in vast areas of the country – including the more prosperous suburbs and seemingly the entire country-side – there were hardly any Muslims at all.

BARELWI AND DEOBANDI ISLAM

The majority of Muslims of sub-continental extraction are followers of the Barelwi reform movement within the moderate Hanafi school of Sunni *shari'ah* law. Many are also influenced by Sufi'ism and may be members or followers of Sufi orders active in the sub-continent. A small minority of Anglo-Pakistani Muslims may be Shi'ite or followers of unorthodox Shi'ite-type movements (see Part 3 – Islamic Sects).

Barelwi Islam dates back to nineteenth-century religious and political disputes in British-ruled India. In some ways the movement can be seen as a reaction to the 'fundamentalist' Wahhabi movement which is now the doctrine of the ruling group in Saudi Arabia, and which also had origins in Muslim resistance to British rule in India (see Part 2 – Islamic History: The Rise of Islamic 'Fundamentalism': The Wahhabi Revolt).

The Barelwis wanted to keep many of the folk practices and Sufi practices which the Wahhabis wanted to do away with. There was a theological disagreement with Whabbi'ism, and a local Indian purist reform called Deobandi'ism, as well. The Barelwis were 'Muhammadan' in the sense that they believed Muhammad maintained a permanent protective metaphysical presence in the universe, somewhat like the Christian idea of the Holy Spirit. The Whabbis and Deobandis puritans rejected this, insisting that Muhammad, like Jesus, had been essentially an ordinary human being, though one chosen by Allah for a special mission.

Finally, there was a political division over the attitude to be taken to British rule. The Barelwi are usually thought of as the originators of the movement for Pakistan – that is, the creation of separate Muslim and Hindu states on the territory of the British Indian Empire. During the British rule the Sufi'ism of Barelwi meant they were also notably pro-Ottoman in outlook, hoping (in the years before the First World War) that the independent Pakistan of their imagination would form part of a revived Ottoman Caliphate. In contrast, the Deobandis wanted to see a united Islamic India emerge from the British Empire. The Deobandi's also shared the Wahhabi's anti-Sufi and anti-Ottoman outlook.

The Hanafi Barelvi/Deobandi divide may be a significant factor in contemporary Pakistani and British Islam. The Deobandi form a small minority of the Sunni Muslims in the UK, probably less than 10 per cent, but they are the ones who are likely to be most receptive to Wahhabi-type evangelising on the part of visiting Saudi and Saudi-backed religious figures. The missionary wing of the Deobani movement, Tablighti Jamaat, is active in the UK, with headquarters in Dewsbury. The movement is said to enjoy support among Muslim students and young Muslims interested in politics.

The Deobandis and other Wahhabi-aligned missionary movements may also play a cult-like role in encouraging young British Muslims to visit Pakistan in order to spend time 're-discovering' the true (Deobandi) faith, lost as a result of time spent in the decadent West. This phenomenom is, of course, in no way specifically Islamic – all religions are prone to developing cults which may be harmful to adherents and to others. Nevertheless, it is true that extremist groups such as al-Qaeda regard the young Muslims of Britain as a potentially fertile recruiting ground, seeing them as the 'lost orphans of Islam' who must be brought back into closer contact with the Muslims of the Middle East, India and the Third World. It is often noted, for example, that relatively few British Muslims can speak Arabic, recite the Qu'ran or understand what is being said in the mosque. They are therefore unusually dependent on the interpretation of their religion by others.

Beyond this, religious participation on the part of British Muslims is high, especially among the older generation, but the religiosity of the community can be overemphasised. It must always be remembered that because Islam does not really separate religion from other aspects of life the mosque is a centre of community life as well as a religious centre.

Concerned over the growing alienation of Muslims from British society, the UK government in 1997 sponsored the creation of the Muslim Council of Britain, a group of supposedly moderate Muslim leaders who are regularly consulted on domestic matters as they affect the British *umma*.

The group has been controversial for its supposed extremism in condemning homosexuality and permissiveness on the one hand, and for its supposedly compliant attitude toward British foreign and educational policies (though the council has condemned British and US policy in the Middle East and opposed British participation in the 2003 attack on Iraq) on the other. More extreme figures in the Muslim community have accused the body of being out of touch with the reality of everyday life for British Muslims.

For a number of years the face of violent Islamic extremism in the UK was the Egyptian-born Sheikh Abu Hamza al-Masri of Finsbury Park mosque in London. Abu Hamaza became a hate figure and easy target for the tabloid newspapers, partly for his rhetorical justification of the '9/11' attacks and partly because of his extraordinary appearance – an eye patch and an artificial hooked hand, the result of injuries sustained while fighting as a volunteer for the anti-Soviet Mujahideen in Afghanistan in the 1980s.

Abu Hamza's organisation, Supporters of Sharia, campaigned for the imposition of *Shari'ah* law in Muslim-majority areas of the UK. He also used a clerical position at the Finsbury Park mosque to propagandise for al-Qaeda and, it was alleged by the American CIA, recruit activists for the terror network. Government attempts to deport Hamza to Yemen failed (he had British citizenship as the result of a short-lived marriage to a British woman). In 2006 he was jailed after conviction on a list of charges including racial hatred and incitement to murder.

More significant than Hamza in some ways was the career of Omar Bakri Muhammed, a Syrian-born Saudi Arabian asylum seeker and radical Islamic thinker sympathetic to al-Qaeda and other violent anti-Western and anti-Saudi movements.

Bakri had formed a movement in Saudi Arabia called Al-Muhajiroun, widely said to be a front for Hizb ut-Tahrir, the international group seeking world Muslim government in the form of a new Caliphate. Al-Muhajiroun or the New Caliphate Movement gained a small followed among some students and young people possibly evangelised by the indigenous Deobandis. Importantly, he may have had an influence on the young British Muslims who carried out the London suicide bombings of 7 July 2005. Beyond this, the influence of his thinking within the notably moderate British Islamic community is likely to have been slight.

In 2005 Bakri went on a trip to Lebanon and while he was out of the country the British government announced he would not be allowed to return on the grounds that his presence in the country was not conducive to the public good. In July 2006 it was reported that Bakri attempted to return to Britain on a warship evacuating British citizens from Lebanon during the punitive Israeli invasion. He was denied a place on the ship.

ISLAM IN WESTERN EUROPE

The Muslim community in the UK is small by the standards of most other European countries. Belgium, France, the Netherlands, Scandinavia, and Germany all have proportionately larger Muslim communities than the UK. Only Spain – ironically given the fact that it was once a great centre of Muslim civilisation – has fewer Muslims than the UK. That may be changing because of the pattern of illegal immigration from Muslim North Africa to Spain – a trend which is being constantly accelerated by economic collapse and crisis throughout the continent.

The US Council on Foreign Relations estimates that the Muslim population of the European Union had reached about twenty million by 2006, representing about 5 per cent of the total population, meaning that there are already more Muslims in the European Union than in Iraq, Syria or Afghanistan. Given current trends in immigration and the differentially higher Muslim birth rate, the Council estimated that the European Muslim population would reach forty million, or 10 per cent of the total, by 2025.

In most European countries Muslims arrived, as in the UK, by way of citizen rights dating back to the period of European colonialism. Thus, the largest group of Muslims in France could trace their origins to Algeria and the countries of French West Africa. There were more than four million French Muslims and, like the Muslims of Britain, they were to a large extent ghettoised in poor housing estates surrounding major cities. In 2005 there was extensive rioting by black and Muslim youths in these areas.

Muslim communities – relatively small in number, but large in proportionate terms – had grown up in Scandinavia as a result of traditional policies of welcoming asylum seekers from oppressive regimes – of which there was never any shortage throughout the Muslim world – and also on the pattern of the German 'guestworker' system.

Germany since the 1960s had allowed large numbers of Turkish Muslims to settle in the country with no citizenship or residency rights, and on the basis of temporary work permits.

Reforms to the system and the steady extension of the principle of human rights allowed increasing numbers of these 'guest-workers' to remain in the country. Through the 1990s they were joined by waves of Muslim refugees from the fighting in the Balkans where Germany felt it had certain historic obligations and interests. The result was that by 2004 Germany, once one of the most narrowly ethnically homogenous countries in the developed world, was home to some 2.6 million Muslims – just over 3 per cent of the total population.

SELECT BIBLIOGRAPHY

Ahmed, Akbar, S., *Discovering Islam*, Routledge, London, 1988.

Ahsan, Manazir, *Islam – Faith and Practice*, The Islamic Foundation, London, 1985.

Ala Mawdudi, Sayid Abdul, *Towards Understanding Islam*, The UK Islamic Mission, London, 1980.

Allworth, Edward, *The Modern Uzbeks from the Fourteenth Century to the Present*, Hoover Institute, 1990.

Al-Qaradawi, Yusef, *The Lawful and the Prohibited in Islam*, Shorouk International, London, 1985.

Brocklemann, Carl, *History of the Islamic Peoples*, Routledge and Kegan Paul, London, 1948.

Cook, Michael, Muhammad, Oxford University Press, Oxford, 1986.

Davidson, Lawrence and Miller, Randall M., *Islamic Fundamentalism*, Greenwood Press, 1998.

El Alami and Hinchcliffe, *Islamic Marriage and Divorce Laws of the Arab World*, London, 1996.

Eliade, Mircea (editor in chief), *The Encyclopaedia of Religion*, Macmillan, New York, 1987.

Endress, Gerhard, *An Introduction to Islam*, Edinburgh University Press, Edinburgh, 1988.

Ervand, Abrahamian, *Iran Between Two Revolutions*, Princeton University Press, Princeton, 1982.

Esposito, John, L., *Islam in Asia: Religion, Politics, and Society*, Oxford University Press, London, 1987.

Esposito, John L., *The Islamic Threat: Myth or Reality?*, Oxford University Press, London, 1999.

Faksh, Mahmud A., *The Future of Islam in the Middle East: Fundamentalism in Egypt, Algeria, and Saudi Arabia*, Praeger Publishers, 1997.

Fuller, Graham E. and Lesser, Ian O., *A Sense of Siege: The Geopolitics of Islam and the West*, Westview Press, New York, 1995.

Glasse, Cyril, *The Concise Encyclopaedia of Islam*, Stacey International, London, 1989.

Hamid, Algar (ed. and trans.), *Islam and Revolution: Writings and Declarations of Iman Khomeini*, Mizan Press, California, 1981.

Haq, Muhammad Abdul, *Sufi'ism and Shari'ah: Muhammad*, The Islamic Foundation, Leicester, 1986.

Hasan, Ahmad (ed. and trans.), *Collections of Hadith According to Abu Dawud and Bukhari*, Lahore, 1984.

Hekmat, Anwar, *Women and the Koran: The Status of Women in Islam*, Prometheus Books, New York, 1997.

Huntington, Samuel, *The Clash of Civilizations and the Remaking of World Order*, Touchstone Books, New York, 1998.

Johansen, Julian, *Sufi'ism and Islamic Reform in Egypt: The Battle for Islamic Tradition*, Oxford University Press, London, 1996.

Khomeini, Imam, *Islam and Revolution*, Mizan Press, Berkeley, 1981.

Marsden, Peter, *The Taliban*, Zed Books, London, 1989.

Montgomery Watt, William, *Islamic Creeds: A Selection*, Edinburgh University Press, Edinburgh, 1994.

Qureshi, Shoaib and Khan, Jahvid, *The Politics of Satanic Verses – Unmasking Western Attitudes*, Muslim Community Surveys No.3, London 1989.

Rashid, Ahmed, *Taliban – The Story of the Afghan Warlords*, Pan Books, London, 2000.

Raza, Syed Ali, *Biography of the Holy Prophet Muhammad*, Peermahomed Ebrahim Trust, Karachi, 1980.

Reuven, Firestone, *Jihad: The Origin of Holy War in Islam*, Oxford University Press, Oxford, 1999.

Robinson, Frederick, *Atlas of the Islamic World since 1500*, Phaidon Press, Oxford, 1982.

Robinson, N., *Islam – A Concise Introduction*, Curzon Books, London, 1999.

Ruthven, Malise, *Islam in the World*, London, 2000.

Sarwar, Ghulam, *Islam: Beliefs and Teachings*, The Muslim Educational Trust, London, 1987.

Shah, Sidar Iqbal Ali, *Selections from the Qur'an*, The Octagon Press, London, 1980.

Shahin, Ermad, E., *Political Ascent: Contemporary Islamic Movements in North Africa*, Westview Press, New York, 1997.

Shireen, Akiner, *Islamic Peoples of the Soviet Union*, Kegan Paul International, London, 1983.

Sicker, Martin, *The Islamic World in Ascendancy: From the Arab Conquests to the Siege of Vienna*, Praeger Publishers, New York, 2000.

Tarsile, Tahrike, *The Qur'an*, Tahrike Tarsile translation, TT Qur'an Inc., New York, 2003.

Trimingham, Spencer, *The Sufi Orders in Islam*, Oxford University Press, Oxford, 1971.

Ziad, Abu-Amr, *Islamic Fundamentalism in the West Bank and Gaza-Muslim Brotherhood and Islamic Jihad*, Indiana University Press, Bloomington, 1994.

INDEX